STRANGE BATTLES

OF THE

CIVIL WAR

WEBB GARRISON JR.

BRISTOL PARK BOOKS / NEW YORK

First Bristol Park Books edition published in 2008

Published by Bristol Park Books
252 W. 38th Street
NYC, NY 10018

Bristol Park Books is a registered trademark of
Bristol Park Books, Inc.

Published by arrangement with Cumberland House Publishing, Inc.

ISBN: 978-0-88486-430-1

Printed in the United States of America.

In memory of my father

Webb Garrison

who dedicated the last twenty years of his life to a pursuit of knowledge of our American Civil War

CONTENTS

PREFACE

MOST IF NOT ALL of the battles of the Civil War had aspects or results that could be considered strange, unusual, or curious. Only a few of those that seemed conspicuously peculiar were selected for inclusion in this book. Each chapter has been written so that it is not necessary to read the book from beginning to end. There is no chronological sequence; each stands alone as an independent entity.

Shortly after my father, Webb Garrison, began writing this book in the spring of 2000, he was diagnosed as having pancreatic cancer. Nevertheless, he was determined to finish what he had begun and insisted on having daily access to his computer until just a few days before he dropped into a coma in mid-July. At the time of his death, the day after his eighty-first birthday, he had completed six chapters and started two others.

During those last two or three months of his life, he had all the support one could ask for from his children and their spouses, who were all anxious to do anything to help him in any way. Everyone respected his need to work and avoided interrupting him while he tapped away on his laptop. He did not want to die in a hospital, so we made changes in his home to accommodate his needs.

For a couple of years my father had encouraged me to write. I was not opposed to the idea, but we did not work well together because he had a set way of addressing the various steps involved in developing a chapter. His ways, however, were foreign to me, and both of us were somewhat bullheaded about how we did things. I wrote some chapters for a couple of his books, but I wrote them at my home—not his.

Of his three children—my sister, Carol; my brother, Bill; and me—I was the logical one to finish *Strange Battles*. The choice was not because I had any innate ability, but because I had the same name as our father and a more flexible schedule that would allow me to concentrate on the book for a few months.

When I started the project I asked Bill if he had the same problem in reading about the Civil War as I had—too many names and too many unit designations. He agreed that it was often confusing to be barraged with so many details, so I decided to limit my name-dropping to only the most important characters involved in the action and to keep the use of unit names and designations to a minimum. After all, the curious will be able to research easily the events recounted here in the multitude of resources currently available on the war.

I decided to produce a book of informative and historically accurate material for leisurely reading, not a scholarly work for the intellectual or knowledgeable Civil War buff. That does not mean, however, that I skimped on the research so I could tell a story in its simplest terms. The research was daunting.

Because my father was a devout reader of the 128-volume *Official Records* compiled by the War Department from 1880 to 1901, he had always begun his work there and then looked to the writings of scholars and others dedicated to studying the conflict. Of course he had wrestled with the *OR* books for decades before the work became available in a more compact form through recent technology. For me the *OR* seemed at first to be too voluminous to wade through—130,000 pages—and the reading was tedious. After a while, though, tracking the correspondence between officers in the field and Washington became extremely interesting, especially when I noticed hints of animosity between the writers and the readers.

As far as the battles, skirmishes, and encounters between Johnny Reb and Billy Yank went, accurate numbers and casualty reports were sometimes difficult or impossible to find. Each side had a tendency to minimize its losses and exaggerate the ranks of the enemy. In some cases in which there was significant disparity between the sources, I intentionally left the numbers vague.

For myself, I prefer to read what the actual participants had to say about a battle rather than a recent interpretation of their words; therefore, I tend to include some very long quotations in these chapters. This is a violation of the canons of good writing and may be generally considered as my cutting corners, but I believe that something is lost when the words of a firsthand witness—at least someone who smelled fear on the field, whose eyes burned with the profusion of powder smoke—are interpreted rather than recounted. Readers are removed further from the source in such instances, and the war becomes too sterile.

Originally, my father had scripted twenty-seven chapters for this book. The desired book length was achieved after twenty-three, so the last four that had to do with the war in the West, addressing the role played by the tribesmen of the Great Plains in the battles of Valverde, Pea Ridge, Newtonia, and Palmito Ranch were omitted. These may yet appear in some future work.

For the purposes of this book, "strange" has been loosely applied to the combat described here. One of the lessons of the Civil War was that there are few "normal" moments in battle, for very little happens according to some logical sequence. Indeed, many veterans commented that their existence in uniform was very boring except for a few intense moments of pandemonium and extreme chaos. Every action on the battlefield elicited a response by the other side. Thus strange occurrences were typical of the violent collisions that ranged along a ten-thousand-mile-long front. Three million men bore arms in this conflict, and each had his own stories to tell when it was all over. This is but a small sampling of those tales.

For me to claim credit for the book without acknowledging the role played by Ed Curtis of Cumberland House Publishing as editor, historian, and contributor would be a grave injustice to him and his tremendous influence on the project. Therefore I consider Ed and his contributions an integral part of this book.

PART 1

SHIPS VERSUS SHORE

1

PORT ROYAL

BROTHERS DID FIGHT BROTHERS

Born in Charleston, South Carolina, in 1808, Thomas S. Drayton was the butt of much schoolboy humor because of his radical political views. Even in his own home, he was a minority of one. Although the rest of the family regularly read the city's moderate newspaper, the *Daily Courier,* Tom would have none of it. Instead he bought the rabidly antigovernment three-times-a-week *Charleston Mercury* and devoured each issue at least twice.

Schoolmates who jeered at him seldom fought with Tom, but they didn't have much to do with him. His younger brother, Percival, however, was universally liked. Their father, an attorney, was high on Charleston's list of eccentrics. He was an outspoken opponent of Sen. John C. Calhoun, *Mercury* editor Robert Barnwell Rhett, and "the rest of the yellow scoundrels who are bent on taking this splendid little state out of the Union."

Having been called on by city fathers to make a speech at a public gathering, the senior Drayton castigated "secessionists who were panting to lead South Carolina from the United States of America for personal, political and financial gain." His discourse generated such sensation that many began to avoid him and crossed the street to evade him. When folk began leaving little hate notes for Tom and Percy's mom, the family immediately made plans to move to Philadelphia.

Tom had already won an appointment to West Point, but moving would mean that he would have to begin the application process anew in Pennsylvania, since appointments were allotted by state. Since no one knew him in the Keystone State, he opted to remain in South Carolina.

As usual, Percy differed with his brother on nearly every point. Fully as eager for a military career as was Tom, Percy also had second thoughts about seeking an appointment to the U.S. Military Academy from Pennsylvania. Instead he applied to the Naval Academy and was accepted at Annapolis in December 1827. At the Naval Academy he won prominence by his opposition to what appeared to be an upcoming North-South sectional split. It took Percy only a year to rise from midshipman to lieutenant, and by 1855 he had become a commander.

While Tom was at West Point, he forged a friendship with Jefferson Davis, but neither man distinguished himself as a cadet. Assignments

The brothers Drayton: Thomas (left) and Percival (right)

after graduation were made on the basis of class rankings. The plum assignments were to the engineers, the artillery, and the cavalry. The remainder were relegated to the infantry. Consequently Tom was made a lieutenant of infantry upon his graduation in 1828. He managed to stay in uniform for the next six years—somewhat beyond the time when his service record cleared him of any obligations to the government for his education.

Tom returned to South Carolina and assumed the life of a planter. Running his big plantation, he won a seat in the legislature and became a director of a railroad. When war broke out in April 1861, he offered his services to the Confederacy. Immediately he was made a brigadier through the good graces of the Confederate president and his friend, Jefferson Davis. Tom was placed in command of the military district of Port Royal.

The other Drayton, Percival, not only had retained his commission in the U.S. Navy, but he publicly asserted that preservation of the Union was more important than his ties with many relatives in the South. Despite this, his loyalty was suspected by his brother officers.

The Union secretary of the navy, Gideon Welles, was a New England newspaper editor who had no naval experience before taking office. He was, however, highly skilled at analyzing complex

Gideon Welles (left) and Samuel F. Du Pont (right)

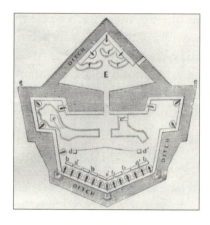

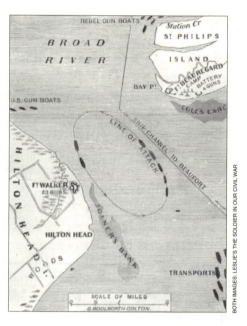

The Federal fleet faced two formidable forts at Port Royal. Fort Walker (plans above) was the more threatening of the two since the battle plan (right) called for the ships to come closest to it.

organizations and finding good minds to solve the problems before him. Many commentators on the war view Welles as one of the most effective members of Abraham Lincoln's cabinet.

Almost as soon as Welles entered his office, he was met with the task of blockading the South. He appointed two boards to study the naval situation and make recommendations. Thus long before the July 21, 1861, battle of Bull Run, Welles pointed out that the Union navy desperately needed a sizable seaport in the Deep South to use as a repair and distribution center for the vessels that would form the blockade.

Most of his colleagues were sure that such an idyllic port did not exist. Those who believed that such a place might be found were also sure that the Southerners would strongly defend it.

Welles awaited the next report from the Blockade Board, which was searching the coast of the Confederacy from North Carolina to Texas for potential ports to meet the need. By the early fall of 1861 he had the board's recommendation—Port Royal—and authorized the creation of a force he called "my Armada."

Unlike Union Gen. Ambrose E. Burnside's secret expedition into North Carolina whose every move was cataloged in the newspapers,

Welles managed to keep a low profile for the Port Royal expedition. In October he put Flag Officer Samuel F. Du Pont in charge of the armada. Incredibly Du Pont soon had seventy-five warships and enough transports to carry twelve thousand men—and only a few perfunctory newspaper stories had been generated.

Welles's agents noted that Port Royal was almost equidistant from Savannah and Charleston—about thirty miles to each. The county seat of Beaufort was at the northern tip of Port Royal, but it was seldom noticed by anyone except those who lived in or near the picturesque little seaport. Nearby Parris Island caused helmsmen to veer their courses slightly, and the inland plantations produced many cotton millionaires; so Beaufort was somewhat prosperous.

Those who had surveyed the region before the war decided that Beaufort's general obscurity was due to its close proximity to Savannah and Charleston. Few took note that the city also had one of the largest and finest natural harbors in the world.

Anticipating that sooner or later the Yankees would recognize the military value of Port Royal, two formidable forts had been built. Fort Walker held twenty-three guns and was only a short distance from the ship channel to Beaufort, to the east. Fort Beauregard mounted sixteen guns and stood across the channel, to the north and east, and was considered the lesser of the pair.

Evidently viewing the two forts as one, the board's confidential report to Welles asserted that Port Royal "has room for all the navies in the world; it is a Fortress Monroe in South Carolina."

The Federal task force was assembled of warships, many small supply vessels, and transports. Named vessels included *Wabash, Susquehanna, Seminole, Mohican, Pawnee Augusta, Bienville, Curlew, Undilla, Ottawa, Seneca, Pembina, Penguin, Isaac Smith, R. B. Forbes,* and *Pocahontas.*

Du Pont planned to hit so hard with his first blow that the enemy could not recover from it. He had not, however, taken into account the fierce storms that dominate the Hatteras area. Four days of howling winds pushed the Port Royal expedition far out into the Gulf Stream. Nearly a dozen ships went down or had to put into port for extensive repairs. With his strength substantially reduced and several days having been lost, Du Pont nevertheless stuck to his original plan.

In October 1861, immediately after rendezvousing near the objective at a point not visible to the Southerners, an order of battle was made. With the *Wabash* in the lead, all the fighting vessels would enter the sound, coming as close to Fort Walker as they dared and directing their whole fire at it.

Swinging around in the three-mile-wide sound, the *Wabash* would then lead the flotilla toward the sea and a regrouping. On its way out, each vessel was to come near Fort Beauregard on Bay Point and fire everything at it as the vessel passed.

This double attack, made possible by the geography of Port Royal with Hilton Head Island on the east and Bay Point on the west, was more than four hours long but proved deadly. Without formal surrender ceremonies, the Confederates abandoned their posts in droves and raced for the mainland. According to one Federal account, "At three a gunboat from the *Wabash,* under Capt. [John] Rogers, landed and planted our glorious Stars and Stripes on the soil of the state that was first to knock it down."

With the North still in a rage at the troops who had panicked at Bull Run, a letter writer at Port Royal rejoiced and observed:

> Our insulted flag was vindicated here. This is a great victory. I don't think you will be troubled anymore about Bull Run, for it was not a circumstance to the stampede that took place here. I almost think they are running yet. They left every thing—clothes, muskets, revolvers, swords, all their camp equipage, fowling pieces; never even spiked their guns. Today the large town of Beaufort, nearly fifteen miles away, is entirely deserted—not a white man in it, and very few blacks.

Several aspects of the battle at Port Royal have received little attention. Because it was a naval venture, Confederate plans for a battle on land often go without mention.

An infantry camp had been established to support Fort Walker within minutes. But on the day of Du Pont's attack, the Southern commanders realized that it would compound the confusion to draw support for the garrison from the sixteen thousand Johnnies, most of whom could not replace fallen gunners because they had never been trained to work the guns.

The man in overall command was none other than Thomas Drayton. His troops failed to take on the Federal landing parties.

Of the Union vessels hit hardest from the Confederate shore batteries was the *Pocahontas,* which was commanded by Percival Drayton. Like the other vessels in Du Pont's attacking fleet, she was a wooden ship. An 80-pounder ball hit the ship's mainmast dead center and cut what an onlooker called "a sawmill-quality hole that was nearly 6 feet wide precisely through her middle."

Du Pont's only naval opposition consisted of six small gunboats, each armed with a single gun. The boats would not have survived a single hit from a Federal gun, so they quickly withdrew.

For the Federals, the problem was one of timing. Although the sound easily accommodated the largest of Du Pont's vessels, low tide would have prevented the ships from navigating the ship channel successfully. So the in-and-out attack was dependent on their successfully gauging the tide.

The Federal victory at Port Royal was even more important than Welles thought. Within a day of the battle, Hilton Head became a coaling station that doubled the range of the Union's South Atlantic Blockading Squadron. Soon machinery, carpenters, gunnery shops, and many other adjuncts to a navy were in place.

Du Pont's fleet heavily bombarded Confederate Fort Walker, where the Southern gunners were frustrated with the task of trying to hit several moving targets.

Union troops landed, but the Confederate forts did not surrender. Instead, Drayton abandoned them and withdrew his men.

Many Union commanders in the eastern theater scoffed at the engagement at Port Royal, discounting the idea that it even deserved to be called a battle. Despite the fact that three brigades of Southern soldiers were at the ready, the Federals suffered no casualties.

The two Drayton brothers continued as enemies for the remainder of the war, with Thomas developing a reputation for being less than brilliant in the field, while Percival distinguished himself as an organizer and administrator within the Union navy—even commanding David G. Farragut's flagship during the August 1864 battle of Mobile Bay.

2

DREWRY'S BLUFF

IRONCLADS THWARTED BY THEIR OWN LIMITATIONS

In DESIGNING THE GUN turret for the USS *Monitor,* John Ericsson had no reason to allow for any greater elevation for the two guns than to achieve the maximum range for the weapons. This proved to be a significant flaw in the battle plans for the May 1862 encounter at Drewry's Bluff, just south of Richmond.

After the March 1862 battle at Hampton Roads, the Confederate ironclad *Virginia* returned to its Norfolk mooring for repairs. She was fitted with a new and stronger prow, more armor, and iron shutters for the gun ports. On April 11, 1862, commanded by Como. Josiah Tattnall and accompanied by six steamers, she set out for Hampton Roads to reengage the Federal ironclad *Monitor.*

The *Monitor,* however, at anchor at Fort Monroe, could not be taunted into a battle. Tattnall ordered one of the accompanying steamers, *Thomas Jefferson,* to capture three nearby ships, two brigs and a schooner. This was accomplished without much resistance from the Federals, and the ships were towed to Craney Island and

The sides of the 950-ton gunboat Galena *were sheathed with iron plate much like the siding on a house. As events were to prove shortly, the metal skin was too thin.*

LIBRARY OF CONGRESS

later to the navy yard. Both brigs carried cargoes of hay for the Union cavalry. Still the *Monitor* never departed the protection of Fort Monroe, so the *Virginia* returned to Sewell's Point, dropped anchor, and later returned to the Norfolk shipyard.

On May 8 the *Monitor* and several other ships approached Sewell's Point and unleashed a barrage on the Confederate batteries there. The *Virginia* left the navy yard to attack the fleet, but as soon as she was in sight the fleet steamed back to Fort Monroe.

Earlier, on May 1, orders were given for the Confederates to evacuate Norfolk and Portsmouth. As a result, the mouth of the James River, which led to Richmond, fell into Union hands. Meanwhile, the evacuation of Norfolk was handled poorly by Confederate Gen. Benjamin Huger—too much property was left intact.

The draft of the *Virginia* was too deep to navigate the James and thus she was trapped. Even if the vessel could run the gauntlet of Federal ships arrayed at Hampton Roads, there was little chance she would survive on the open water, because the ironclad was not designed to function at sea.

On May 10 some river pilots assured Tattnall that he might be able to get the *Virginia* to Richmond if he could lighten the vessel and shorten her normal draft of twenty-two feet to eighteen feet. When the task was done, however, the wooden hull of the vessel was

This illustration of the inside of the Monitor's *turret subtly depicts the elevation limits of the twin guns. They were the heaviest weapons available at the time and were noted for their range.*

LESLIE'S THE SOLDIER IN OUR CIVIL WAR

exposed and vulnerable. Making matter worse, westerly winds had affected the tide, making the river too shallow for the vessel to get past the Federal-occupied portion of the James.

Believing that there was no other course of action, Tattnall had the ship grounded near Craney Island then ordered the vessel's destruction. The crew saturated the decks and roof with oil before abandoning ship. Powder trails were laid as fuses were set to ignite the oil. When these were ignited, the ship burned fiercely for almost an hour before the fire reached the ship's magazine. A little before 5 A.M. on May 11—two months after her maiden voyage—the *Virginia* exploded with a deafening roar. A court of inquiry subsequently found her destruction unnecessary and premature since no Federal attempt was made to move into the James.

The three-hundred-man crew of the nonexistent *Virginia* marched twenty-two miles from Craney Island to Suffolk, arriving that same evening. From Suffolk they traveled by railroad to Richmond. Several crewmen were then dispatched to what at one time had been known as Fort Darling but later, after falling into disrepair, became known as Drewry's Bluff. Situated only seven or eight miles from Richmond, it was the best if not the only place to stop any Union advance on the Confederate capital by water. The Southerners made camp in the woods upriver from the bluff.

In January 1862 a company known as the Southside Heavy
Artillery of Virginia Volunteers enlisted. The men had elected their
own commissioned and noncommissioned officers and left their
homes in Chesterfield County for training and subsequent duty. One
of the enlistees, Cpl. Samuel Mann, observed: "The ages of the men
of the company ranged all the way between seventeen to about forty-
five or fifty years, and were, by occupation, mostly farmers, with a
sprinkling of carpenters, cotton-mill hands, with some gentlemen."

Augustus H. Drewry had recruited the company and was elected
captain and commander. He was first assigned to Battery No. 19 on
the turnpike between Richmond and Drewry's Bluff. Believing that
battery to be unimportant to the defense of Richmond, he asked permission of Brig. Gen. George Washington Custis Lee (Robert E.
Lee's oldest son) to scout a better spot on the James River for a battery of guns. Quickly he determined that the best site on the river for
such a battery was on his own property. Drewry and his men began
construction of a fortification on March 18 at Drewry's Bluff, on the
south bank, ninety feet above the river. Two engineers were assigned
to the company as advisers.

Log cabins were erected for living quarters, and the battery was
prepared for the mounting of guns—two 8-inch Columbiads and
one 10-inch. The 8-inch guns fired a 64-pound shot and the 10-

*Columbiads such as this
one were emplaced by the
Confederates at Fort
Darling at Drewry's Bluff.*

inch hurled 128-pound shells. The guns were brought downriver to a wharf that had been erected to receive them. They were then hauled up the steep incline on a railway to the battery where they were emplaced.

When these preparations were completed, training commenced in heavy artillery tactics and drill became the primary focus for some of the Southside Heavy Artillery of Virginia Volunteers. Consultants were employed by Captain Drewry at his own expense to train his men. One was Scottish, the other English. Intense drilling took place every day.

At the same time, the remainder of the company either worked on obstructing the channel of the river below the wharf or dug rifle pits downriver from the fortification. Piles were driven into the river bottom, and cribs were built and loaded with stone. Finally two steamers were sunk to make the river more impassable.

On May 13 a steamer retreating from Federally occupied waters warned the small Confederate force at Drewry's Bluff that five Yankee gunboats, including two ironclads, were headed up the river to attack them. By this time the refugee crewmen of the *Virginia* had arrived and were busy mounting a gun on the bluff west of the fort and covering it with a casement of logs. Another gun position was placed upriver but too far away to be of any use in the approaching battle.

This view of the battle at Drewry's Bluff shows the near ninety-degree angle of the river as well as the deployment of the Federal flotilla. The Galena *is in the lead, and the* Monitor *is depicted as veering close to the right bank of the James River.*

An early morning rain on May 15 undermined the casement over the navy gun just west of the battery and caused the heavy logs to collapse on top of it, but not completely disabling it.

At about 6 A.M. a signal shot was fired indicating that the five ships were not far off. The Confederates rushed to their stations.

On the river, the Federal ironclads *Galena* and *Monitor* led the wooden-hulled *Aroostook, Port Royal,* and *Naugatuck* toward Richmond. Southern sharpshooters in the rifle pits along the river annoyed the Union gunners as the ships approached Drewry's Bluff. About three-quarters of a mile from the bluff, the three wooden boats dropped anchor and the two ironclads steamed to within six hundred yards with *Galena* in the lead. Exchanges between the battery and the ships began at about 7:45, and all five ships participated in the firing.

The first shot from the 10-inch Columbiad on the bluff almost dismounted it. It was not used again until the battle was near its end. The bluff was left with only two 8-inch guns against what appeared to be a formidable arsenal. What was not quickly realized at the time was that the *Monitor* was too close to elevate her two 11-inch Dahlgrens adequately to have much effect on the bluff. Had she been able to aim her guns accurately, the battle would have had a much different ending. The commanding officer of the *Monitor,* Lt. William Jeffers, offered this report:

> The *Galena* having anchored at about 1,000 yards distant from the fort, and being warmly engaged, I endeavored to pass ahead of her to take off some of the fire, but found that my guns could not be elevated sufficiently to point at the fort. I then took position on the line with the *Galena* and maintained a deliberate fire until the close of the action, when in company with the other vessels, I dropped down to the anchorage of the morning.
>
> The fire of the enemy was remarkably well directed, but rarely toward this vessel. She was struck three times; one solid 8-inch shot square on the turret, two solid shot on the side armor forward of the pilot house; neither caused any damage beyond bending the plates.

The ironclad (more appropriately, iron-shingled) *Galena,* which was perfectly capable of elevating her guns, became the main target in the ensuing battle that lasted close to four hours. Toward the end

U.S. NAVAL HISTORICAL CENTER

This contemporary drawing of the battle illustrates that Fort Darling had virtual command of the bend in the river. The Confederate gunners struck every vessel several times.

of the battle those manning the guns on the bluff were ordered to cease fire for thirty minutes to conserve ammunition. Perhaps believing that ammunition was very short or exhausted, the *Monitor* signaled for the other Federal gunboats to advance upriver and take up positions behind the ironclads.

All five ships did their best to disable the battery, and during this period the Confederates sustained most of their casualties. The 100-pounder Parrott Gun aboard *Naugatuck* burst, leaving her vulnerable and unable to strike back.

The following account from a Confederate volunteer describes the rest of the battle:

> About this time a naval officer walked down and said to me "we must commence to fire again, as the boats are now firing into our men." So without further waiting we all resumed our posts for action at the guns. When Captain Drewry, on seeing how the boats had been concentrated, commanded in a very confident tone of voice: "Fire on those wooden boats and make them leave there," when both of our guns resumed fire, and put some shot through them broadside, when shortly, I think I saw a shell from the ten-inch

U.S. NAVAL HISTORICAL CENTER

Galena was hit twenty-eight times; eighteen shells penetrated the hull and deck. A crewman said, "The ship began to fly all to pieces and in a short time we were a complete wreck."

gun—which had at last been remounted, burst on the deck of the Galena, and I am not sure, but that Captain Tucker's naval gun also began to lend its aid at the "eleventh" hour.

A few more rounds were fired before the Union boats and ironclads retreated downriver. *Galena* was almost out of ammunition by 11 A.M. and had suffered the most damage of any of the ships, receiving twenty-eight hits from the Southern guns, most of it 8-inch round shot. Thirty of the ship's crew were either killed or injured.

The notion that iron-plated vessels such as the *Galena* were impervious to heavy damage was now disproved in blood. The prototypical *Monitor* was hit only three times and suffered no damage other than dented armor.

Confederate casualties were seven killed and eight wounded, mostly naval personnel trying to remount their gun. Although the central battery on the bluff was hit by enemy fire, no one there was killed or badly injured.

The battle demonstrated to both sides that lacking support from troops on land or a redesign of the *Monitor*'s gun-openings, ironclads alone would never get past Drewry's Bluff.

3

FORT FISHER

WHEN BUTLER FAILED TO FIGHT

WITH FORT FISHER GUARDING its harbor, Wilmington, North Carolina, was the most active port still open in the Confederacy in late 1864. This harbor was still used by blockade-runners that continued to bring desperately needed goods to the South. In the fall of 1864, Union Lt. Gen. Ulysses S. Grant, determined to staunch the flow of supplies into that port, devised a joint army-navy expedition that would eliminate the formidable fort. Originally he planned to place Maj. Gen. Godfrey Weitzel to lead the land forces; however, Benjamin F. Butler insisted that he, being the senior officer, should command the expedition rather than Weitzel. Butler's political clout was such that Grant acquiesced to the demand.

Butler arrived near Fort Fisher with sixty-five hundred men in transports, but it was too late in the day on December 24 to attempt a landing. A Union fleet of fifty-one warships had already begun hammering the fort with an incredible storm of shells. The next day Butler did little with his men other than amuse the enemy before he

21

retired from a potentially deadly battle. Upon returning to Fort
Monroe and giving his report to Grant, he was relieved of command
and sent home to Massachusetts.

Prior to the war, Butler had specialized in criminal law and
played an active role in politics. He had been elected to the Massachusetts House of Representatives and subsequently to the state
senate. As a delegate to the Democratic National Convention in
Charleston in 1860, he did not increase his popularity at home by
endorsing Vice President John C. Breckinridge's bid for his party's
nomination. When the war broke out, Butler was among the first to
answer Abraham Lincoln's call for volunteers. He was made a
brigadier and given command of the Eighth Massachusetts Regiment and promoted to major general shortly afterward.

During the early weeks of the conflict, his men protected the
routes to Washington through Maryland and kept them open for
incoming troops. In April 1862 his troops followed David G. Farragut's fleet into New Orleans, and Butler was made military commander of the Crescent City. The captive populace made no secret of
their contempt for all things Federal and despised Butler for what they
perceived as his tyrannical rule. In response to a general order that the
citizens, and especially the women of New Orleans, comport themselves with civility toward his troops, Butler became one of the most

Benjamin F. Butler (left) and David D. Porter (right)

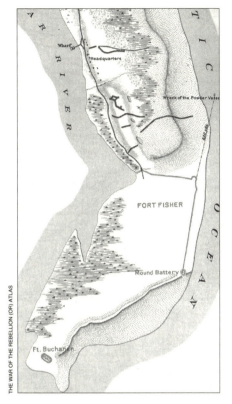

Fort Fisher was but a single installation in a series of defenses erected to protect the port of Wilmington, North Carolina. By late 1864 it had been enlarged to form an L-shaped fortress with one half-mile leg spanning the finger of land between the Atlantic Ocean and the Cape Fear River. The other leg was at least a mile long and ended at a huge mound on which two heavy seacoast guns were placed. Along this perimeter at least forty-four guns were installed.

notorious Northerners in all the South. Jefferson Davis issued an order that if Butler were ever captured, he was to be hanged. At the time of the first battle of Fort Fisher, Butler was in command of the Army of the James.

In July 1862 Col. William Lamb was ordered to Fort Fisher to assume command. Situated on the southern tip of Smith Island where the Cape Fear River enters the Atlantic, about fifteen miles south of Wilmington, the fort was a small work with protection for much of its perimeter consisting of sandbags. Only two of its six guns were suitable for seacoast defense. Other batteries were adjacent to it, bringing the total battery up to seventeen guns. The entire defensive works, however, could be destroyed by the enemy with little difficulty.

Lamb immediately began construction of a new Fort Fisher, a structure of such defensive strength and magnitude that the enemy would never be able to penetrate it. He obtained permission from Gen. Samuel Gibbs French, and construction continued until the morning of December 24, 1864. Lamb claimed:

> I never ceased to work, sometimes working on Sunday when rumors
> of an attack reached me, having at times over one thousand men,
> white and colored, hard at work. In the construction of the mound
> on the extreme right of the seaface, which occupied six months, two

inclined railways, worked by steam, supplemented the labor of men. Although Fort Fisher was far from completed when attacked by the Federal fleet, it was the largest sea coast fortification in the Confederate States. The plans were my own, and as the work progressed were approved by French, Raines, Longstreet, Beauregard and Whiting. It was styled by Federal engineers after the capture, the Malakoff of the South. It was built solely with the view of resisting the fire of a fleet, and it stood uninjured, except as to armament, two of the fiercest bombardments the world has ever witnessed.

On that fateful Christmas Eve in 1864 the fort had forty-four guns but was short on ammunition. The largest gun in the place was a prized Armstrong gun, and Lamb had only a dozen rounds for it. The rest of the magazine held only thirty-six hundred shot and shell for the other forty-three guns.

The plan devised by the Federals to capture the fort was straightforward and simple: assault. To this, however, Butler added his own special touch. He proposed that the flat-bottomed steamer *Louisiana* was to be loaded with 350 tons of gunpowder and exploded near the fort, causing at least a breach in the walls and stunning the defenders sufficiently for Butler's troops to storm the fort. The actual engagement did not take place as planned.

As part of the planning for the so-called powder ship plot, Adm. David Dixon Porter, commanding the fleet involved in the operation against Fort Fisher, on December 8 went about determining the depth of the water near the fort. He prefaced a request to the senior officer with an outline of the intended venture: "[We] propose running a vessel drawing 8½ feet (as near to Fort Fisher as possible)

This view of the interior of the seaface traverses gives some idea of the size of the installation. Butler hoped that his exploding powder ship would vaporize these defenses.

with 350 tons of powder, and exploding her by running her upon the beach outside and opposite Fort Fisher. My calculations are that the explosion will wind up Fort Fisher and the works along the beach, and that we can open fire with the vessels without damage."

The *Louisiana* left New York on December 8 and headed for Craney Island, near Hampton Roads, where she was loaded with explosives. The USS *Sassacus* towed her to Beaufort, North Carolina, on December 13, where additional powder was added to bring the total to 235 tons, which was all that Porter could get at that time.

On December 17 the admiral sent instructions to A. C. Rhind, commander of the *Louisiana:* "You will proceed when ready, with the *Louisiana,* under your command to the east bar, New Inlet, and place the vessel as close to Fort Fisher as the water will permit, even to running her on the beach. When she is there she is to be exploded by means of clocks, slow matches, etc., which have been furnished you, at such time as your judgement may seem best." He noted, "I think that the concussion will tumble magazines that are built on framework, and that the famous mound will be among the things that were, and the guns buried beneath the ruins." As an after-thought Porter added that a controlled fire might guarantee an explosion better than the clocks and fuses.

There was, of course, a plan of escape for the officers and crew of the *Louisiana,* and all ships were warned to reduce their steam prior to the explosion and to stay at least twelve miles away.

On December 6 Butler sent a message to Porter asking when he should leave with his troops from Fort Monroe. Porter's reply was that much of the preparation would be completed by the next morning but

This was one of the many bombproofs at Fort Fisher. Earthwork forts proved to be far more resilient than traditional brick-and-mortar edifices.

The powder ship had no effect on the fort's defenses. Federal naval gunners did far more damage in mid-January 1865 prior to a massive coordinated land assault.

that he should wait for another message that would pinpoint an accurate departure date.

On December 16 Porter sent word that his ships would leave the next morning for the rendezvous near Confederate Point (the juncture of the Cape Fear River and the Atlantic). Butler, however, had already arrived there a day earlier and was running low on coal and water. Forced back to port at Beaufort, ninety miles north of the target, violent weather prevented him from joining Porter until December 24.

On December 18 the admiral sent a letter to the general telling him that he had ordered the explosion of the *Louisiana*. Weitzel, still with Butler at Beaufort, was dispatched to request that the detonation be postponed until Butler's army could join in the attack. Porter called back the *Louisiana*.

On December 23 Porter felt that he could wait no longer. The sea was calm and the weather was ideal for the operation. He gave orders for Rhind to carry out the instructions for the destruction of the fort.

Lookouts at the fort spotted the burning vessel well after midnight at a distance of about a mile. Lamb assumed that it was a blockade-runner, paid it little attention, and went to bed. He recalled:

> I had hardly lain down before I felt a gentle rocking of the small
> brick house [formerly the light keeper's], which I would have

attributed to imagination or to vertigo, but it was instantly followed by an explosion, sounding very little louder than the report of a ten-inch Columbiad. The corporal of the guard was called for in every direction by the sentinels, and the officer of the day reported the blowing up of the magazine of the vessel which had been on fire. I telegraphed General Whiting, at Wilmington, of the explosion, and retired to rest. In the morning the explosion was the subject of conversation among the officers, and some had not even been aroused by the commotion it created. I thought so little of it that the only entry I made in my diary was "a blockader got aground near the fort, set fire to herself, and blew up."

On the morning of December 24 the Federal fleet approached Fort Fisher, and Lamb, to conserve ammunition, instructed all of the guns to fire only on his command and, even then, only once every thirty minutes.

According to Porter's report to Gideon Welles, the Federal fleet kept up a shower of shells at the rate of 115 per minute for five hours; however, that rate must have been for a shorter period of time than five hours for that would make the total number of shells fired to exceed 34,000. Apparently though, between just two of the ships, the *Minnesota* and the *Colorado*, 3,500 shots were fired.

Lamb estimated that around 10,000 shells were received from the enemy, making the rate more like 33 per minute. Regardless of the actual count, it was a fierce bombardment. After the first hour and fifteen minutes, Porter noticed that the guns at the fort had become silent with only an occasional shot thrown in their direction. Smoke and fire could be seen rising from it, and the Federals assumed that the magazines were on fire.

Although Fort Fisher had inflicted some damage on the fleet, the real casualties came from the bursting of five 100-pounder Parrott guns, killing or wounding forty-four officers and men. Butler arrived around sunset that day with some of his transports, and the rest of his men arrived for the landing the next day.

The real situation at Fort Fisher was much different from the image in the minds of those aboard the ships at sea. Minimal damage had been sustained. The garrison flag had been shot away, and the wooden quarters behind the flag had been set afire by exploding shells. The fires had spread to some tar and pitch stored near the quarters, causing more flames, but the most severe damage was the loss of overcoats that the defenders had left in their quarters on a balmy December day.

During that first day of battle, Lamb's men expended 672 projectiles, and twenty-three men were wounded. Only one was mortally injured. Three were seriously hurt, and nineteen only slightly.

Renewed offensive maneuvers began around 7 A.M. on Christmas morning. There were about 120 small boats available to carry Butler's troops from their transports to the beach. A landing place was chosen about three miles up the coast from the fort. Seventeen gunboats escorted and protected the transports while the soldiers went ashore in the rowboats. The *Ironsides,* closest of the ships, held her fire until around 10 A.M. Afterward the fleet maintained a constant but less vigorous fire than the preceding day's while three thousand men landed.

Reinforcements for Lamb arrived that morning, bringing the garrison to almost fourteen hundred, including three hundred teenage junior reserves. Gen. W. H. C. Whiting—who had been in overall command of the defenses of Wilmington until the newly arrived Braxton Bragg took control—was responsible for the additional men. Bragg, at Sugar Loaf, about five miles away and less than two miles from where the Federals landed, did nothing to repel the advancing infantry. The last message sent to Bragg that day, prior to the telegraphic communication's being lost at 4 P.M., was: "A large body of enemy have landed near the fort, deploying as skirmishers. May be able to carry me by storm. Do the best I can. All behaving well. Order supports to attack." There was no response.

Sharpshooters trying to pick off gunners were spotted at 4:30 in an abandoned work nearby. A few shots of canister put a quick end to their intentions. At 5:30 a brutal assault against the land face by the Federal fleet commenced. The Southerners were ordered to seek protection but to be ready to man the parapets as soon as the firing ceased, since a heavy line of skirmishers was ready to attack the fort as soon as the navy finished its work.

When the guns fell silent, eight hundred men and boys took their positions while grape and canister awaited the advancing troops. It was dark, and targets within the fort were difficult to see. Federals fired their weapons without doing any damage, and just when they appeared to be ready for a general assault, they were called back.

Butler had determined that the fort was too well protected to be taken by storm. The troops headed back up the beach to the boats and on to the waiting transports. Butler left seven hundred men behind in his haste to return to sea. Those men waited there unmolested until they were picked up by the navy two days later.

In the two days of action fewer than thirteen hundred projectiles were thrown at the Federal fleet, and total casualties for the garrison were sixty-one killed or wounded. Porter did not have a casualty list when he sent his report of the battle to Gideon Welles, but these losses were not considered to be of any significance.

Part of the difficulty Butler experienced with Grant after the battle may have originated with Porter's attitude toward the entire affair. Butler's assessment of the strength of Fort Fisher may have been more accurate than the admiral's. In Porter's report to Welles he stated:

> When I started on this expedition, you may remember, I said how the place could be taken, viz, with the navy attacking it by water and 12,000 troops properly provided to work on the land. Well, sir,

Each gun position was well protected. Thus when Butler's powder ship was detonated at 1:30 A.M. on Christmas Eve 1864, there was no effect. Most of the defenders assumed a boiler had exploded on one of the Union ships and went back to sleep.

it could have been taken on Christmas with 500 men, without losing a soldier; there were not 20 men in the forts, and those were poor, miserable, panic-stricken people, cowering there with fear, while one or two desperate men in one of the upper casemates some distance above Fort Fisher managed to fire one gun, that seldom hit anyone.

I feel ashamed that men calling themselves soldiers should have left this place so ingloriously; it was, however, nothing more than I expected when General Butler mixed himself up in this expedition, starting his troops out from Hampton Roads with only a few days' provisions, and without water, trusting to the steamers to make it, which they could not do. The transports were so frail that they should never have left Hampton Roads; the result was, when the time arrived for action the troops were all in Beaufort. He had time then to get enough of them to New Inlet; he and three transports arrived on the first day while we were firing, when the beach was smooth, and having 2,000 men on the ground, all he had to do was to land and take possession of the panic-stricken garrison. Almost every man in the work was stunned by the explosion and unfit for duty; this we heard from the prisoners.

The entrance to Fort Fisher is at the far left of this image, marked by the break in the palisade fence. Only one of the guns installed here was still in place when the fort was taken.

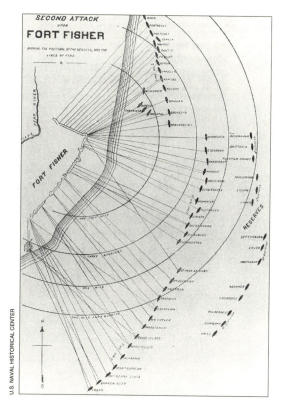

When the Union fleet returned to Fort Fisher in January 1865, the attack assumed less inventive measures and relied on a heavy bombardment to set the stage for a complex coordinated assault. The fifty-nine warships brought more than six hundred guns to bear on the huge fort made of sand and reinforced with wood.

It is scarcely worthwhile to be impatient under these disappointments; the Navy will have to meet them throughout a war like this, where so many incompetent men in the Army are placed in charge of important trusts. General Butler only came here to reap the credit of this affair, supposing that the explosion would sweep the works off from the face of the earth. Had he supposed in the first instance that there would have been difficulties he would never have joined the expedition.

General Weitzel went on shore, determined what the report of the defenses would be, for General Butler had made an opinion for him. The Department, sir, has no cause to be dissatisfied with the share the Navy has taken in this affair; the ships did their work so beautifully that you will hear of but one opinion expressed by lookers-on.

If this temporary failure succeeds in sending General Butler into private life, it is not to be regretted, for it cost only a certain amount of shells, which I would expend in a month's target practice anyhow.

Three weeks later in a battle ending in hand-to-hand combat, high in casualties for both sides, Fort Fisher fell.

The naval bombardment began on January 13, 1865, and was more focused than earlier bombardments. First the gunners attacked the landface of the fort, opening the way for an assault there, and then shifted their guns to the seaface. On January 15 the fort capitulated.

Butler was unhappy with the treatment he received from Grant after returning empty-handed from his expedition to Confederate Point. This can be clearly seen in a letter to Whiting dated February 22, 1865. It contained twenty-four questions regarding the wisdom of his own decisions in the assault against Fort Fisher. The essence of the last question was whether or not the general thought Butler had acted prudently in removing his men. Whiting, then a prisoner of war, answered each question thoroughly and agreed that he had made the right decision in withdrawing his troops. He couldn't resist elaborating further that if Bragg had been competent, Butler's men would have never made it to the fort.

4

SABINE PASS

AGAINST TERRIFIC ODDS

On THE MORNING OF September 2, 1863, Maj. Gen. William B. Franklin called for his officers to assemble at headquarters in occupied New Orleans. He announced that the command had received orders from Washington that it had been chosen to execute a secret but highly important mission.

The general detailed which divisions should embark immediately "with orders to assemble at some convenient point on the [Mississippi] River below this city." The men were to rendezvous with a fleet of transports, and the officers were to confer with Lt. Frederick Crocker, who had been assigned to head the naval portion of the expedition. The naval contingent consisted of twenty-seven vessels, which were mostly small and in bad repair.

Franklin's assembled officers learned that they were to take tiny Fort Griffin on the Sabine River. They were not told anything about the political results that the Washington planners hoped would stem from this action. France was already deeply involved with Mexico,

33

and the Lincoln administration wanted to discourage the French from heading north.

The Sabine River, protected by Fort Griffin, was only seven miles long, but in earlier times it had served as one of the boundaries between the United States and Mexico. Situated about halfway between Galveston and Beaumont, Texas, the fort was considered highly vulnerable because its walls were made of mud. Capturing the fort would accomplish at least three objectives.

First, Federal forces would be in position to strike at Houston and at lightly defended Galveston, thereby facilitating Union control of southwestern Texas. From bases that would be established after taking this position on the Sabine, Federal forces could move forward and take all of the Lone Star State.

Second, Union occupation of the Texas coast would stem the illicit flow of cotton from Sabine City. Despite the ongoing blockade of Southern ports, this enterprise was believed to be quite large.

Third, and perhaps most important, the French in Mexico would be strongly discouraged from moving over the border that was barely seven miles from the point at which the Sabine River emptied into the Gulf of Mexico.

Shortly after meeting with his officers, Franklin read in the *New York Herald* a detailed account of the "vast armada assembled for the purpose of taking a Confederate post on the coast of Texas." He fumed because he knew that only one of his officers could have leaked the story of the expedition.

Gen. Nathaniel P. Banks was to head the army contingent of the expedition. He was quoted by the *Herald* as regretting that he had transportation for only six thousand troops. The newspaper, which circulated throughout the North but also found its way south to Richmond, correctly listed the more important vessels of the flotilla: *Clifton, Arizona, Sachem,* and *Granite City.*

Banks was quoted as being confident that "rumor had been kept entirely at fault, and that the blow will fall on the enemy in a quarter unexpected by them." A few days later his pronouncement was found to be dead wrong.

Possibly the newspaper story influenced Confederate Gen. John B. Magruder to send couriers up and down the coast of Texas. Members of the garrison of Fort Griffin pondered alternatives, decided that the blow would probably fall on them, and made hurried preparations to engage the oncoming Federal force. Youthful Lt. Richard W. "Dick" Dowling, formerly a saloon keeper in Houston and now an officer of the state militia, warned the men of his company to be ready to take a very hard blow.

At the time, neither Dowling nor Banks knew that the approaching Union expedition was relying heavily on the word of an unknown informer who actually knew very little about Sabine Pass. This man did not alert the Federals to the mud flats that lay on both sides of the Gulf near their objective. A fully equipped soldier would sink to his waist in the goo. Most likely the informer did not know that additional problems awaiting the Northerners included shallow water and a huge oyster bed that divided the mouth of the Sabine River in such a way that it would be impossible for several ships to enter the area simultaneously.

Dowling and his men, who were predominantly Irish, had been organized as the independent Davis Guards, named in honor of Jefferson Davis, the Confederate president. Ordinary folk, however, preferred to call the unit the Dockwallopers, since many of the men had worked on the docks before the war. In the autumn of 1861 the unit was absorbed by the First Texas Heavy Artillery and designated as Company F. The men had participated in the recapture of Galveston

Nathaniel P. Banks (left) and David G. Farragut (right)

early in 1863. Despite this limited combat experience, they were regarded as one of the toughest units in the state.

Meanwhile, the Federal flotilla, working with poor and limited geographical information, sailed past their target and had to turn around. All eyes had been scanning the water for the blockading gunboat *Owasco*, but without success. What Banks and the naval commanders did not know was that the gunboat had withdrawn without leave and was miles away, nearing Galveston to replenish its supply of coal and oil. Lacking the identifying vessel on station, none of the ships' captains was sure where their objective was. As a result, *Clifton, Arizona, Sachem, Granite City*, and the line of transports proceeded farther west until a prominent landmark thirty miles south of their objective made them realize their mistake.

A planned attack at dawn was now impossible. Because of the confusion over the position of Fort Griffin, it was not until midafternoon on September 8 that the Federal flotilla weighed anchor and the ships took their places in the line of battle.

Aboard the first of the seven heavily loaded transports was West Point graduate Gen. Godfrey Weitzel, who headed a special band of five hundred veterans and a group of sharpshooters. Banks accompanied him and expressed a profane disgust that the line of warships ahead of them did not seem to be moving at their best speed.

John Bankhead Magruder (left) and Richard "Dick" Dowling (right)

Armed with 32-pounders, 9-inch Dahlgrens, and 30-pounder Parrott rifles, the strongest ship in the squadron, *Sachem,* steamed slowly up the east channel (also known as the Louisiana channel) and presented herself broadside to the little fort at about 3:45. Shots were exchanged at close quarters, and one of the Confederate shells struck the warship's boilers. She quickly hoisted a white flag. Numerous seamen and officers jumped from the disabled vessel into the water, anticipating that the ship was about to explode. No accurate count of the Federal dead was ever made.

During much of this action, *Arizona* was firmly and helplessly grounded.

Soon the 892-ton *Clifton* reached the west channel (or Texas channel) in company with the tugboat *Uncle Ben.*

Weitzel's advance contingent, scheduled to keep close to the *Clifton,* were ordered into small boats as soon as the *Clifton* reached full speed in the channel. Once ashore, these picked men were to advance on the fort as skirmishers and keep the Southern gunners too busy to man their guns. These small boats, however, became stuck in the mud, and the men were prevented from going ashore by the mud flats, which trapped the few who tried to get ashore.

In his report, Weitzel furiously summarized why he and his men did not get more involved in the action:

> I was at the mouth of the Sabine Pass with seven transports. These carried 1,200 infantry that could be landed; 12 guns and 50 wagons that could not be landed. The enemy had a heavy battery of six guns, two gunboats, and a field battery within six miles, and was being rapidly reinforced. We had nothing to protect us except the fire from the guns on our transports, which would have been of little use against the enemy's gunboats. The enemy's battery commanded the whole landing, and he could, with his battery and gunboats, have destroyed us at any time. The remainder of my force was outside the bar in vessels, all of which had to be lightened, and at least three days would have been required to land it.

Weitzel embellished the facts. No other firsthand account of the battle mentions Confederate gunboats. No reinforcements reached the fort while its guns were firing.

Asst. Surgeon George H. Bailey, who well knew that his corps did not take an active role in battle, ignored convention. After his early arrival he pulled off his coat with its identifying insignia and soon—in Dowling's words—"was administering Magruder pills" to the enemy.

Skilled Rebel gunners and the oyster beds and the mud flats proved that overwhelmingly superior Federal firepower didn't necessarily mean much.

In less than forty minutes, the invasion of Texas ground to a halt. Those Union vessels still able to retire hurriedly withdrew. The plans to take Texas out of the Confederacy were scrapped.

Dick Dowling and his forty-three gunners captured two Federal gunboats and all aboard them, including the commander of the naval portion of the expedition. They damaged at least three other vessels and repelled the transports, which returned to New Orleans.

Sabine Pass was the most astonishing Confederate victory in Texas during the war. When Jefferson Davis was given an account of the brief but decisive action, he dubbed it "the Thermopolae of the West."

No accurate count of Federal casualties was ever made public. In addition to the capture of the naval commander and several hundred

The scene of the action of September 8, 1863. The radius of the circle is one mile.

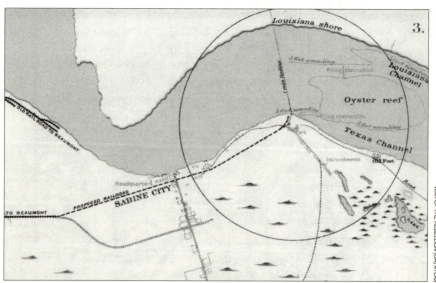

LESLIE, THE SOLDIER IN OUR CIVIL WAR

The two Union gunboats Clifton *(left) and* Sachem *(right) drew heavy fire from the guns at Fort Griffin (in the far background).* Clifton *escaped, but* Sachem *was captured.*

members of the attacking force, many of the seamen and sharp-shooters aboard the *Clifton* drowned.

In a lengthy letter to the president, Banks dismissed the loss of the two gunboats as "unimportant, except for their armament." Guns lost with the *Clifton* were of considerable importance, he admitted. In this letter, nothing was said about having thrown two hundred mules overboard to lighten the fleeing *Laurel Hill.* Neither did he mention having jettisoned two hundred thousand rations from the grounded *Crescent* in trying to get her afloat. Failure of the expedition, he insisted, was due solely to "the insufficient naval force with which the attempt was made."

Franklin's official report said two officers and seventy-five men aboard the *Clifton* were lost. In addition he knew of one officer and twenty-five men aboard the *Sachem* who did not return to New Orleans. Having no idea how many were killed or wounded or captured, Weitzel ignored simple arithmetic and solemnly wrote, "My total loss is, therefore, 3 officers and 94 men."

Raging at what he knew of the others' reports, Crocker asserted that the loss was entirely due to "army forces and their leaders." He demanded a formal court of inquiry. Adm. David G. Farragut went on record as believing that a court-martial was warranted; however, the demands upon the West Gulf Blockading Squadron were so great that "great inconvenience" would be caused by such a hearing. In Washington elaborate plans for the conquest of Texas were pushed aside and never revived.

Richmond's reaction was predictable. The Confederate Congress passed a formal resolution of thanks to Dowling and his men. According to the congressional document, the officers and forty-one enlisted personnel made a daring, gallant, and successful defense and defeated "a fleet of five gunboats and twenty-two steam transports that carried a land force of fifteen thousand men."

In the village of Sabine, jubilant citizens collected funds with which to commission the only Confederate medal to be awarded during the war. Known as the Davis Guard Medal, forty-one were made from Mexican silver dollars whose two sides were smoothed and engraved. These were awarded to the enlisted men. For the officers, two were cast in gold from jewelry and watches donated for the purpose. The letters D.G. and a Maltese cross were engraved on one side, and the other was inscribed: Sabine Pass / Sept. 8th / 1863. A presentation ceremony was held one year after the battle.

The forty-fourth medal was sent to Richmond and solemnly presented to Jefferson Davis—who wore it until his captors stripped it from him at Fort Monroe when he was imprisoned after the war. Ten years later Davis attended a session of the Texas State Fair. He was reportedly overwhelmed when the two surviving members of the Davis Guard presented him with a medal worn by one of their comrades until his death.

In one of the strangest battles of the Civil War, forty-three men stood off an assault force of seven thousand men. The odds were something like 163 to 1 in favor of the Federals. The mud walls of tiny Fort Griffin—and the mud flats of the Sabine River—withstood and repelled the attackers. No Confederate lives were lost.

PART 2

WAR ON THE WATER

5

THE CSS ALBERMARLE

A DOSE OF REBEL MEDICINE

WITH COASTAL NORTH CAROLINA under blockade and all but the port of Wilmington being virtually closed, desperate Southerners had to resort to unusual means to pursue any kind of shipbuilding program to counter the enemy gunboats and warships steaming in their waters. The Confederates awarded contracts for eighteen construction projects, including three to the firm of Gilbert Elliott and William Martin for two ironclads and a gunboat. Elliott and Martin set up shop in a former cornfield that was well inland, which was to keep the project beyond the raiding range of the Union navy. Elliott and Martin, however, managed to build only one of the ships, but it was a beauty and it was huge—at least by the standards of the day. With this ship, Southern sailors could attack Plymouth, North Carolina—a Union navy base—and from there the Confederates would be able to cruise up and down the coast, taking out enemy ships every day.

Before construction started, the vessel was named the CSS *Albemarle*. Naming of ships followed no pattern in either navy.

Many ordinary citizens thought that the pride and joy of their state should not have been named for an inlet of the Atlantic Ocean or for a small textile town. They much preferred grander names, such as *Raleigh* or *Charlotte* or *Greensboro.* By the time the general public of the state knew what was going on, however, it was too late for anyone to offer any opinion.

The cornfield in which the 158-foot vessel, a ram, was built was near Edwards Ferry on the Roanoke River. Initially the work was guided by John L. Porter, a naval architect and one of the three men involved in the design and construction of the CSS *Virginia.* Porter, however, lacked certain people skills and was replaced by Cmdr. James W. Cooke. One of Cooke's first tasks was the job of scouring the countryside for scrap iron, which was needed by the thousands of tons. One part of the *Albemarle* story, probably devised to rankle the Federals, was that the superintendent of construction, Gilbert Elliott, was a barely literate teenager.

As soon as the last big shipment of iron plate arrived and was bolted in place, the ship was given a lengthy formal inspection by Confederate Lt. Robert D. Minor and pronounced fit for duty. When floated on April 18, 1864, the vessel did not give the usual quiver when she hit the river. No wonder. Her timbers were select eight-by-eight-inch pine. She went into combat almost immediately.

The vessel's raised sixty-foot-long midships were plated with two layers of iron to a thickness of four inches. In addition to two 7-inch Brooke pivot guns, an immense iron-covered oak ram projected from the bow. Under special circumstances, this ancient armament was considered to be as formidable as the guns.

Big as she was, the iron-plated ram was driven by a pair of four-hundred-horsepower engines. Yet the most remarkable thing was that the ship could navigate in only six feet of water.

Union Gen. Benjamin F. Butler, in overall command in coastal North Carolina, knew that an ironclad was being completed by the enemy but gave her little thought. "I don't believe in ironclads," he noted in one of his dispatches.

Butler's attitude probably contributed to the success of the Rebel vessel in her first engagement. Although small, Federally occupied Plymouth, North Carolina, was an important port. She was noticed even in the Executive Mansion, where Lincoln turned

Construction of the 158-foot Albemarle *ironclad ram began in January 1863, but she was not commissioned until April 1864. Almost immediately the vessel went into action in the North Carolina sounds.*

down a plan for a massive strike in which the port would have played a significant role.

Gen. Robert E. Lee personally directed the Confederate ironclad to join forces with soldiers led by Robert F. Hoke and "liberate" Plymouth by driving away the Union garrison. Still hoping to regain control of the North Carolina coast, Jefferson Davis delegated the planning of the operation to Gen. Braxton Bragg, then his military advisor.

Bragg, whose views on ironclads in general were diametrically opposite to those of Butler, sent a coded telegram to Hoke in which he said: "After your forces plus the ram have captured Plymouth and opened the river, your attention should immediately be directed to New Berne and Washington."

The battle for Plymouth began about 4 P.M. on April 17. Union Gen. Henry W. Wessels had about three thousand foot soldiers and numerous batteries. His naval flotilla consisted of *Miami, Southfield, Whitehead,* and *Ceres.* From New Berne, Gen. John Peck wrote, "I feel entirely sanguine that the iron clad in the Roanoke [River] will be destroyed if she attacks Plymouth." His optimism was based in part on the knowledge that a very long and heavy boom had been built to prevent the Confederate ram's coming close to the town. A Southern

In her initial combat on April 19, 1864, Albemarle *was confronted by two Union gunboats. The Confederate ironclad sank one,* Southfield *(in the foreground above), and drove off the other,* Miami *(in the background).*

reconnaissance found that enough sunken vessels and other junk had been towed into the river to create a barrier that could only by breached during daylight hours. A large number of torpedoes—developed by the Southerners and called "infernal machines" by both sides—made the barrier extremely dangerous.

On the morning after the preliminary inspection of the river, it was found that unusually heavy rain had raised the water level nearly ten feet above the obstructions. Aboard the *Albemarle* Cooke rejoiced briefly then ordered battle stations and got under way. At about 3 A.M., as the ironclad neared Plymouth, two vessels showing no lights converged on her.

Cooke called for full speed and steamed directly toward the pair of ships that lay so near to one another that he correctly guessed that they had been lashed together with chains. They were the Union gunboats *Miami* and *Southfield.*

Albemarle gave *Miami* only a minor blow at her bow then immediately drove straight into *Southfield.* The Confederate's ram penetrated all the way to the ship's boilers.

Union sailors aboard *Miami* worked feverishly to separate from the sister vessel and watched it go to the bottom of the rain-swollen

river. Gunners opened fire on the Southern ship and scored numerous hits at very close range. Yet their impact didn't seem to damage
the enemy. One of the balls shattered against the slanted side of *Albemarle*, and fragments flew back into the gun crew aboard the *Miami*,
instantly killing Capt. Charles W. Flusser. Horrified and suddenly
frightened, the Yankee crew turned the vessel and withdrew downriver. For the remainder of that day, *Albemarle*'s pair of Brooke rifles
pounded at the Federal positions around Plymouth.

Confederate infantry struck simultaneously from two sides.
Moving slowly, *Albemarle*'s guns raked the enemy on both sides. A
Union officer recalled "the rebel ram had possession of the river,
thus enfilading the entrenchments right and left and exposing rear
of the garrison to merciless broadsides."

Surrender of the port at 10 A.M. ended what many have dubbed
"the most successful of many Confederate combined operations in
which military and naval forces cooperated, always under military top
command."

The huge *Albemarle* returned to its anchorage, about eight miles
above Plymouth. Meanwhile, in Washington the Southern ironclad
became the subject of several high-level consultations. All agreed that
the ship had to be taken out of commission—and soon. Although she
had not yet begun to prowl the waterways in search of Federal shipping to destroy, she had already proved to be a significant threat.

The skipper of USS Miami *(below), Capt. Charles W.
Flusser (left), was killed in the action against the*
Albemarle. *He was with the gunners at the
front-mounted 9-inch Dahlgren. Pieces from
the third shell fired at the Southern ship flew
back into the gun crew; Flusser was struck in
the chest. His ship withdrew.*

Union commanders set out to destroy the Confederate ironclad. In their first attempt, they tried to demolish the vessel near its dock. Five crewmen—coxswain John W. Loyd, firemen Allen Crawford and John Laverty, and coal heavers Benjamin Loyd and Charles Baldwin—from USS *Wyalusing* volunteered to mine the waterway in front of the ironclad.

Toward sunset on May 25 the party ascended the Middle River to its near junction with the Roanoke. They carried the torpedoes on litters across the swamps to the river. Their explosives were to be laid near the bow of *Albemarle* and another ship, *Crawford*, then the men were to swim back to the swamps from where they could detonate the ordnance.

All went as planned until just before the torpedoes were to be fixed in place. A line fouled a patroling schooner, and a lookout saw the swimmers and opened fire on them. Abandoning their torpedoes to save their lives, the Federals made it to dry ground and safety—but *Albemarle* was undamaged.

More alarmed than ever when told of the fiasco, Rear Adm. Samuel P. Lee, who headed the North Atlantic Blockading Squadron, dispatched seven gunboats—*Mettabesett, Sassacus, Wyalusing, Miami, Whitehead, Commodore Hull,* and *Ceres*—under Capt. Melancton Smith to the waters off the mouth of the Roanoke River. When the

In action late in the day on May 5, 1864, the Union gunboat Sassacus *rammed the* Albemarle. *The collision did more damage to the Federal ship than the Rebel ironclad.*

Confederate ram next emerged into the Atlantic, the Federals were waiting for it. The inevitable happened on May 5, 1864.

While *Miami* and several gunboats attacked and occupied the attention of *Albemarle, Sassacus* seemed to pursue one of the iron-clad's accompanying vessels but then veered suddenly and rammed *Albermarle* very hard on her starboard side. With the vessels inter-locked, gunners traded shots at point-blank range.

Fifty-four shots from Smith's flotilla bounced harmlessly off the side of the Rebel ram, but a single shot from *Albemarle* blew up the boiler of the *Sassacus.* Soon engulfed in clouds of steam, many aboard the badly wounded vessel jumped into the water. Action for the day ended then and there. The Confederate ram withdrew and returned to its dock on the river, and the Federals acted to prevent *Sassacus* from going to the bottom. The captain of the wounded Union ship pronounced *Albemarle* more dangerous than either of the two most notorious Confederate ironclads, *Atlanta* and *Virginia,* but scoffed at the notion that his appraisal meant little, "coming from the mouth of a poor loser."

On July 5 Lt. William B. Cushing was called to Hampton Roads. He had distinguished himself in at least two battles and was considered capable of undertaking a dangerous mission. He also submitted two proposals for dispatching *Albemarle.* In a meeting with several officers in the headquarters of the North Atlantic Blockading Squadron, he was first offered their condolences for the loss of his brother during the battle of Gettysburg. Then Cushing was told that his proposal to attack the Confederate ship with torpedo launches had been approved.

From Virginia, Cushing hurried to New York to secure the neces-sary equipment. Finally he located two steam launches with nearly noiseless motors and, with a band of handpicked men, departed New York for North Carolina. Along the way he lost one of his tiny vessels near Chesapeake Bay, but he continued on in the remaining boat. Half-jokingly, Cushing told his tiny crew that they would soon give the Confederate behemoth "a little dose of Rebel medicine," refer-ring to the fact that spar torpedoes and torpedo launches were a Southern innovation. Once Cushing arrived in position, he waited for a dark night on which to launch his attack.

About midnight on October 28 the tiny steam launch reached the mouth of the Roanoke River; her objective lay about eight miles

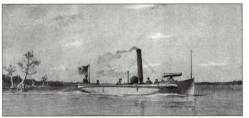

To destroy the Albemarle, *Lt. William B.
Cushing (right) proposed that torpedo
launches attack the Confederate ironclad at
its moorings. With the approval of the navy,
Cushing obtained two steam-powered picket
boats and fitted each with a 12-pounder
howitzer and a side-mounted torpedo boom. Only
one (above) survived the trip to North Carolina.*

ahead. Reducing speed so as to eliminate noise and light from the
motor, which he covered with a tarpaulin, Cushing pursued his
objective despite a sudden heavy storm.

At a point about two hundred yards from the *Albermarle,* a dog
on shore began barking loudly. The element of surprise had been
compromised. Moving directly forward, with speed now greatly
increased, the attackers soon saw that heavy logs, bound together by
chains, were being used to form a thick protective boom around the
Confederate vessel.

The Federal raiders drew close enough to see that their little boat
could not penetrate that boom. Cushing swept around in a wide
curve, then headed toward the boom at full speed. He desperately
hoped it had been there long enough to accumulate a heavy coat of
slime, which formed very rapidly in these waters. Hitting it with the
bow of his vessel very high, he gambled that his light craft would skid
and slide over the top.

It was, after all, a suicide mission, as he had carefully explained
to his men. When his small boat hit the logs at full speed and went
over, Cushing realized that he was within ten feet of his target. He
quickly yanked a tripwire that lowered the spar torpedo, steered it
against the side of the Confederate ship, and detonated it. The
explosion blew a lethal hole in the *Albemarle*'s hull. A resulting
geyser of water swamped Cushing's boat, and the Federals took to

HARPER'S PICTORIAL HISTORY OF THE GREAT REBELLION

On the night of October 27–28, 1864, Cushing and seven volunteers attacked and sent the Albemarle *to the bottom of the Roanoke River. The vessel was later salvaged by the Federals.*

the river. Two or three drowned. Except for Cushing and a single unidentified sailor, the others were quickly captured.

For three days Cushing hid in the swamps, but with the help of a local freedman, he managed to find a Union ship.

From Washington he received the rare Thanks of Congress. His portion of the prize money awarded for the sinking of *Albemarle* was sixty-five thousand dollars. At the same time, he was promoted to lieutenant commander.

Postwar evaluations indicate wide approval of these actions. Adm. David G. Farragut commented to Gideon Welles, the secretary of the navy, "While no navy in the world had better or braver officers than ours, young Cushing was the hero of the war."

Writing in 1884, naval historian James Russell Soley observed:

When it is reflected that Cushing had attached to his person four separate lines—the detaching lanyard, the trigger line, and two lines that directed all movements of the boat, one of which was fastened to an ankle and the other to a wrist; that he was also directing the adjustment of the spar by the halliard; that the management of all these lines, requiring as much exactness and delicacy as a surgical operation, where a single error in their employment, even a pull too much or too little, would render the whole expedition abortive, was carried out directly in the muzzle of a 100-pounder rifle, under a fire of musketry so intense that several bullets passed through his

LIBRARY OF CONGRESS

The Albemarle *was refloated after Plymouth, North Carolina, was occupied by Union troops. The vessel was taken to Norfolk Navy Yard. She remained there until she was sold in 1867.*

clothing—with the expedition carried out with perfect success—it is safe to say that the naval history of the world affords no other example of such marvelous coolness and professional skill as were shown by Cushing in the destruction of the *Albermarle.*

Once more, a David had vanquished a Goliath.

6

ALABAMA VERSUS HATTERAS

A THIRTEEN-MINUTE VICTORY

ON THE AFTERNOON OF January 11, 1863, the USS *Hatteras* steamed out of Galveston's harbor to seek the identity of a ship that could just barely be seen on the horizon. Twenty miles out and too late to go back, Union lookouts identified the unknown vessel as the CSS *Alabama*. The Confederate ship was lying in wait for the *Hatteras*, which was an approach differing from Capt. Raphael Semmes's usual tactic of flying a false flag to draw his quarry in and then raising the Confederate colors.

Semmes was born in 1809 in Maryland and must have been a likable and charismatic character or he might have been hanged for his shenanigans. He was one of those rare individuals possessed of a daring and keen sense of humor that entertained others rather than evoked their censure.

He began his naval career as a midshipman at the age of seventeen. Ten years later Semmes was a lieutenant and subsequently served as an aide on the staff of Gen. William Worth during the

Mexican War. During his ten years before the mast he studied for the bar and became a lawyer. The only interesting duty he pulled in the prewar years was on the navy's Lighthouse Board, however. On February 5, 1861, he resigned his commission after Alabama seceded from the Union.

His first command was the CSS *Sumter*, distinguishing his service to the South as something approaching a pirate by steaming against the enemy's commerce ships in the West Indies in 1861. The Confederate secretary of the navy, Stephen R. Mallory, described the task as commerce raiding. By attacking Northern shipping, Mallory hoped to turn New England's maritime industry against the Lincoln administration. To accomplish that, the South needed several commerce-raiding ships, but the primary shipbuilding ports in the South were all but bottled up by the Northern blockade. So Mallory sent a select group of men to Europe to have the necessary ships built abroad.

It seemed a fairly simple thing to do as long as there was money to pay for it and no international laws were broken. Execution of the task, however, was anything but simple, and each project became

The CSS Sumter *was a converted merchant ship purchased by the Confederate government in April 1861. It was the first commerce raider, and in its only year of service, under the command of Raphael Semmes, the ship took eighteen prizes.*

something of a clandestine operation. British law forbade assistance to a belligerent nation. Mallory's people stayed within the limits of the law; the ships they had built did not have armament—that was added later. Of course the U.S. ambassador protested vehemently that the spirit of the law was being broken, and Federal warships frequently appeared whenever one of the Southern ships was scheduled to launch.

Nevertheless, a handful of commerce raiders were built in Great Britain. Construction of the CSS *Alabama,* christened the *Enrica* but also known as Hull No. 290, was completed at the Laird shipyard in Liverpool in May 1862. She was 211 feet long, 32 feet wide at maximum width, drew 14 feet of water, and was equally adept at sailing or steaming with a screw propulsion system. A device called a "condenser," which was really a distillery that converted salt to fresh water, was among her strengths in terms of staying at sea for prolonged time periods.

After building the ship, the next great task was getting the ship out of Liverpool, recruiting a crew, and equipping her with supplies and guns. Escaping the watchful eye of the USS *Tuscarora,* Capt.

Semmes's successful cruise with the Sumter *led to his receiving command of the CSS* Alabama, *one of the first British-built cruisers. Her two-year career commenced on August 24, 1862, and she captured sixty-four U.S. merchantmen.*

Matthew J. Butcher and a crew of Englishmen and Irishmen steamed from Liverpool under the cover of bad weather with a destination of Terceira in the Azores off the coast of Portugal. If the vessel were stopped at sea or near the Azores, there was really only one Confederate aboard, and he was instructed to say that he was the purser of a private ship.

A second ship, the *Agrippina,* was scheduled to rendezvous with the rogue ship at Terceira and to supply her with everything except men. A third ship, the *Bahama,* carrying Semmes and some officers and crewmen, was to also join them there. Semmes hired many men from the European crew, but many were reluctant to join the ship's company without an increase in pay. All of this was accomplished by August 20, 1862. As soon as Semmes took command, he renamed the vessel *Alabama* after his adopted state.

The next several days were spent breaking in the ship, caulking leaks, finishing the mounting of the guns, and taking other steps designed to make it seaworthy. On the fifth day out, a ship was spotted and Semmes raised a Spanish flag. A couple of days later he showed French colors to a Portuguese brig.

No one could better describe the beginning days of this campaign than Semmes himself. Although this is a lengthy quotation, it's but a snippet of his chronicle. At the time the word "parole" defined a prisoner who signed an agreement stating that he would not bear arms against the Confederacy for the balance of the war. In return for his parole, the prisoner was freed.

Friday, September 5.—Cloudy, with the wind light from the eastward. Soon after daylight gave chase to a brig which outsailed us, and soon afterwards made a ship, which we soon discovered to be lying to, with her fore-topsail to the mast. As we approached, discovered her to be a whaler. Hoisted the English colors, which was returned by the ship hoisting United States colors. Having come within boarding distance, sent a boat on board and brought the captain on board with his papers, hoisting our own colors as the boarding officer got alongside. She proved to be the ship *Ocmulgee,* of Edgartown, the captain being a genuine specimen of a Yankee, Abraham Osborn. Captured her and brought the crew on board, and a quantity of rigging of which we were in need, and some beef and pork, and small stores. At 9 P.M. hove her to, with a light at the peak, and brought

U.S. NAVAL HISTORICAL CENTER

Raphael Semmes (foreground) and his executive officer, John McIntosh Kell, were photographed aboard the Alabama *during a stopover at Cape Town, South Africa.*

away our own officer and crew, and lay by her during the night. Number of prisoners, 37.

Saturday, September 6.—Cloudy, clearing off fine toward night. At 9, having descried a bark, set fire to the prize, and gave chase. At meridian came up with and showed the United States colors to the chase, which proved to be a Frenchman bound to Marseilles. Kept away N. 1/2 W., and in a couple of hours afterwards made the island of Flores ahead. A beautiful night.

Sunday, September 7.—A fine, clear day, clouding towards evening. Running in for the island of Flores. At 11 A.M. mustered the crew for the first time, and caused to be read the articles of war, to which the crew listened with great attention. At 3:30 P.M., having approached sufficiently near the town of Lagens, on the south side of the island, we sent all the prisoners on shore (having first paroled them) in the three whaleboats belonging to the prize *Ocmulgee;* and at 4, filled away on the starboard tack to head off a schooner that appeared to be running in for the island. Having approached her within a mile, we hoisted the English colors. The chase not showing her colors in return, fired the lee bow gun. Still paying no attention to us, but endeavoring to pass us, fired a shot

The battle between the Alabama *and the USS* Hatteras *took place approximately thirty miles from Galveston, Texas.*

HARPER'S PICTORIAL HISTORY OF THE GREAT REBELLION

athwart her bow. Not yet heaving to, or showing colors, fired a second shot between her fore and main masts. She then hoisted the American colors, and rounded to. Sent a boat on board, and took possession of her. The captain coming on board with his papers, she proved to be the *Starlight,* of Boston, from Fayal to Boston, via Flores. She had a number of passengers, among others some ladies. Put a prize crew on board of her, brought on board all the United States seamen, seven in number, including the captain, and confined them in irons; and ordered the prize to remain close to us during the night. Some dark clouds hanging over the island, but the wind light and the sea smooth. Among the papers captured were a couple of dispatches to the Sewards, father and son, informing them of our operations at Terceira. This small craft left Boston only six days before we left Liverpool in the *Bahama.* How strangely parties meet upon the high seas. The master was the cleverest specimen of a Yankee skipper I have met; about 27 or 28. He avowed his intention of trying to run the gauntlet of my shot, deprecated the war, etc.

Monday, September 8.—Weather fine, with the wind from the southward and eastward. At 7 A.M. stood in to the town of Santa Cruz [island of Flores] in company with the prize, and lowered the cutter and sent the prisoners on shore, with a note addressed to the governor. In the meantime the governor himself, with several citizens, came on board of us. The governor offered us the hospitalities of the island, etc., and in return I expressed to him the hope that his fellow-citizens who were passengers on board the prize had suffered no inconvenience from her capture. In the afternoon gave chase and showed English colors to a Portuguese brigantine. We then wore ship and chased a bark in the N.W., with which we came up about sunset. She proved to be the whaling bark *Ocean Rover,* from Massachusetts, forty months out, with a cargo of 1,100 barrels of oil. Laid her to for the night, and permitted the captain and his crew to pull in to the shore [Flores] in his six whaleboats, the sea being smooth, the wind light offshore, and the moon near her full. This was a novel night procession.

With her two prizes at her side, the next morning started with similar maneuvers for the *Alabama.* A large barge was spotted nearby, and an English flag was hoisted. When the vessel failed to respond, a blank was fired. The barge showed U.S. colors and was captured.

From August 24, 1862, to January 4, 1863, Semmes captured twenty-six ships and paroled 492 prisoners. Of those ships, five were released on ransom bond, meaning that the captain, on behalf of the ship's and cargo's owners, agreed to pay a certain sum to the Confederacy within thirty days of the end of the war. Semmes resorted to this whenever it was impractical to detail a prize crew from his men to sail the ship to a friendly port with a prize court, where the ship and cargo could be sold.

Similar in size to the *Alabama,* the *Hatteras* was a side-wheel steamer that had been purchased by the Union navy in 1861 and converted from a passenger ship into a ship of war. During her first year of service, she was credited with capturing fourteen blockade-runners. When the Confederates took and occupied Galveston, *Hatteras* was ordered to rendezvous with four other Federal ships near the city.

In the early afternoon of January 11, *Alabama* was cruising off the coast of Galveston and Semmes was trying to determine the strength of the Federal fleet in the area. When the Confederate ship was spotted, *Hatteras* gathered steam to investigate the appearance of the unknown vessel.

Noting that he had attracted the attention of a Federal ship, Semmes ordered that his ship's propeller be lowered and that the boilers be fired so that he too would have steam power with which to maneuver. Over the next few hours, while tracking the *Hatteras*'s slow approach, Semmes gradually nudged his ship out to sea, trying to get far enough away from shore so that the engagement would be delayed until after nightfall and his guns would not be heard in the harbor.

As he approached the unidentified steamer, Lt. Cmdr. Homer C. Blake, the Federal ship's captain, suspected that she might be the infamous *Alabama* and ordered his men to battle stations. It was after dark, around 7 P.M., when the ships were within hailing distance.

When asked to identify his ship, Semmes responded that the Confederate raider was a British vessel, the merchant steamer *Petrel.* He inquired what ship the other was but could not understand the reply. The response did not make much difference since he knew she was a Federal warship.

Blake ordered a boat to be lowered for a boarding party of six to inspect the other ship, but before they reached their destination the first lieutenant of the suspect vessel called out the ship's true identity, and in the same moment *Alabama*'s guns opened on the *Hatteras*.

Both ships maintained a rapid fire for thirteen minutes, and then the battle was over. *Hatteras* had received fatal wounds at her waterline.

The Alabama *approached Galveston on January 11, 1863, and noted five blockading ships nearby. When the ship was seen, the* Hatteras *was dispatched to investigate. Semmes avoided the vessel until night fell, then turned on her.*

U.S. NAVAL HISTORICAL CENTER

The Confederate gunners fired a broadside at point-blank range that tore huge holes into the hull of the Federal ship. The vessel surrendered in sinking condition, and Semmes rescued survivors.

The Federal captain ordered a gun to be fired and a light to be shown as evidence of his defeat. Semmes immediately offered assistance and lowered some boats to ferry the men of the sinking ship to safety. The Confederates considered searching for the Federals' small boat with the boarding party but felt that it would be difficult to find it in the dark; they would make it to safety without any help.

While Blake surrendered his sword, Semmes welcomed him aboard and offered to make his stay as comfortable as possible. Blake and John M. Kell, the executive officer of the *Alabama,* had worked together prior to the war, and their reunion increased the warmth of his reception.

Only one had been wounded aboard the Confederate ship, but the Union ship had suffered two killed and five wounded, one severely. In a report filed by Edward S. Mathews, a U.S. naval surgeon, it was noted, "Although destitute—owing to the rapid sinking of the *Hatteras*—of all medical stores, and even of sufficient covering for the wounded, yet no difficulty was experienced in their proper treatment. An ample supply of medicines and surgical appliances was placed at my disposal for the use of the sick and wounded of the *Hatteras* by the medical officers of the *Alabama.*"

The 108 men of the sunken vessel were placed in irons, but the 18 officers were allowed free access to the ship. Encumbered by so many captives, Semmes cruised to Jamaica where all were paroled and given their freedom. Also put ashore was a Confederate sailor who had been accused of drunkenness and theft. Unfortunately, he was also knowledgeable of the Confederate shipbuilding enterprise in England. In time the Federals found him, and he disclosed everything he knew. Thus Semmes's victory over the *Hatteras,* in a way, affected his government's overseas shipbuilding enterprise as well as the commerce-raiding program.

7

The Hunley and the Housatonic

DEATH TO THE VICTOR

THE 107-FOOT-LONG USS *Housatonic* was armed with eleven guns, including a 100-pounder Parrot rifle and an 11-inch Dahlgren. It was sunk on February 17, 1864, by the tiny 30-foot-long *Hunley*, a submersible ship only four feet wide and five feet tall. The nine men within this new-fangled "submarine propeller" with a spar torpedo at her bow may have suspected that they would never return to land.

The word "submarine" as applied to an underwater vessel or ship was not in use at the time of the Civil War even though experiments had been conducted with such craft as early as the Revolutionary War. Thus in the parlance of the records of the war one finds reference to the 47-foot-long USS *Alligator* as a "submarine propeller," and Confederate naval records refer to the *Hunley* as a "submarine torpedo boat" as well as a "submarine propeller."

In New Orleans, early in the war, James McClintock and Baxter Watson undertook the task of building a submarine torpedo boat to go against the Federal blockade of the Mississippi. With expenses straining their resources, they allowed Horace Hunley and others to join them in late 1861. The boat made it past its first stage of development in the calm waters of Lake Pontchartrain. It could submerge and surface and slowly move forward while on or below the surface of the water. Concurrent with these successful tests, the Federals took advantage of an opportunity and seized New Orleans. The submarine was scuttled, and Watson, McClintock, and Hunley headed for Mobile to renew their efforts to build an underwater weapon.

Maj. Gen. Dabney Maury assisted the three in finding an appropriate machine shop, Park and Lyons, and additional manpower was supplied by the Twenty-first Alabama Regiment, already working there on other projects. Lts. George Dixon and William A. Alexander, both engineers of the Twenty-first Alabama, were assigned to supervise the construction work.

The first attempt to recreate the vessel destroyed in New Orleans was an iron boat about twenty-five feet long, six feet high, five feet wide, and tapered at both ends. She was towed to Fort Morgan for a test, but rough weather sank her before she could be manned for the first trial run.

The workers at Park and Lyons began work on another boat. This time an iron boiler provided the basis for their creation. About twenty-five feet long and about four feet in diameter, it was split into half-cylinders that were worked and tapered separately into the final form. Then the pieces were joined and riveted together. This craft was dubbed the *H. L. Hunley.* Hatches were placed on both fore and aft sections, and viewing portals were set into the raised area around the hatches and eight tiny skylights were set in the top half of the hull as a means of providing outside light.

This side-view drawing of the Hunley *was prepared from sketches made by Lt. William A. Alexander, one of the men who directed her construction.*

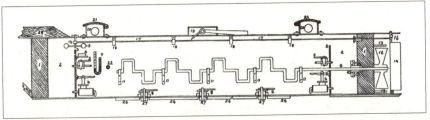

According to Lieutenant Alexander, "Two men experienced in handling the boat, and seven others composed the crew. The first officer steered and handled the boat forward, and the second attended to the after-tank and pumps and the air supply, all hands turning on the cranks except the first officer. There was just sufficient room for these two to stand in their places with their heads in the hatchways and take observations through the lights of the combings."

Alexander further described the operation of the *Hunley:*

> All hands aboard and ready, they would fasten the hatch covers down tight, light a candle [to monitor the amount of air within the vessel], then let the water in from the sea into the ballast tanks until the top of the shell was about three inches under water. This could be seen by the water lever showing through the glasses in the hatch combings. The seacocks were then closed and the boat put under way. The captain would then lower the lever and depress the forward end of the fins very slightly, noting on the mercury gauge the depth of the boat beneath the surface; then bring the fins to a level; the boat would remain and travel at that depth. To rise to a higher level in the water he would raise the lever and elevate the forward end of the fins, and the boat would rise to its original position in the water.

In the calm waters of Mobile Bay the *Hunley* looked impressive as it dove under an old ship and towed a floating torpedo into the target vessel. In the rougher waters of the Gulf it did not fair so well. The dragging torpedo had a mind of its own at the maximum speed of four miles an hour, and no one could be certain what ship would be hit.

This top view depicts the placement of the crew along the starboard side of the craft and also highlights the diving planes.

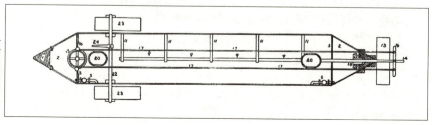

By the summer of 1863 it was decided that the craft could best serve the South in Charleston rather than Mobile. So the *Hunley* was loaded onto flatcars and transported to South Carolina.

At the same time the prototype of a new kind of torpedo boat was being developed with the encouragement of Confederate Gen. P. G. T. Beauregard. This was a steam-powered boat that lay low in the water and carried a crew of four and a spar torpedo. The torpedo was rammed against the side of an enemy vessel and detonated. Its small size and large mission lent the prototype and subsequent vessels like it to be named after its biblical counterpart, *David.*

In a paper published in the Southern Historical Society Papers in 1878, Beauregard described the inequities that existed between the defenders and the Federal blockaders at Charleston. In particular he described the October 5, 1863, attack on the *New Ironsides:*

> Shortly after this bold attempt of Captain [J. C.] Carlin, in the summer of 1863, to blow up the *New Ironsides,* Mr. Theodore Stoney, Dr. Ravenel, and other gentlemen of Charleston, had built a small cigar-shaped boat which they called the "David." It had been specially planned and constructed to attack this much-dreaded naval Goliath, the *New Ironsides.* It was about twenty feet long, with a diameter of five feet at its middle, and was propelled by a small screw worked by a diminutive engine. As soon as ready for service, I caused it to be fitted with a "Lee spar-torpedo" charged with seventy-five pounds of powder. Commander W. T. Glassell, a brave and enterprising officer of the Confederate States Navy, took charge of it, and about eight o'clock one hazy night, on the ebb tide, with a crew of one engineer, J. H. Tomb; one fireman, James Sullivan; and a pilot, J. W. Cannon; he fearlessly set forth from Charleston on his perilous mission—the destruction of the *New Ironsides.* I may note that this ironclad steamer threw a great deal more metal, at each broadside, than all the monitors together of the fleet; her fire was delivered with more rapidity and accuracy, and she was the most effective vessel employed in the reduction of Battery Wagner.

The *David* rammed its target at 9 P.M. that night, with the torpedo about six feet under water. Tomb, the engineer aboard the Confederate craft, offered this account:

The torpedo exploded, and the big frigate was shaken from stem to stern, but the explosion produced a bad effect on the *David*. The volume of water thrown up, passing down the smokestack, put out the fires and filled the body of the boat, as well as disabled the engine. Lieutenant Glassell then gave orders for each man to look after himself, and we all went overboard. Lieutenant Glassell was picked up by a transport schooner, Sullivan by the *Ironsides,* and Canners [Cannon], who could not swim, stuck to the *David*. I swam some distance down the harbor; but finding that my clothing was impeding my progress, and looking back and seeing that the *David* was still afloat, I concluded to return and try to save her. After getting aboard I adjusted the machinery, started up the fires once more, and, helping the pilot aboard, proceeded up the harbor, turning between the *Ironsides* and a Monitor to prevent them from using their heavy guns on us in passing. The *Ironsides* fired three shots from her heavy guns, which passed over us.

Although the *New Ironsides* was not sunk, enough structural damage was sustained that she was retired from Charleston Harbor

Charleston boat builders devised these small four-man steam-powered torpedo launches, known as Davids, to drive off the Union blockading fleet. Although the first of these to attempt such a mission succeeded in damaging one of the premiere vessels of the Federal fleet, subsequent successes were very rare. Thus the Hunley *was brought to South Carolina to try where these had failed.*

During trial runs in Charleston Harbor, the Hunley *sank several times. At least thirty-two men lost their lives trying to master control of the craft in the active waters. The high number of deaths brought the craft the moniker "the peripatetic coffin." One of those killed was H. L. Hunley, one of the vessel's designers and the namesake of the boat.*

for repairs. The concept of the *David* had been a good one, and Beauregard welcomed the addition of the *Hunley* to his arsenal of torpedo boats.

The *Hunley*'s shape caused it to be given the nickname of "the fish torpedo boat." Confederate naval Lt. J. A. Payne was given charge of the vessel, and she was manned by a crew of navy volunteers. Their target was to be the *New Ironsides.*

While moored to the steamer *Etiwan* at the wharf at Fort Johnston, the steamer pulled away and dragged the smaller ship on its side. The hatches were open and the little *Hunley* quickly filled with water and sank. Five men were lost on the submarine, but three escaped, including Payne. Beauregard reported that two had drowned in the mishap; William Alexander claimed that six had perished. Alexander also claimed that a previous swamping of the vessel in Charleston Harbor had taken eight lives.

The submarine was raised. On September 21, 1863, H. L. Hunley and a former crew that had served the vessel in Mobile took over the refitting. One of the men was Lt. George Dixon.

Originally, "the fish boat" was designed to tow a floating torpedo into a target vessel by diving beneath the vessel and resurfacing on the other side. On October 15, 1863, Hunley (substituting for Dixon) successfully made several dives under the naval receiving ship at anchor in Charleston Harbor; however, after a few dives the craft failed to surface. All aboard were lost.

Again the small vessel was raised. The scene inside the boat, however, was a tormented tableau of death. Beauregard described it: "When the boat was discovered, raised and opened, the spectacle was indescribably ghastly; the unfortunate men were contorted into all kinds of horrible attitudes; some clutching candles, evidently endeavoring to force open the man-holes; others lying in the bottom tightly grappled together, and the blackened faces of all presented the expression of their despair and agony."

William Alexander also described the scene:

> The boat, when found, was lying on the bottom at an angle of about 35 degrees, the bow deep in the mud. The holding-down bolts of each cover had been removed. When the hatch covers were lifted considerable air and gas escaped. Captain Hunley's body was forward, with his head in the forward hatchway, his right hand on top of his head (he had been trying, it would seem, to raise the hatch cover). In his left hand was a candle that had never been lighted, the seacock on the forward end, or Hunley's ballast tank, was wide open, the cock-wrench not on the plug, but lying on the bottom of the boat. Mr. Parks' body was found with his head in the after hatchway, his right hand above his head. He also had been trying to raise his hatch cover, but the pressure was too great. The seacock to his tank was nearly empty. The other bodies were floating in the water. Hunley and Parks were undoubtedly asphyxiated, the others drowned. The bolts that held the iron keel ballast had been partially turned, but not sufficient to release it.

After Alexander and Dixon directed the reconditioning of the *Hunley,* they could only get permission from Beauregard to ask for volunteers for a new crew, but the general ordered that the vessel could not dive again. Too many lives had been lost. Beauregard instead authorized it to be used as a torpedo boat, much like the *David.*

It was a seven-mile walk from the crew's quarters in Mount Pleasant to Battery Marshall where the vessel was moored. Four days a week the crew would journey to the battery, decide on a likely target, put the spar torpedo in place, and go out toward the chosen victim until conditions forced them back to land. Then they removed the torpedo and walked back to Mount Pleasant. The basic problem was that the intended targets were too far away, usually about twelve miles, and the men—who had to operate a crank propeller—would get exhausted long before they could reach their destination.

In spite of Beauregard's prohibition that the boat not submerge again, Dixon and Alexander experimented with her as a submarine, once keeping her down for two and a half hours.

On February 5, 1864, Alexander received orders to return to Mobile and begin work on a breechloading repeating gun. He was disappointed that he had to abandon work on the submarine, but the reassignment spared his life.

George Dixon remained in Charleston as captain of the *Hunley.*

On the night of February 17, Dixon and his crew of eight set out to attack the USS *Housatonic,* which was the closest Federal ship outside of Charleston Harbor. The attack was successful. A hole was blown into her side and she sank quickly, but the *H. L. Hunley* was never seen again until more than 131 years later, when the wreck was discovered in 1995. The small boat was raised in August 2000.

In a letter from Capt. M. M. Gray of the Office of Submarine Defenses to Maj. Gen. Dabney Maury regarding the loss of the *H. L. Hunley* and her crew, five sailors and one soldier were named as crewmen with George Dixon. That letter leads us to believe that only seven men were aboard when the boat struck the *Housatonic,* but the excavation of the recovered submarine proves that the submarine's last mission was undertaken with a full complement.

The experience aboard the *Housatonic* described by Acting Ens. Edward A. Butler:

> The night of February 17, 1864, was clear and very cold for the latitude of Charleston, S.C. The "Housatonic" was lying at anchor in six fathoms of water off Beech Inlet, near the extreme north end of the line of the blockading fleet. Captain Taylor had been succeeded in command by Captain Charles W. Pickering of Portsmouth, N.H., a tall, fine looking officer, with many years of naval experience. He was said to be one of the handsomest men in the service.
>
> A fresh north-westerly breeze was blowing, and the ship was heading toward the inlet. I had returned from deck duty in the second dog watch, and near nine o'clock was reading aloud to such as were present in our room, when the sharp roll of the drum, calling

WAR OF THE REBELLION (ONR)

The 1,930-ton Ossipee-class steam screw sloop of war Housatonic *was the victim of the first successful submarine attack in history. Union casualties in the action were five lost, mostly because the water was shallow and the masts of the sunken ship remained above the surface. H. L.* Hunley, *however, did not return to port until 136 years later, when the vessel was recovered from the ocean floor.*

"all hands to quarters," disturbed our pastime. Seizing my side arms I rushed on deck with others, and made my way forward toward my station, which was the command of the thirty-pounder Parrott gun, near the bow of the ship. Before I could reach the place, the cause of the summons appeared. Through information from refugees, and from other sources, we were aware that the rebels were trying every device for destroying the ships, and at this time great caution and unusual vigilance was being maintained for our own preservation. Double lookouts, fore and aft, were kept day and night, with an officer on the bridge, and another on the forecastle. On the evening named, the officer forward reported to the officer of the deck a suspicious looking object, apparently drifting out with the wind and tide in our direction. It appeared at first like a snag or drift log, thirty or forty feet long, with a slight projection above it, about a third of the way from the end. Ordinarily this would have excited no particular attention, but it was promptly reported to the captain, who gave the order "All hands to quarters." The alarm by drum beat must have been heard on board the torpedo boat, for such it proved to be, as its speed quickened, and it moved rapidly toward us, and was soon along our starboard side, too close for the depressing of our broadside guns to be worked in the short interval. A few musket shots were fired at the object, but without apparent damage. This unwelcome visitor steered for our magazine, but having too much headway the point of contact came under our starboard quarter, and the torpedo, being evidently exploded by concussion, sent the whole stern of the ship flying into the air for a hundred feet or more, in a dense smothered column of smoke, water and wreckage. Our chains were slipped, and the engines had made a few revolutions astern, when this occurred.

The ship had just returned from Port Royal, and was heavily laden with coal and stores. She sank like a stone, as rapidly as she could fill, with her stem entirely gone. Fortunately we were in shoal water, but for this fact I should probably not be here tonight, giving you an account of one of the most exciting incidents of my life in the United States Navy.

As the ship went to the bottom, she rested quietly on her port bilge, her masts at an angle of forty-five degrees, the hull entirely submerged. One of the cutters on the starboard side was hanging to the davits, and remained so that it could be cleared for use. As the ship began sinking, many were thrown into the water, and others most distant from the explosion climbed into the fore rigging, myself being among the latter.

There was very little excitement, or apparent confusion, arising from this sudden change in our plans and daily habits. We at first thought our boilers might explode, and that many must be killed and drowned as a natural result. The boat spoken of was soon afloat, and with it was picked up our captain, who had been thrown into the water from the bridge, and was considerably cut about the head, and other officers and men, who were overboard, were rescued from drowning. The boat, with the captain, was then dispatched to the USS "Canandaigua," a vessel of the same class as our own, and the nearest to us, about a mile and a half distant. As we lay to the windward of her, and the explosion being deadened by the volume of water, no one outside of our own company had seen or heard anything of the disaster which had overtaken us.

The death toll for the *Housatonic* was low; only five men were killed in the explosion. It was, nonetheless, a great victory for all defending Charleston except for those brave men who had gone down aboard the *Hunley*.

8

HAMPTON ROADS

THE BATTLE THAT COULDN'T BE WON

N O OTHER BATTLE OF the Civil War had a greater influence on the future of naval design and construction around the globe than the duel between the *Monitor* and the *Virginia,* also known as the *Merrimack,* at Hampton Roads on March 9, 1862. For four hours the two ironclad warships pounded each other at close range to no avail. No significant damage was inflicted to either ship.

Months earlier, on May 8, 1861, the newly appointed Confederate secretary of the navy, Stephen R. Mallory, wrote: "I regard the possession of an iron-armored ship as a matter of the first necessity. Such a vessel at this time could traverse the entire coast of the United States, prevent all blockades, and encounter, with a fair prospect of success, their entire navy."

In the summer of 1861 the Confederate navy moved ahead in designing and building such a vessel. The work occurred at the Gosport Navy Yard near Norfolk and was completed eight months later. The hull of the USS *Merrimack,* which had been scuttled and sunk by the Federals during the evacuation of the facility in April 1861, was salvaged and reconditioned to be the skeleton of the *Virginia*. A combination of thick planking and iron covered an armored casemate, and ten guns were mounted, one at the bow, one at the stern, and four on the port and starboard sides. Perhaps the deadliest weapon added to the ship was an iron ram attached to her prow. Propulsion was provided by a steam-driven screw system, and this was perhaps the vessel's Achilles' heel for the engine was woefully weak for the heavy ship.

A July 18, 1861, report from Mallory offered some details of the project:

> The frigate Merrimack has been raised and docked at an expense of $6,000, and the necessary repairs to hull and machinery to place her in her former condition is estimated by experts at $450,000. The vessel would then be in the river, and by the blockade of the enemy's fleets and batteries rendered comparatively useless. It has, therefore, been determined to shield her completely with three-inch iron, placed at such angles as to render her ball-proof, to complete her at the earliest moment, to arm her with the heaviest ordnance, and to send her at once against the enemy's fleet. It is believed that thus prepared she will be able to contend successfully against the heaviest of the enemy's ships, and to drive them from Hampton Roads and the ports of Virginia. The cost of this work is estimated by the constructor and engineer in charge at $172,523, and, as time is of the first consequence in this enterprise, I have not hesitated to commence the work, and to ask Congress for the necessary appropriation.

The Federals knew exactly what was going on at the Gosport base and took steps to counter the Confederates with a fleet of Yankee ironclads. On July 4, 1861, Gideon Welles, the Union secretary of the navy, asked Congress for an appropriation to build one or more of these ships. One and a half million dollars were authorized.

John Ericsson, a Swedish-American naval engineer, had long been interested in the concept of a rotating gun turret. His design for an ironclad whose hull was mostly underwater and whose only armament was a twin-gunned nine-foot-tall turret was a hard sell to Welles and the Ironclad Board, but Ericsson was convincing—especially when he pledged to pay for the ship himself if he missed the

Franklin Buchanan (left) was an old navy man when he was given command of the CSS Virginia *(above). At his first opportunity, on March 8, 1862, he took his ship into action and engaged the Federal blockading fleet at Hampton Roads.*

delivery date. In the meantime, the navy authorized the construction of two other ironclads of a more conventional design.

When work began on Ericsson's odd little ship, he had one hundred days in which to have a vessel ready for action. The work was subcontracted to three companies. The hull was built by the Continental Ironworks of Green Point, New York. The engines were consigned to Delamater and Company of New York. And the turret, appropriately enough, was to be created by the Novelty Ironworks, also of New York.

Work commenced on the keel in late October. One hundred days later, on January 30, 1862, the ship was launched. Ericsson named it the *Monitor*. The craft was described by James Russell Soley:

[It] consisted of a small iron hull, upon which rested a large raft, surmounted by a revolving turret. The hull was 124 feet long and 34 feet wide. The raft projected at the bow and stern, its total length being 50 feet greater than that of the hull. Its overhang amidship was 3 feet 8 inches wide, gradually increasing toward the bow and stern. The raft was 5 feet deep, and was protected by a side armor of five 1-inch iron plates backed with oak. The deck was covered with two ½-inch plates, over timber laid on heavy wooden beams. The turret was armored with eight 1-inch plates, and its roof was protected by railroad iron; in it were two 11-inch Dahlgren guns. The pilot house, in front of the turret, was built of square iron bars, notched together, with a bolt through the corners. On top of the pilot house was an iron plate, 1½ inch thick, set in a ledge without fastenings.

In anticipation of the imminent launching of the *Virginia,* the Federal navy was anxious to get the *Monitor* into position at Hampton Roads before the Confederate ship could attack. Beset by many delays, the awkward-looking ship finally left the Brooklyn Navy Yard on March 6. John L. Worden was placed in command of the ship, and the vessel was towed out to sea with the *Currituck* and *Sachem* as escorts. Despite the efficiency with which the ship was built, she arrived too late to prevent the havoc wreaked by the *Virginia* on the Federal fleet at Hampton Roads two days later.

At about 11 A.M. on March 8, the unfinished Confederate ironclad cast off from the Gosport Navy Yard for the first trial of her steam engines. Drawing twenty-two feet of water, the vessel's top speed was only five knots. Her crew of three hundred was not aware of the offensive intention of Capt. Franklin Buchanan, the ship's captain, until they reached Hampton Roads. Accompanying her were the gunboats *Raleigh* and *Beaufort.*

Despite the many guns in action on that first day of battle at Hampton Roads, Virginia's *front-mounted ram did the most damage in sinking the USS* Cumberland.

U.S. NAVAL HISTORICAL CENTER

Lolling at anchor ahead lay the USS *Cumberland,* which was armed with twenty-four guns. When the *Virginia* appeared and steamed toward her, the ship's gunners were called into action and opened fire on the Southern vessel at a distance of about one mile. The *Virginia* veered neither to port or starboard but patiently knifed through the water toward her objective.

Passing within three hundred yards of the USS *Congress,* a broadside struck the Confederate ship and the balls bounced off the iron-and-wood sides. *Virginia*'s gunners returned the broadside. Heavy fire also came from Federal shore batteries, but nothing deterred the Southern ironclad's straight-as-an-arrow course for the *Cumberland,* whose 9-inch Dahlgrens continued to search for a weak spot in the Confederate's armor.

Despite the torrent of shot and shell, the *Virginia* rammed the side of the *Cumberland,* pressing the deadly ram well into the interior of the ship. Immediately the ship began to founder, almost pulling the Confederate vessel under as well. The Southern ship reversed engines and withdrew, but its deadly prow broke off inside the sinking Federal ship. The gunners aboard the *Cumberland,* however, maintained their fire until the decks were awash.

The only damage done to the ironclad—aside from the loss of the iron ram—either that day or the next was done by the *Cumberland*'s guns. A midshipman aboard the *Virginia* reported, "The broadside fired by the *Cumberland* just as the *Virginia* rammed her cut one of the *Virginia*'s guns off at the trunnions, the muzzle off another, tore up the carriage of her bow pivot gun, swept away her anchors, boats and howitzers, riddled her smokestack and steam-pipe, and killed or wounded nineteen men."

Meanwhile, the captain of the *Congress,* now aware of the futility of taking on the armored ship head-on, steered his vessel into shallow water, knowing that he could not be pursued beyond a certain point. He went too far, however, and grounded the ship. The *Virginia* took a position about two hundred yards from the *Congress* and unleashed barrage after barrage until the Federals hoisted a white flag.

The Confederate gunboat *Beaufort* was signaled to remove the wounded from the *Congress* but was driven away by Union sharpshooters on land. Unaware of this change of events, Buchanan ordered a boarding party dispatched to the stricken Federal ship.

Halfway to their destination, the boarding party took fire from the sharpshooters ashore, who then turned their attention to the *Virginia*. Buchanan called for a rifle and fired on the men who had violated the truce he was observing to aid the *Congress*. and he was wounded for his troubles. Before relinquishing the fight, he ordered that incendiaries and hot shot be unleashed on the *Congress*. He pulled back as the Federal ship caught fire and burned.

The next ship to draw *Virginia*'s attention was the *Minnesota*, which had grounded some distance away while trying to avoid the Southern ship. At least the shallow water prevented the Confederates from getting too close, but several broadsides were fired before the Rebel ironclad retired for the night. Buchanan passed command of the ship to his executive officer, Catesby ap Roger Jones.

Around midnight that night the *Monitor* arrived, too late to be of any help that day but in time to write a new chapter in the annals of naval warfare the next day. While Hampton Roads was eerily lighted by the burning *Congress*, the *Monitor* moored near the grounded *Minnesota* and awaited the battle of the next day.

As the sun rose the next morning, the *Virginia* steamed into view, approaching the mouth of the Elizabeth River to inspect the *Minnesota* and complete her destruction. From the far side of the Northern ship, a shape on the surface of the water began to circle into sight. The Federal ironclad showed itself to the Confederate ship. The "floating barn" met the "cheesebox on a raft."

A massive battle commenced between the two ships. Guns blazed for four hours, but neither ship sustained significant damage. All the while, the *Virginia* attempted to destroy the stranded *Minnesota* and received fire from her and the Union shore batteries. The *Monitor* retired at noon, but only because her captain had been temporarily blinded by a hit to the pilothouse. The Confederate ship, unable to get close enough to the *Minnesota* to deliver a deathblow, also withdrew.

The May 10, 1862, issue of *Scientific American* does not mention the battle of Hampton Roads in its page 2 "Notes on Military and Naval Affairs," but it did devote one column of a three-column editorial page to the ironclads later in the magazine, after more important issues were discussed, such as statistics on sewing machines in America and Europe, a subterranean railroad in London, minks as

Capt. John L. Worden (left) commanded the USS Monitor *(above) in his vessel's initial action against the* Virginia. *When the ship arrived at Hampton Roads during the night of March 8, the scene was illuminated by the* burning Cumberland.

insect catchers, the colors of coal tar, an improved coasting sled, and other equally significant articles. A short excerpt from that editorial—a reaction to the attention given the battle—gives the gist of it:

> To a person who has kept even moderately informed in regard to the experiments on iron plates, there is something amusing in the excitement caused by the fight between the Merrimack and Monitor. That action showed the power of certain kinds of plates to resist certain kinds of shot fired from certain kinds of guns with certain charges of powder, but did not show what would be the result, when any of these conditions were materially changed. The idea that it settled the whole question of the invulnerability of iron-plated ships is ridiculous, and the assumption that it showed harbor fortifications to be worthless is more ridiculous still.
>
> In the first place neither the Merrimack nor the Monitor was furnished with the heaviest artillery which is manufactured at our arsenals, and which has been proved to be practically safe and serviceable. The Monitor had 11-inch guns firing shells weighing 169 lbs. and it is stated that the charge was 12 lbs. of powder. Now Rodman's 15-inch gun has been fired more than 500 times, with shells ranging from 315 to 330 lbs. in weight, and with charges of powder ranging from 35 to 50 lbs. giving initial velocities to the projectile varying from 902 to 1,328 feet per second. What the effect of such a missile would be upon iron plates cannot be even conjectured, plausibly, from the results of the firing on board the Monitor.

The battle between the ironclads ended as a standoff. Both captains were forced to relinquish command after they were injured in action, although not against each other.

There is something to the skepticism expressed by the editors. Fearful that a two-gun ship was all that stood between the *Virginia* and Washington, Union authorities had issued orders for the gunners not to use the strongest charge in firing the *Monitor*'s guns. As it was, the plank-and-iron casemate of the Southern ship was cracked during the engagement; a full charge might have brought about a different outcome to this first battle between ironclads.

Both the North and the South had created and tested a new type of warship, one that seemed impervious to bombardment. The concept of the ironclad had become a reality, but neither proved to be the ultimate weapon its advocates had preached. For both sides to have two equally strong vessels, neither gained an advantage—except for the one day when the *Virginia* roamed Hampton Roads unmolested.

The duel at Hampton Roads may not have proven anything about the invulnerability of ironclad warships, but it did mark the beginning for the obsolescence of wooden ships of war all around the world.

PART 3

COVER-UPS AND BLAME SHIFTING

9

COLD HARBOR

GRANT'S WORST BLUNDER

IN MARCH 1864 ABRAHAM LINCOLN promoted Ulysses S. Grant, making him the nation's first lieutenant general since George Washington. The president explained this action by saying only, "He fights!"

For almost three years Lincoln had little success with the generals in the eastern theater, and especially in northern Virginia. The list of names was long—Irvin McDowell, George B. McClellan (twice), John Pope, Ambrose E. Burnside, and Joseph Hooker. George Gordon Meade had been hurled into action at the beginning of the Gettysburg campaign then stalled when the front once again moved below the Potomac River. The Union war machine was frozen in place.

Grant's star rose and his general's stars multiplied following critical victories at Forts Henry and Donelson, Shiloh, Vicksburg, and most recently at Chattanooga. His selection as overall commander, however, was somewhat controversial, and with an election coming in November, Lincoln's political future was intertwined with the battlefield exploits of his army and the accomplishments of his generals—especially this new supreme commander of all Union armies.

Once the ceremony was concluded in Washington, Grant was, like his predecessors, expected to move on Richmond—the longtime goal of the Union army in the hope that the seizure of the Confederate capital would end the war. Meade was still in command of the Army of the Potomac, and he expected to receive orders from Grant in the same manner in which he had received instructions from Henry W. Halleck, who had been general in chief prior to Grant's appointment. When Grant arrived at Meade's headquarters in the field, Meade was somewhat unsure of who was in charge of the army. Grant confirmed that Meade was still the head of his army, but Grant would dictate orders from the field, not from Washington.

The Grant command got off to a bad start. Before he could strike a blow against Robert E. Lee's Army of Northern Virginia, Lee struck first. A three-day battle ensued; Grant lost seventeen thousand men and Lee suffered seventy-five hundred casualties. Union losses were as great as those that had ended the campaigns and commands of McDowell, McClellan, Pope, Burnside, and Hooker. The Federal ranks had not seen much worse action than what had just transpired in the marshy land of woods and underbrush known as the Wilderness. All anticipated that the army would withdraw to its previous camp above the Rapidan River. Lee had flummoxed another Yankee general, and Lincoln had yet to find a commander who could win a battle against the Virginian, much less win the war.

Surprisingly, Grant ordered an advance. The soldiers in the ranks cheered when they heard the news. Lee noted that he now faced an adversary who seemed to know how to fight. Several more bloody encounters occurred. Almost immediately the armies clashed at Spotsylvania Court House; Grant lost eighteen thousand, and Lee ninety-five hundred. When the action resumed at the North Anna River, Grant suffered nineteen hundred casualties and Lee lost two thousand.

Obviously, victory was not decided by one's losses; instead, it was awarded to Grant on the basis of his grinding progress toward Richmond. At the same time, little was said officially regarding his casualty lists, which collectively exceeded the strength of the Army of Northern Virginia.

Regardless of how hard Grant struck at Lee and tried to maneuver around the Confederate army toward Richmond, Lee struck back and detoured Grant along an arc from west to east above the Rebel capital. By the end of the first month of Grant's campaign, the armies found themselves on the familiar ground where McClellan's Peninsula campaign had faltered in 1862, shortly after Lee had been given command of the Southern army.

After the engagement at the North Anna, dozens of Rebel units converged on Cold Harbor, about eight miles east and four or five miles north of the capital. The settlement—which was little more than a clearing, a tavern, and an intersection—appeared on less than a dozen maps of Virginia. Its only significant feature was its name, and few seemed to know where the name came from. The temperature was rarely very cold there, and there was no harbor, unless one viewed the tavern as a shelter from the woods all around it.

Lee anticipated that Grant would take this route to Richmond, and he concentrated his army along the banks of the Chickahominy. The impending clash held the fate of two governments in the balance.

Very little distinguished the crossroads at Cold Harbor other than five roads met here.

News of Grant's huge casualties began to unnerve his backers in Washington. Earlier, as the battle of the Wilderness was concluding, Lincoln and chief of staff Henry W. Halleck had met with an unidentified agitated general from the field. Since the general did not want to be relieved of duty as the campaign was progressing, he said nothing directly critical of Grant. He did, however, suggest that "our forces are decidedly deficient in the reconnaissance department." This was not the first time Lincoln had heard such concerns about Grant's lack of preparations for battle. The president thanked the officer for his concern and urged him and his fellow commanders to do everything "to prevent anything being done in desperation or rashness."

The first action at Cold Harbor occurred between Union and Confederate cavalry on May 31. Lee knew that the path through Cold Harbor led to Richmond for Grant, so he dispatched a division of horse soldiers to the crossroads to hold the town. In the meantime, Grant sent a division of troopers to the area to protect his left flank, which was anchored at Bethesda Church, three miles away. Lee's cavalry got there first, but Grant's men were not long in forcing them back—at least as far as some breastworks. The Southerners held on throughout the day, expecting reinforcements. But the rein-

One of the hallmarks of the Army of Northern Virginia after Spotsylvania was the speed with which rifle pits and breastworks were thrown up. Thus Robert E. Lee's troops quickly assembled a formidable line opposite the Army of the Potomac at Cold Harbor.

LESLIE'S THE SOLDIER IN OUR CIVIL WAR

As soon as the Federal Sixth Corps arrived on the scene after a long march under a broiling summer sun, the troops were hurled against the Confederate line. They broke through, but they could not hold the position.

forcements, coming up from the area of Bermuda Hundred, got lost. By the time they arrived, the Yankee cavalry had forced the Confederates to withdraw.

Federal support came up to occupy and hold the position on June 1, but the cavalrymen spent a nervous night reinforcing the breastworks and anticipating a Southern counterattack. Lee was determined to resecure the crossroads town. His troops reached Cold Harbor before Grant's, but these Confederates arriving on the scene were untested, green troops. During the first moments of the fighting that followed, their commander was shot down and the men panicked. By the time the Southerners had reformed to attack, fresh Union soldiers arrived and bolstered the line.

Meade urged Grant to attack, and Grant concurred, believing that a significant gain could be made if not a complete breakthrough; the breakthrough might occur the next day. Six Union divisions fell upon four Confederate divisions. One soldier likened the fighting to "hell turned sideways." After three hours the shooting stopped as night fell. No one looked forward to the sunrise.

Grant tried to rush more troops to the scene. He decided to focus the next day's assault on the right side of the Confederate line. The fighting had been particularly heavy there, and he reasoned that the Southerners would have little time under the cover of darkness

In the fighting of June 3, one division broke through a southern segment of the line and took prisoners but was driven back by a counterattack.

to enhance their defenses in that sector of the field. To preclude any shift of Confederate reinforcements from the left side of their line to the right, two Union corps were to strike that part of the line.

Lee indeed was shifting his men to his right side. He was shifting a lot of men along a seven-mile arc from the Totopotomoy to the Chickahominy Rivers.

Federal commanders saw this and urged an early morning attack. The attack did not happen, because significant numbers of Union soldiers failed to arrive until 6:30 on the morning of June 2. They were exhausted and incapable of attacking that day. The assault was scheduled for the next morning. June 2 was not a quiet day, however. Confederates attacked at Bethesda Church but were hurled back. Then it rained.

The time did not pass lightly for the Union soldiers in the ranks. They had all day to gauge the strength of the Confederate position opposite them. Southern soldiers were not idle either; they spent all day reinforcing their position. Skillfully the Confederates masked their defensive works by blending the positions with the contours of

Combat artist Alfred Waud depicted a moment of the June 3 fighting in which a Zouave regiment charged the line and its colonel was shot down carrying the colors of the unit.

the surrounding land. Trenches were dug, and artillery was emplaced with deadly crossing fields of fire over every imaginable approach.

Sites for the Confederates' defensive works were selected with great care. End to end, they stretched for about eleven miles and were sheltered by a dense growth of trees. In front of the trees was an open meadow whose width varied from about one-half to four miles.

Since the month had been very dry, most of the creek beds held very little water. The overnight rain changed that. Instead, the banks of most of these streams, one of which lay directly in front of the serpentine Rebel line, were now mostly soft mud and slime. The Federals faced a formidable task in breaking Lee's line at any point—sharpshooters and small batteries aside.

In one of the strangest group activities of the war, most of the Union soldiers in the front lines sewed or pinned their names to their uniforms so their bodies would be identifiable should they fall the next day. This act was far more orderly than the preparations of their commanders, however. Grant's headquarters issued no specific orders for the attack. No one scouted the Confederate positions. All such preparations were left to the discretion of the corps commanders—who had no attack plan other than to fling their men toward the Southerners.

At 3:30 A.M. the Union ranks were dressed for battle. The mood was funereal. As sunlight crept up from the horizon, the Federals looked across an expanse of land that seemed abandoned. At 4:30 fifty thousand men began to move out. A few hundred yards separated the two armies, and the Confederates held their fire until the Northerners were well within range. Then they loosed a deadly fire on them that no one seemed able to describe later. The carnage was as bad as any of the war. Many Federal soldiers said they never saw the Southerners, only the smoke and flame of their rifles.

By 5:30 the Federals not shot down were hunkered on the ground for safety. As many as seven thousand were dead. It was a stunning defeat for Grant, but he was not anxious to end the fighting. Meade sent inquiries about halting the assault; Grant urged him to exploit any opportunity to break through the Confederate lines. Meade ordered another attack, and the order was refused from the commanders on down the line to the soldiers in the field. No one was going to charge the breastworks again.

At noon Grant visited three corps headquarters. He canceled all operations in the field but ordered his people to hold their positions. On the basis of their communications that day, apparently neither Grant nor Meade understood what had happened.

Neither side called for a truce to bury the dead; each commander believed there was an opportunity to exploit here. So the artillerists

Lee and Grant took a great deal of time to negotiate a truce to claim the dead and wounded from the battlefield. As a result, burial details were not allowed onto the field until four days after the fighting. The number of Yankee dead far exceeded that of the Rebels, and the dead on the field greatly exceeded the number of wounded.

BATTLES AND LEADERS

Cold Harbor was the worst defeat of Grant's career, and he admitted to his staff, "I regret this assault more than any one I have ever ordered." In his report to Washington, he downplayed the situation: "Our loss was not heavy, nor do I suppose the enemy to have lost heavily." It was hardly accurate in the face of seven thousand casualties to Lee's fifteen hundred.

exchanged shots for three days and occasional shooting erupted between the two lines. Finally, Grant decided to withdraw and swing his army to the southeast, across the Virginia Peninsula, and strike at Petersburg. The movement began during the night of June 12. It was the end of the Overland campaign and the beginning of the siege of Petersburg.

Grant was not a man to dwell on failure. Apparently his generals also chose not to emphasize the negative; as far as possible they offered objective accounts of the campaign without criticizing Grant's unfortunate blunder. For his part, Grant confessed to his officers, "I regret this assault more than any one I ever ordered."

Some years after the war, having turned down earlier inquiries regarding his impressions of the battle, Union Gen. Martin T. McMahon published a lengthy, detailed account of the battle from start to finish. His first three sentences jolted many old-timers out of their rocking chairs:

In the opinion of the majority of its survivors, the battle of Cold Harbor never should have been fought. There was no military reason to justify it. It was the dreary, dismal, bloody, ineffective close of the Lieutenant-General's first campaign with the Army of the Potomac and corresponded in all its essential features with what had preceded it.

Although Grant had correctly believed that the Confederate defenses around Cold Harbor made up the "last formidable Confederate works before Richmond," the commanding general was anxious to push through them before Lee could get the bulk of his army in position. According to McMahon, these movements "brought us in front of the most formidable position yet held by the enemy." The aging general also noted that no single position offered a good overview of the battleground in front of the army. McMahon concluded: "The time of actual advance was not above eight minutes. In that little period more men fell bleeding as they advanced than in any other like period during the war."

As the powder smoke cleared from the tiny crossroads settlement of Cold Harbor, the end of the war was coming into view. Within a month's time, Grant had lost fifty thousand men—as many casualties as the Army of the Potomac had sustained in all the action preceding his direction. Lee had lost thirty thousand. Grant's ranks were refilled; Lee's army never recovered.

10

SECOND MANASSAS

PORTER BECOMES THE SCAPEGOAT

THE AUGUST 29–30, 1862, battle of Second Manassas (or Second Bull Run) branded John Pope as an incompetent general and marked the end of the military career of Union Maj. Gen. Fitz John Porter. The results of the battle also opened the door to Confederate operations north of the Potomac in the early fall of that year, taking the war onto Federal soil.

In July 1862 Pope had been named to head the newly formed Army of Virginia, created out of the uncoordinated and varied commands scattered across western and northern Virginia. Pope had caught the eye of the military planners in Washington after impressive victories in the western theater at New Madrid and Island No. 10. Many saw him as an antidote to the cautious and intractable George B. McClellan, whose Peninsula campaign had halted abruptly in the face of Robert E. Lee's robust and daring Seven Days' battles, which then pushed McClellan's army across the peninsula and bottled it up at Harrison's Landing. At first, the War Department hoped that Pope and McClellan might work together to hit Lee from two sides, crushing his army and then moving in force against Richmond. Instead, Pope joined the anti-McClellan faction in Washington and campaigned to replace him. In the end, McClellan fell victim to his own procrastination as much as the behind-the-scenes chicanery in the Federal capital.

Pope established a supply base at Manassas Junction for his army, but the elements of this force were slow in coming together. His first offensive act—other than some infuriating pronouncements regarding the superiority of western troops to eastern soldiers—was to order on July 12 a raid in force against the railroad junction at Gordonsville. Unfortunately for him, the commander of the attack ponderously executed his orders as if he were conducting a campaign. By the time the Federals finally approached the area, they found elements of Thomas J. "Stonewall" Jackson's corps defending the rail center. Lee had shifted the men there from the peninsula when it became apparent that McClellan was content to remain safely within the defensive works around Harrison's Landing.

Within a short while it became apparent to Lee that McClellan no longer posed a threat to Richmond. It was more likely that Pope would be moving on the Confederate capital. Lee decided to strike first and in early August dispatched Jackson's full corps and A. P. Hill's division to Gordonsville.

Jackson determined to strike Pope's southernmost units at Centreville. Instead he ran into Nathaniel Banks's army near Cedar Mountain on August 9. Chaos ruled the day, but by the time the sun set, the Federals had withdrawn. Jackson, however, advanced not much farther and returned to Gordonsville.

By August 13 McClellan began to vacate his position at Harrison's Landing. In Richmond, Lee was relieved that the threat to Richmond was being removed, but he was apprehensive that McClellan might join forces with Pope and move on the Rebel capital from the north. Since parts of Jackson's corps were already in the area, Lee decided to send James Longstreet's corps to link up with Jackson and strike Pope before the Union armies could merge into a single force and roll over the Confederate opposition in northern

Stonewall Jackson's flanking march to get behind John Pope's army ended with his pillaging the Union supply depot at Manassas (above left) and then attacking the Federals near the old Manassas battlefield (above right, a scene from a Union perspective).

Virginia. Again Lee gambled that alacrity and audacity would thwart the Federal threat.

Initial plans called for an ambush of Pope between the Rapidan and Rappahannock Rivers. Then a dispatch case with a copy of Lee's orders fell into Union hands. Pope moved rapidly to consolidate a position above the Rappahannock and denied Lee the opportunity.

On August 22 Confederate Gen. Jeb Stuart's cavalry swooped down on a Federal camp at Catlett's Station. It turned out to be Pope's headquarters, and the horse soldiers found a dispatch case with news of McClellan's movements, including information on the anticipated movements and timetables for the Third, Fifth, and Sixth Corps of the Army of the Potomac.

Lee decided to split his army again. Jackson's corps was to swing to the west and north, to get above Pope's army and appear to be moving toward the Washington area. Longstreet's corps would occupy Pope's front along the Rappahannock—where the Federals expected him to strike. If all went well, Pope would have to fall back toward the Federal capital. Longstreet would follow Jackson a day later, link up with himm and catch Pope off guard, possibly causing him to withdraw from his strong position on the heights overlooking the Rappahannock.

On August 25 Jackson's corps began its march. Federal observers dutifully noted the numbers of men and reported the information to Pope, who concluded that the evidence indicated that Jackson was returning to the Shenandoah Valley.

The battle of Second Manassas occurred slightly north of the scene of the first battle fought there just thirteen months prior. An unfinished railroad provided Jackson's corps with a ready-made earthwork and proved formidable.

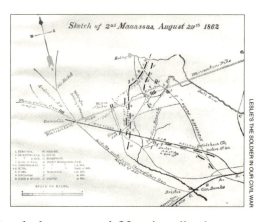

LESLIE'S THE SOLDIER IN OUR CIVIL WAR

Jackson pushed his men hard; they covered fifty-six miles in two days. By sunset on August 26 the force of twenty-five thousand men was approaching Bristoe Station, roughly twenty miles behind Pope's lines. One of the general's goals was to strike at the Orange and Alexandria Railroad and cut off Pope's communication with Washington. His men easily overwhelmed the Federal force there, cut the telegraph line, and wrecked a section of track that claimed at least two trains. Jackson sent a small force from there to the Union supply base at Manassas Junction, four miles to the north. They swarmed the small guard detail there, and Jackson arrived with all but three brigades, which were left at Bristoe Station with Richard Ewell.

At the huge supply depot the Confederates captured three hundred prisoners, eight artillery pieces, fifty thousand pounds of bacon, one thousand barrels of corned beef, two thousand barrels of salt pork, and two thousand barrels of flour. In addition to such general supplies, there were delicacies such as wine, whiskey, and cigars. For an army that had been subsisting on corn and apples for two days, the buffet before them was quickly enjoyed. Jackson was most fearful of the liquor and ordered it destroyed.

Pope still had about sixty thousand men in the area, so Jackson knew he had to move. While his men enjoyed the smorgasbord of captured supplies, a New Jersey brigade blundered into the depot in response to news that a Confederate raiding party had struck. Both groups were surprised by the other. The Federals found themselves at a great disadvantage. Shots were exchanged, and the Union commander, Gen. George W. Taylor, was killed. His men withdrew, but A. P. Hill's division pursued and captured most of them.

In the meantime, large numbers of Union soldiers approached Bristoe Station. Fighting broke out, and Ewell pulled his men north to join Jackson at Manassas. Before Jackson's men left the supply depot, they torched it. To confuse the Federals, the general divided his force into three units and sent each by a different route to an area seven miles north of Manassas Junction and just above the old Manassas battlefield. There he waited for Longstreet's arrival.

Confusion reigned in the Union ranks. In addition to the chaos at Bristoe Station and Manassas Junction, the army's general officers were divided in their loyalties between McClellan and Pope. In their eyes, matters were drawing to a head, because McClellan was supposed to be moving his army to join up with Pope's. Many wondered who would command once both generals were together. For his part, based on his experience at Corinth, Mississippi, Pope anticipated general in chief Henry W. Halleck's imminent arrival to command both armies in the field.

Meanwhile, Pope initiated a search for the Confederates. Slowly he realized that the action around Manassas was not the work of a raiding party, but a Confederate army. In fact, it was Jackson's army, and Pope was all but intoxicated with the idea that he would be the Yankee general to destroy the Confederate legend. By annihilating Jackson, he would also cripple Lee. The idea overshadowed everything Pope could imagine, and he momentarily forgot about Longstreet, despite news from his cavalry that Longstreet was fighting through the mountain passes behind the Union lines. Then word arrived on August 28 that Jackson had attacked a Federal column on the Warrenton turnpike, north of Manassas.

Jackson's corps occupied a two-mile position along an unfinished railroad. The site was known as Stony Ridge. Pope's people swarmed into the area, but his divisions were spread out all over the area. Battle lines formed on the morning of August 29, and the Federals struck at various points along Jackson's line in piecemeal fashion. Longstreet's corps arrived in the late morning, around 10:30 A.M., and took a position to the south of Jackson, forming an L-shaped line. Artillery was positioned at the junction point of the two corps.

Pope arrived on the battlefield early that afternoon, but he took no notice of Longstreet. When he saw reports of movement behind the Confederate line, he interpreted them as evidence of a retreat.

Union Gen. Fitz John Porter's division of about twelve thousand men was one element of Pope's army that had been reassigned from McClellan's army. During the Peninsula campaign the division had been attached to Ambrose E. Burnside's corps of the Army of the Potomac. The unit had distinguished itself in the fighting at Mechanicsville, Gaines's Mill, and Malvern Hill. For his part in the campaign, Porter was promoted by McClellan and thereafter was fiercely loyal to McClellan. With the realignment of the armies, Porter's division hoofed it westward from Aquia Landing then north to Culpeper and Warrenton Junction. During the two days in which Pope issued several orders to his temperamental commanders to march to various points to isolate Jackson, Porter's corps was dispatched from Warrenton Junction to Bristoe Station.

In the early morning hours of August 29, orders arrived directing Porter to Centreville, ten miles distant, because Confederates—A. P. Hill's division, which was temporarily lost—were reported to be moving into the area. Pope hoped to trap Jackson with the two corps

The fighting took place along a two-mile front on August 29, 1862, with Pope focusing all of his army against Jackson. As in many other battles, the Union commander sent his army

commanded by Porter and Irvin McDowell. The latter had been in reserve near Washington during McClellan's Peninsula campaign.

Porter's men had been on the march all day; he knew they needed more sleep than one or two hours, so he did not move until shortly before dawn. McDowell, however, failed to respond at all. His corps was scattered, and he could not execute the commander's orders. Pope was furious. He had lost an opportunity that, in truth, did not exist. In time, the matter would return to haunt Porter.

Meanwhile, Pope directed his units to converge on Jackson at Manassas. Porter's corps arrived on the southern end of the field on the morning of August 29. He was in an ideal position to hit at Jackson's right just before Longstreet arrived, but his divisional commanders proceeded with extreme caution. Orders arrived from Pope at that moment, directing Porter to move toward Gainesville, which was behind and beyond Jackson's position, but to get there Porter would have to march through Longstreet. Confusing the matter even more was Pope's ambiguity; he issued joint instructions to Porter and

into battle unit by unit rather than strike in force. While Jackson kept Pope occupied, James Longstreet's corps arrived and formed to attack the flank of the Federals.

McDowell to advance and be ready to attack—but he did not tell them to attack. Instead Pope warned that the situation was in flux and that they should be prepared to withdraw.

As Porter pondered how he might proceed, the long-lost McDowell appeared with his corps. The situation they faced was not what Pope's orders described. A vast body of Southern soldiers was before them, and Pope's orders gave no indication that he knew there were any other Confederates on the field in addition to Jackson's corps. Porter and McDowell chose to hold their positions; McDowell moved across the field and joined Pope as soon as the latter appeared on the battlefield early that afternoon.

Pope expected that Porter would attack that afternoon, and Porter awaited instructions. Finally Pope issued the order to attack, but Porter—five miles south of Pope's headquarters—did not receive the order until 6:30 P.M. Still Pope did not seem to appreciate the situation in which Porter found himself; he still seemed ignorant of Longstreet's presence. Due to the lateness of the hour, Porter elected not to attack. Pope would never forgive or forget that.

The fighting ceased around 9 P.M. The brunt of the battle had fallen on Jackson, so Lee shifted troops to fill in the gaps wrought by the Federal attacks.

Pope continued to misinterpret these movements as Jackson retreating. To do so, he also chose to ignore reports that Longstreet had arrived. In a message to Halleck on the morning of August 30, Pope exaggerated the situation:

> We fought a terrific battle here yesterday with the combined forces of the enemy, which lasted with continuous fury from daylight until dark, by which time the enemy was driven from the field, which we now occupy. Our troops are too much exhausted yet to push matters, but I shall do so in the course of the morning, as soon as Fitz John Porter's corps comes up from Manassas. The enemy is still in our front, but badly used up. We have lost not less than 8,000 men killed and wounded, but from the appearance of the field the enemy lost at least two to one. He stood strictly on the defensive, and every assault was made by ourselves. Our troops behaved splendidly. The battle was fought on the identical battle-field of Bull Run, which greatly increased the enthusiasm of our men. The news just reaches me from the front that the enemy is retreating toward the moun-

LIBRARY OF CONGRESS

Fitz John Porter's corps had come up near the site of Longstreet's position, but the Federals did not attack. So Pope, ignoring reports of Longstreet's presence, moved Porter against Jackson on the morning of August 30, but the Confederates still maintained their line.

tains. I go forward at once to see. We have made great captures, but I am not able yet to form an idea of their extent.

On the morning of August 30, the armies were in virtually the same positions they had held the preceding day. Lee kept his corps where they were. Pope continued to refer to the imminent Confederate retreat. He ordered Porter to move up into the Federal line in front of Jackson. In doing so, he removed the only element of his army that had held Longstreet in check.

The reorganized Federal line consisted of McDowell on the left, Samuel P. Heintzelman on the right, and in the center were Porter, Franz Sigel, and Jesse L. Reno. Artillery fire from both sides began early and dominated the fighting for most of the day. At 1 P.M. Pope was informed that Longstreet was advancing, but he chose to disregard the news as inaccurate.

At about 3 P.M. the Federals advanced against Jackson's line again. Some Southern regiments exhausted their ammunition and resorted to hurling rocks at their attackers. James Garnett, one of Jackson's men, recalled: "The Irish battalion of the second brigade

Longstreet attacked and crushed Pope's weakened left flank, which had been occupied the day before by Porter's corps.

had fought with stones after their ammunition gave out, and it is credibly stated that my friend and old college-mate, Lewis Randolph, a lieutenant in the Irish battalion [First Virginia battalion], killed a Yankee with a large stone."

Confederate artillery exacted a heavy toll on Porter's men, the only element of the Federal line to make any headway on Jackson's position. Then Longstreet struck the left side of the Union line and rolled over any and all obstacles in his way. Jackson's men emerged from the unfinished railroad line and swept toward Chinn Ridge to link up with Longstreet. The Federals fell back. While various units provided rear-guard protection, Pope's army withdrew to Bull Run and then to Centreville.

Fighting continued until about 10 P.M., when the appearance of nineteen thousand reinforcements gave the Federals the confidence to stop for the night. Pope's army had suffered sixteen thousand casualties, more than 25 percent of his total force. Lee lost ninety-two hundred men, about 17 percent of his army.

On September 2 Pope lost his command and was reassigned to Minnesota to put down a Sioux rebellion and protect frontier settlements. A few days later the Army of Virginia was merged with the Army of the Potomac, and command was given to McClellan.

The battle of Second Manassas was not yet over, however. Pope never waged war more successfully than he did in blaming the loss at

Manassas on Fitz John Porter. For his part, Porter did nothing to endear himself to Pope. Like many officers in the Army of the Potomac prior to the battle, Porter had voiced his displeasure about having to fight under Pope. Porter, however, exercised the bad judgment of putting his thoughts to paper and including such grumbling in his dispatches. In particular, on August 28 Porter had sent a message to his former commander, Burnside, in which he expressed his contempt for Pope. Unfortunately for Porter, Burnside did not edit out such comments from the dispatches that were forwarded to Washington.

Charges of disobedience, disloyalty, and misconduct were subsequently submitted against Porter, and a court-martial convened on November 27, 1862. In reality, however, Porter was not on trial but rather George B. McClellan.

To the politicians in Washington it appeared that the officers of the army were in a state of near revolt. Too many were devoted to McClellan and contemptuous of Pope. The latter had called upon the former to rush his twenty-five thousand men to the battle, which was possible since McClellan had returned to Alexandria, but McClellan chose not to join the fight. He argued that a rout was inevitable and that his men were needed to defend Washington should the Confederates get past Pope's withdrawing army. Thus it appeared plausible for many to suspect that McClellan and the generals "loyal" to him conspired to deprive Pope of any chance of victory.

After the battle of Second Manassas, McClellan had successfully stalled Robert E. Lee's first invasion of the North at the September 17 battle of Antietam, but he had not tried to follow up the battle and weaken Lee's army even more, possibly destroying it.

By McClellan's side on the battlefield that day was Porter, whose command was held in reserve and never saw action. His troops' inactivity was mostly due to Porter's observation to the overly cautious McClellan, "Remember, General, I command the last reserve of the last army of the Republic." This counsel was given at the crucial moment following the timely arrival of the A. P. Hill's division, which thwarted the Federal attack on the right side of Lee's line. So the Union assaults ceased, and Lee held his position for the rest of the day and the next, expecting another attack, before withdrawing.

In the weeks following the battle, the Army of the Potomac remained encamped on the Antietam battlefield in Maryland. Not even a visit by Abraham Lincoln could dislodge McClellan. Finally, the president replaced McClellan, and a political campaign commenced to discredit the general from returning.

Edwin M. Stanton, the secretary of war, was in the forefront of those who believed that any other general would be a better commander than McClellan. So he seized this opportunity to pillory the former commander of the Union army by persecuting one of his most outspoken supporters, Porter. There was no better weapon to use against Porter and McClellan than Pope, who had his own ax to grind for McClellan's tacit refusal to come to his aid during the August fighting at Manassas.

The court that was convened on December 3, 1862, to try the case was stacked against Porter. Testimony was selectively accepted to validate the case against the accused. Furthermore, the defense was restricted, because any questions regarding the wisdom of the commanding general's orders were disallowed.

Perhaps one of the most damaging witnesses was Irvin McDowell, whose reputation was also at stake stemming from allegations made against him and publicized in the press. At the same time that testimony was being taken in the Porter trial, McDowell was also facing a court of inquiry in the same building to defend his own actions at Second Manassas.

Although no official charges had been made against McDowell, the general had insisted on a court of inquiry into his own competency as a general officer based on accusations of "McDowell's treason" made in a letter written by a dying officer, Col. Thornton Brodhead, of the First Michigan Cavalry. This court met in sixty-seven sessions to satisfy the general's ego. Testimony and deliberations took sixty-seven days. In the end, the court ruled there was no reason to delve further into the matter. McDowell's reputation, however, was destroyed, and he never again held a field command in the war against the South.

In general, McDowell's testimony at the Porter trial was self-serving at best and perjury at worse. The gist of his appearance before the Porter inquisitors was the assertion that had Porter executed Pope's orders of August 29, the results of the battle would have been a Federal victory.

While the Porter court-martial was ongoing, the Federal army was again bloodied and routed, sustaining nearly thirteen thousand casualties. The Union commander at the battle of Fredericksburg was Ambrose E. Burnside, another McClellan disciple. In the weeks that followed, rumors circulated around Washington that command of the army was to be returned to McClellan, or that he might possibly be given the position of general in chief. This, however, was not the deepest desire of the Lincoln administration. Politically, a judgment against Porter would be a repudiation of the McClellan party.

Thus, after forty-five days of proceedings, the finding of the court on January 21, 1863, was that Porter was guilty of two counts of disobeying orders. The court sentenced him "to be cashiered, and to be forever disqualified from holding any office of trust or profit under the Government of the United States."

Porter did not accept his fate meekly. He appealed the conviction and, for the rest of his life, he campaigned to clear his name, which would be only natural since his cousin was David Dixon Porter, one of the naval heroes of the war and four-time recipient of the Thanks of Congress.

The government took fifteen years to review the case. In large measure, Porter's cause was supported by Democrats and Pope's by

Longstreet's attack rolled up the left side of Pope's army and generated a panic. As the Federal army pulled back, Jackson moved up, and the battle ended with a kind of orderly rout.

Republicans. The latter viewed any attempt to reverse the verdict to be, in some sense, a judgment against Lincoln. Porter first approached the Andrew Johnson administration, but the matter was left for Ulysses S. Grant to address. Grant refused. The next attempt was directed by friends of Porter to William T. Sherman, then the commanding general of the army. Sherman was at first favorably inclined to pursue the matter, then Pope launched a subtle campaign in the press that under-cut Porter but also surfaced Confederate accounts of the battle, which tended to support Porter's interpretation of the facts. The potential review was dismissed by Sherman.

Finally a review was ordered in July 1878 by President Ruther-ford B. Hayes, himself a general during the war. Public interest in the battle of Second Manassas had been revived in 1876 by the publica-tion of a history of the campaign, not by an American author or his-torian, but by the Comte de Paris, Louis-Philippe d'Orleans, who had been on McClellan's staff. His popular account painted a drasti-cally different image of the battle than what had been accepted as fact heretofore and lent credibility to Porter.

The president's instructions to the review board (known as the Schofield board because it was chaired by Gen. John M. Schofield)

Pope's army withdrew across Bull Run Creek in an orderly fashion, stabilized by a stubborn rear guard that kept the Confederates at bay. The withdrawal was completed by midnight.

BATTLES AND LEADERS

recognized the faulty nature of the evidence accepted by the court-martial, which favored Pope's understanding of the progress of the battle, that is, Longstreet's presence on the battlefield did not exist until Pope decided that Longstreet was there. Furthermore, the testimony of Confederate commanders was also accepted by the review board. This included testimony from Longstreet, who stated that while his men were blocking Porter from coming to Pope's aid, Porter's presence prevented him from going immediately to Jackson's assistance.

In its findings, the Schofield board stated: "Justice requires such action as may be necessary to annul and set aside the findings and sentence of the court-martial in the case of General Fitz John Porter and to restore him to the position of which that sentence deprived him." Publicity garnered by the review, however, created a hotly debated political issue. Interestingly, Porter's loudest supporters were former Confederate soldiers. The nation was immersed in refighting the battle of Second Manassas, and the old wounds and allegiances arose anew.

In Washington the judgment of the Schofield board was not well accepted. Politically, President Hayes could not approve the findings, so he submitted the report to Congress without endorsement and the matter was debated for almost a decade. In the meantime, Porter gained the support of Grant, who wrote openly of his change of heart following the findings of the review board and also apologized publicly to Porter for not having reviewed the case when the matter first came to his desk in the White House.

Porter's conviction was not finally set aside until August 1886, twenty-three years after the verdict had been announced. President Grover Cleveland, who had avoided service during the war by hiring a substitute and who was the first Democrat to occupy the White House since James Buchanan, restored Porter's good name and rank as a colonel, dating from May 14, 1861. Thus ended the second battle of the battle of Second Manassas.

Five days after his rank had been restored, Porter was officially retired from military service. With the stigma of his court-martial removed, he once again became the police commissioner of New York.

Many historians concede that Porter was dealt with unjustly at his court-martial. At the same time, many historians point out that, in large measure, Porter was a victim of his own indiscretions. While

Fitz John Porter (left) drew a court-martial for his actions at Second Manassas, but he contested the findings for the rest of his life. John Pope (right) believed that Porter's court-martial redeemed his honor, but that verdict was reversed twenty-three years later.

he may not have been capable of executing the attack Pope ordered on the morning of August 29, Porter had no significant proof of Longstreet's presence. Indeed, Longstreet was there, but Porter did not probe the Confederates to ascertain their strength or position. Instead he was as content as his mentor, McClellan, to assume that he was greatly outnumbered by the enemy before him and, thus, should not do anything to evoke a confrontation.

This passive approach to war making had gained very little for the North and would gain nothing in the face of the pugnacious Lee in northern Virginia. Many in Washington saw that the Union cause was better off without generals who, in the words of the *Springfield Republican,* "cannot fight except on particular days and under particular generals." In short, Porter was not entirely undeserving of his court-martial. McClellanism had to be rooted out if the war aims of the North were to be realized, and Porter's removal was a major step in that direction.

11

BALL'S BLUFF

A COMPLETE MUDDLE OF AN EXAMPLE

IT WAS A BATTLE that need never have happened. Afterward, Federal losses amounted to almost half the seventeen hundred men who had fought there. One of them, Col. Edward D. Baker, had been a close family friend of the Lincolns and a national figure in his own right. How he and so many others came to die were questions that perplexed and angered the Northern public and fueled one of the darkest episodes in Civil War history.

During the anxious and awkward months following the Confederate victory at Manassas in July 1861, the Lincoln administration took steps to address the military shortcomings exposed on the battlefield. A new commander, George B. McClellan, was brought to Washington from western Virginia, and he demonstrated a profound ability to organize and train the citizen soldiers of the republic, transforming them into a disciplined army. At least the orderly ranks looked like an army if one gauged such things by demonstration drills and parades.

In the South, Jefferson Davis was shaking up his army, not for any shortcoming on the field, but because egos were clashing and there was an election to be won. At the moment, Davis was only the provisional president. P. G. T. Beauregard was making noises that he might seek the office, and he was beloved by the people for both the taking of Fort Sumter and the Manassas victory. Davis shipped him west to join Albert Sidney Johnston's army. Left to command in northern Virginia was Joseph E. Johnston, a man who many viewed as never anxious to advance when he could retreat. Johnston began to consolidate commands around Richmond and abandoned several sites close to the Federal capital at Washington.

Union troops, of course, were only too happy to accommodate the withdrawing Southerners and occupy their former positions without firing a shot. The area between Washington and Fairfax Court House was all but devoid of Confederate forces. McClellan, however, noticed that the Southerners seemed to remain in place around Leesburg, about thirty-five miles upstream from Washington. A show of force, he reasoned, should be all that was necessary to send them farther south.

On October 19, 1861, McClellan ordered a reconnaissance of Dranesville, Virginia, about thirteen miles from Leesburg. The Federal force would be comprised of Brig. Gen. George A. McCall's thirteen thousand men. News of such a movement would be reported by Confederate scouts, and the Southern commanders might interpret the marching Federals as preparations for an attack on Leesburg. Given the series of withdrawals engineered by Johnston, the Confederates might pull back. Thus much could be gained by maneuver rather than assault. It was a gambit.

The next day McClellan ordered a surveillance of Leesburg by Brig. Gen. Charles Pomeroy Stone, whose command was based in Poolesville, Maryland, about eight miles east of Leesburg. If the appearance of McCall's men wasn't sufficient to dislodge the Southerners, perhaps Stone's ten thousand men might confirm the imminent Federal threat.

Stone moved his men toward the Potomac River and erected batteries at Edwards Ferry, Maryland, southeast of Leesburg, to shell the Virginia side of the river. He then sent a force of one hundred men over in three boats, and they returned after a short time. As evening

LIBRARY OF CONGRESS

To encourage the Southern army to abandon Leesburg, Virginia, Gen. George B. McClellan suggested "a slight demonstration." Thus Brig. Gen. Charles P. Stone ordered his artillery to shell the Confederate side of the Potomac from Edwards Ferry, Maryland, and set in motion the events that climaxed with a Federal assault at Ball's Bluff.

fell, Stone dispatched a twenty-man patrol to scout the activity around Leesburg and note any responses to the presence of the Federals.

The patrol moved three miles upstream to Harrison's Island to cross the river. Opposite the island was an area known as Ball's Bluff, named for the family of George Washington's mother. The men ascended the steep bluff by a timeworn cow path and moved inland. About three-quarters of a mile from the river, they halted when they came across what they believed was a Confederate camp. They returned to Harrison's Island around 10 P.M. and sent a report about the camp to Stone at Edwards Ferry.

Stone interpreted the patrol's information as an indication that the Southerners were withdrawing from Leesburg. He decided to send two reconnaissance groups in force across the river and into Virginia. The first crossed at Edwards Ferry and was led by Stone personally. The second was led by Col. Charles Devens at Ball's Bluff.

Devens had three hundred men and only three ten-man boats to get them across the river. Thus the crossing required four hours. Once on Virginia soil, Devens was to attack and destroy the camp discovered by the earlier patrol. At that point Devens had discretion whether to return to Harrison's Island or to hold out in the Leesburg area and call for reinforcements. Once Devens was ashore and had consolidated his force, he was joined by Col. William R. Lee's Twentieth Massachusetts Regiment, which Stone had dispatched to cover Devens's possible withdrawal.

Moving inland, the Federals found no camp. The evening shadows had likely tricked the patrol into construing corn shocks for tents.

Nevertheless, Devens pushed on until he was within a mile of Leesburg. From a ridge he glimpsed a few bona fide tents. He sent word to Stone that he would hold his position and await reinforcements.

Beyond Devens's view, however, was a lot more than a few tents. A short distance southeast of the town was a camp of two thousand Confederates commanded by Col. Nathan G. Evans. They had been moved into the area in response to McCall's occupation of Dranesville the day before. Evans had, in the meantime, sent out patrols, and one of these had heard Devens's men crossing the river.

At 7 A.M. forty Confederates, trying to avoid encountering the Federals and report back to Evans, blundered into Devens's position. Shots were exchanged. The battle of Ball's Bluff began when both sides called for reinforcements.

Evans was now aware of the two Federal crossings. He decided the incursion at Ball's Bluff was the more threatening and directed his men toward that position. At the same time, he dispatched three regiments

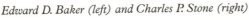

Edward D. Baker (left) and Charles P. Stone (right)

to block the road leading to Leesburg from Edwards Ferry. Seven companies went to support the forty men engaging Devens.

Unsure of what numbers he might be up against, Devens fell back toward the bluff. Ten more Federal companies were moving up the bluff, however. So he turned back to rejoin the fight against Evans. The Confederate commander responded by shifting more men toward Ball's Bluff.

Devens began to fall back again. By 2 P.M. the fighting occupied a large open field atop the bluffs. Entering the scene at this time was Col. Edward D. Baker, a man with more political skills than military talent.

Baker had been born an Englishman and had been an early law partner of Abraham Lincoln's in Springfield. His only battle experience had come during the war with Mexico. He was also an acquaintance of Stone, whose trust in Baker was far greater than it should have been. Stone placed command of the Harrison's Island operation in Baker's hands.

Once Baker was in the area, he focused his efforts on securing a large flatboat to handle the crossing from the Maryland shore to the island. The segment between the island and the Virginia shore was still limited to a few small boats. The battle had been going for many hours by the time Baker eventually made it to the top of the bluff.

Fatefully, Baker's inexperience came into play early. He arranged his battle line across the lower area of the open field and anchored his flanks in the surrounding woods. The Federals were now highly susceptible to Confederate snipers in the cover of the woods.

Union Col. Milton Cogswell arrived with his regiment at about 2:30 P.M. He surveyed the position and suggested to Baker that some men occupy the higher ground to the left of the Federal line. Baker ignored him.

Evans, however, immediately sent men to the higher position. Moreover, Confederate reinforcements arrived, and an effective converging fire was laid on the Union line. Numerically, Baker's force outnumbered Evans by a hundred men or so. The Southerners, however, were mostly veterans of the battle of Manassas; all the Federals were untested, unblooded troops.

The best thing going for the Federals was the three cannon that Baker had brought with him to the scene—two mountain howitzers and a 12-pounder James. The price for their presence was that the flow of men up the bluff had been halted to allow the gunners to carry their dismantled weapons and manhandle the James to the top. For a while an effective fire was laid on the Confederate positions, but Baker positioned the big guns in front of his line without sufficient infantry support. The gun crews were picked off by Southern sharpshooters. Baker's line was also weakened because the troops behind the guns did not have a clear field of fire.

Around 4:30 that afternoon Baker attempted to push forward. To do this he tried to inspire his men to follow him in the only manner he knew—he went in front of his men to lead by example. Four bullets ripped into him, and he was dead before he hit the ground. A fierce fight became even fiercer as both sides fought to take possession of the body. Baker's men claimed the corpse, but the Confederates now moved in on three sides and pushed the Federals toward the edge of the bluff.

Command of the Union troops fell to Cogswell. Rather than fall back immediately to the island and the Maryland shore, he tried to swing left and follow the river to link up with the Edwards Ferry contingent led by Stone. It was a good plan, but its execution led to disaster. While two companies were shifting from the right side of the line to the left, the men became disoriented and surged forward. They were cut down where they stood.

Cogswell was not aware than one thousand men waited on Harrison's Island and two thousand waited on the Maryland shore to be ferried into the fighting. Farther south, Stone had two thousand men on Virginia soil. No one not at the scene of the fighting knew the situation at the bluffs—Baker had not sent any messengers to anyone with reports of what was going on. As far as Stone knew, all was well.

By 5 P.M. Stone had decided to move toward the bluffs, but his way was blocked by the regiments sent by Evans to secure his line. Stone was apprised that the Southerners had set up breastworks and artillery between Baker and him and that as many as ten thousand Confederates were in the area.

Immediately Stone withdrew from Virginia, crossing back into Maryland, and marched to the site of the Harrison's Island crossing. At 6 P.M. he sent word to McClellan that he desperately required assistance from McCall, who he believed was in Dranesville.

Three miles upstream from Edwards Ferry was Ball's Bluff, a rocky height that had been named for a former landowner, the family of George Washington's mother, Mary Ball Washington. Atop the bluff were eight acres of open field bordered by thick forest. The only way to the top from the river was by a narrow path up a steep bank densely covered with tangles of mountain laurel.

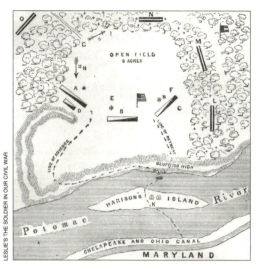

In fact, McCall was nowhere near Dranesville. He had executed his orders exactly and had withdrawn from the area as soon as he had completed his reconnaissance. At the time of Stone's call for help, McCall was more than twenty miles away from Stone.

McClellan was very much surprised to hear the news of the fighting at Ball's Bluff. He had heard nothing because Stone had heard nothing because Baker had sent word of nothing.

Meanwhile, at the scene of the fighting, Cogswell's command fell back to the edge of the bluffs under the pressure of repeated Confederate assaults. In the shadows of the setting sun the Southerners penetrated the Union line. Panic broke out. Some Federals made it down the cow path to the river, but most of the men hurled themselves over the bluff and fell into the river and sank under the weight of their equipment. For the Northerners who made it to the riverbank, there were no boats. The large flatboat used to ferry the wounded to the rear was swamped by panicked men and capsized. A small group of eighty Federals managed to march upstream along the shore and establish a ferry to the northern tip of Harrison's Island. While the macabre scene played itself out on the river, the Southerners clustered along the edge of the bluffs and maintained a deadly fire on anyone in a blue uniform.

When the fighting was over, the Federal losses were devastating: 49 killed, 198 wounded, 529 captured, and well over 100 lost to the river. For the next several weeks, bodies washed ashore around Washington. Confederate losses were 36 killed and 117 wounded.

News of the battle that should never have been fought shocked the Northern public. The defeat three months earlier at Manassas had been a blow to Union morale, but that was viewed as a clash of titans with the fate of the nation in the balance. In contrast, the battle at Ball's Bluff was over nothing. No strategic goal was at hand. Baker's death only emphasized the needlessness of the engagement.

Most embarrassed by the affair was McClellan. He had not wanted to fight a battle because he knew that his army was not yet ready—although in his eyes it would never be ready. He had hoped to gain a foothold in the Leesburg area by maneuver, not by force of arms. The affair only illustrated that the Union command was too loose to engage the Confederates when units went into combat and failed to communicate effectively from the field. The chain between McClellan and Stone and Baker had been too slack. The latter were the victims of vague orders from McClellan, and Baker—a prominent politician and confidant of the president—was dead on the field. Baker was dead because he was a poor field commander, but the brunt of the blame and judgment that should have fallen on him was borne by Stone.

Out of the ashes of the tragedy at Ball's Bluff came the Joint Committee on the Conduct of the War. Someone had to answer for

Baker arrived at the top of the bluff around two o'clock. Although he was a veteran of the Mexican War, he had little combat experience and made several tactical errors, which included failure to notify Stone of the situation. He was killed around 4:30 in front of his troops. The Federals began to withdraw shortly after six o'clock.

the Union disasters, and the politicians in Washington decided that they should police the military commanders. Failure now had a price beyond casualty lists and public censure. The seven-member committee established in December 1861 was controlled by Radical Republicans. It was a star chamber, holding hearings in secret, denying legal counsel to witnesses, and prone to accepting as fact any allegation of treasonous behavior. The commanders most susceptible to the Joint Committee were those who had ties to the Democratic Party or were nonabolitionists.

In fact, McClellan was the committee's primary target, but he was protected by the president. So the committee attacked him by investigating some of the generals who were unfortunate enough to be involved or were close to the scene of a military embarrassment. First on the list was Charles Pomeroy Stone.

For his part, Stone was a remarkably loyal soldier of the republic. A member of the West Point Class of 1845, he had served in the Mexican War and been breveted twice for gallantry. He stayed in the army until 1856 then returned in January 1861 when summoned by general in chief Winfield Scott to command the volunteers defending the national capital. His men were posted across Washington during Lincoln's inauguration, watchful of any attempt to assassinate the new president. When McClellan was brought to Washington to command the armies of the republic, Stone was assigned to command a division.

Despite the fact that Stone was a son of Massachusetts, he was not an abolitionist. If anything, he was severely conservative in political matters and did not blur the line between political beliefs and military rectitude. Such personal discipline proved to be potent when his division was stationed in Maryland, a slave state that was held in the Union largely by the strong-arm maneuverings of the Lincoln administration.

As a commander, Stone was something of an old army martinet, and some of the New England troops serving under him were not pleased to be ordered to return fugitive slaves to their Maryland owners. To make matters worse, Stone issued an order against "advising and encouraging insubordination among the negro servants in their neighborhood." Stone's version of military discipline also did little to endear his men to him.

The Ball's Bluff matter came back to haunt Stone when his official report of the battle was leaked to the *New York Tribune* in late October 1861. In it Stone praised Baker's bravery but elucidated the politician's shortcomings as a commander in the field. Many rose up to defend the dead hero and to point fingers at Stone.

In the brouhaha that followed, one of Stone's soldiers wrote to Massachusetts Gov. John A. Andrew of the orders to return fugitive slaves to their owners. The governor and Sen. Charles Sumner of Massachusetts denounced the order and the man behind it. Congressmen began to call for an investigation, which the Joint Committee was only too happy to oblige.

All testimony before the committee was delivered in secret. In January 1862 Stone was among the first witnesses called, and he restated his version of the battle much as it had appeared in the newspaper, although he was forbidden by orders from McClellan—who had much to lose—from divulging anything of the nonplanning that preceded the movements of October 19–21. At best, the vagueness of McClellan's orders would be damning of the commanding general. McClellan was torn between the injustice coming toward Stone and protecting himself. McClellan won that battle of conscience.

The opinion of the committee turned hard against Stone when members of a New York regiment testified that the general had communicated with Confederates and exchanged many sealed packages with them during numerous—too numerous to their liking—white-flag truces. They also added that Stone had permitted civilians to pass freely between the lines and that most "secession-minded" Marylanders had a good opinion of the man. Stone was also charged with allowing the Southerners to erect a fort to defend Leesburg. Almost a third of the thirty-six witnesses called during the investigation were men from this regiment.

Stone was quizzed on these accusations, because treason had been implied more than ineptitude. Regarding the matter of fugitive slaves, the inquiry went something like this:

QUESTION: It is said of you that you take slaves and return them to secessionists. . . .

ANSWER: That is a slander that has been circulated very freely, and, I am sorry to say, by men in official position.

QUESTION: Do not understand that I mean it as a reflection upon you. But I have seen that statement in the papers.

ANSWER: It has been uttered on the floor of the Senate. I am sent with a military force into a certain county in Maryland. I was told when I was sent there that I was to give full and complete protection to that county. I have tried to obey every order of the War Department I have ever received; and, upon the other hand, I have insisted upon my troops obeying every law of the State of Maryland. I do not allow them to harbor the slaves, or the free employed negroes, or the apprentices, or the sons and daughters of the farmers in that neighborhood in my camps. If a negro runs away from a farmer into my camps and lounges around there, he is turned out of the camps. . . . The slaves that run away from the enemy and come over are got to my head-quarters as rapidly as possible; they are then questioned carefully, and all the information I can get from them is taken. They are made as comfortable as they can be, and put to work in the quartermaster's department, or have been until lately. If they can take care of themselves, they have been allowed to do so the best way they could. If they have needed assistance, they have been fed and clothed and put to work by the quartermaster or commissary. I am not aware of any slaves coming over from the enemy's lines having been given up to any claimant.

Fugitive slaves were one thing; passing information to the enemy was another. Or so the testimony of the New Yorkers had implied. The regimental commander, Col. George W. B. Tomkins, had come to the committee on his own. He may have been motivated to slander Stone given that Stone had pressed charges against Tomkins in September 1861 for what amounted to fraud and also cowardice in the face of the enemy. The matter was not yet resolved when Stone encountered his own troubles. This information was subsequently brought before the committee to offset the testimony of the New Yorkers against Stone.

The committee seemingly disregarded the motivation of the New Yorkers now that it had the tantalizing specter of treason. Members of the committee also ignored any testimony that explained the exchange of packages as correspondence from prisoners. In the mind of the committee, Baker was not done in by his own folly; he was betrayed by his commanding officer.

This interesting distortion of Stone's case was taken to the new secretary of war, Edwin M. Stanton. When the committee suggested that Stone be investigated by the War Department, Stanton was very anxious to gain the committee's confidence. He ordered Stone's arrest and imprisonment at Fort Lafayette in New York Harbor. Most of the political prisoners of the Lincoln administration were sent there. Stone himself allegedly exclaimed when informed of his destination, "Why, Fort Lafayette is where they send the secessionists!"

At this point McClellan acted to protect Stone. He held the secretary's arrest order for several days, and he went to the committee to ask that Stone be allowed to respond to the charges that had been laid against him. On January 31 Stone appeared before the committee again and again justified his actions on October 21. When the allegations of disloyalty were mentioned, Stone was thunderstruck. He explained the exchange of prisoner parcels and denied that a fort had been built within range of his guns.

After this appearance before the committee, the recommendation to Stanton was not changed, and the arrest order was reissued. McClellan tried to find alternatives, but in the end he justified the arrest on the flimsiest evidence his chief of intelligence, Allan Pinkerton, could devise: The Confederates and Maryland secessionists thought Stone was "a very fine man." Collusion, at least in McClellan's mind, was "proven." The arrest was made during the early morning hours of Saturday, February 8, 1862.

Stone was transported by train the next evening to New York. Some confusion at the depot in Philadelphia forced the prisoner to pay for his own ticket to the place of his incarceration. As soon as he arrived at Fort Lafayette, he was placed in solitary confinement.

News of Stone's imprisonment made headlines throughout the North. Stanton ensured that enough information leaked to imply that Stone had been charged with disloyalty. He was quickly tried, convicted, and sentenced in the court of public opinion. The general consensus was that hanging was too good a fate for a man like Stone.

Stone retained counsel and awaited a formal serving of the charges against him, which, according to the articles of war, were to be filed within eight days of the arrest. When the deadline came and passed, nothing was delivered to the prisoner or his attorney. Stone sent inquiries to McClellan's headquarters, the adjutant general's office, and the secretary of war. No substantive information was conveyed back to the prisoner. McClellan's staff responded that the matter was still under investigation. Stanton indicated that the charges were being reviewed prior to being publicized. The adjutant general's office did not respond at all.

In the meantime, the Joint Committee on the Conduct of the War heard nine additional witnesses in the Stone matter. Since they corroborated Stone's account of the incident, the committee chose to ignore it. Pinkerton chose to continue interviewing Marylanders and amassing information for a file he titled, "Further information concerning Gen. Stone's treachery."

For weeks nothing was done in Washington regarding the case. The War Department was content to have a villain behind bars. The Joint Committee believed it had demonstrated its value by investigating the Ball's Bluff matter and finding the culpable culprit behind the tragedy. McClellan was relieved that his failings in the matter had not been exposed.

During the withdrawal from the fight, many Union soldiers fell into the river and drowned or were shot by the Confederates massed on the heights. The bodies were retrieved from the Potomac throughout the following week.

Stanton found that Stone's imprisonment communicated to the generals beneath him the ruthless measures he was prepared to take if they did not prosecute the war aggressively and to his satisfaction. For his part, Lincoln allegedly told Stanton, "To hold one commander in prison untried is less harmful in times of great national distress than to withdraw several good officers from active battlefields to give him a trial." To pursue the matter in court would be to lose it. The evidence against Stone was hearsay at best and imaginary at worse. For as long as the general was behind bars, the generals in the field would know that the war would be fought not just militarily but with regard to the goals and policies of the administration.

To be sure, Stone had his defenders, not the least of which was Winfield Scott. The old general thundered from retirement at West Point, "If he is a traitor [then] I am a traitor, and we are all traitors." A petition from Massachusetts found its way to the White House. It was signed by representatives of many of the Bay State's most prominent families, Boston politicians, Harvard luminaries, and hundreds of others. Voices were raised on Capitol Hill, and a measure was passed urging the president to report on Stone's arrest. Politically, the validity of the Joint Committee was called into question, and the committee members responded that their investigation had raised no question of Stone's guilt.

In New York Harbor, after seven weeks of confinement in Fort Lafayette, Stone was transferred to Fort Hamilton, which was supposedly less oppressive. His inquiries to the War Department remained unanswered. To a friend, Stone wrote, "I am in a complete muddle."

Stone's advocates continued to press for his release. In the early summer, Sen. James A. McDougall of California added a rider to a military pay bill. The matter addressed officers under arrest and repeated the stipulation of the articles of war that required charges to be filed within eight days of an arrest but added that imprisoned officers were entitled to a trial within thirty days of their arrest. Crucial to the legislation, at least in regard to Stone, was that the proscriptions would be applicable to anyone currently under arrest and awaiting trial.

The measure passed, but Stanton exercised his prerogative and did not act until thirty days after the measure had become law. Stone was released from confinement on August 16, 1862, following 189 days behind bars. The release order stated succinctly, "The necessities of the service not permitting the trial, within the time required by law, of Brigadier General C. P. Stone, now in confinement in Fort LaFayette [*sic*] awaiting trial, the Secretary of War directs that he be released from arrest."

Freedom, however, meant little to Stone without clearing his name. He continued to press for information on what charges had been filed against him and by whom. General in chief Henry W. Halleck's letter of reply stated, "I have no official information of the cause of your arrest, but I understand that it was made by the orders of the President. No charges or specifications are, so far as I can ascertain, on file against you." Yet Halleck had no orders for Stone.

In a face-to-face meeting with Stone at the White House, the president said that if he could tell him all he knew about the matter, he could tell Stone very little.

Stanton claimed that the arrest order came from McClellan.

McClellan insisted that he had acted only on Stanton's orders and had consistently appealed for Stone's release.

When the Confederate army invaded in September 1862, precipitating even more chaos in Washington and (following John Pope's defeat at Second Manassas) leading Lincoln to turn back to McClellan when he needed a commander for the army, McClellan submitted a request to Stanton to reinstate Stone. The request was denied.

In early 1863, when Joseph Hooker, the latest general to be named to command the Army of the Potomac, nominated Stone to be his chief of staff, Stanton denied the request.

Stone was persistent nonetheless. During a meeting with members of the Joint Committee in February 1863, he was allowed to hear the damaging testimony that had been offered against him and to respond. Stone answered each accusation to the committee's satisfaction, and since McClellan was no longer in command of the army, Stone could relate in detail the vague orders he had received from McClellan that led to the debacle at Ball's Bluff. The committee revised its report on the matter to include this testimony. To all intents and purposes, the blot on Stone's record was expunged. All was not forgiven, however.

For a brief time Stone was given a post in the western theater. Out of the blue, Stanton ordered that he be mustered out of the volunteers;

his rank reverted to that of a colonel in the regular army. In August 1864 Stone was given a brigade in the Army of the Potomac, but he was a pariah. Questions of loyalty were raised anew, and Stone saw no recourse other than to resign his commission.

Stone turned to commercial pursuits but was heavily in debt in the immediate postwar years. In 1870 he and about fifty former commanders of the war, including Confederates, found military positions in Egypt. Stone was made a chief of staff. One of the expatriates with him was Walter H. Jenifer, a Southerner who had fought at Ball's Bluff. Stone remained in Egypt for thirteen years, returning to the United States after Britain conquered the ancient land in 1882.

Lacking military pursuits, Stone returned to engineering. His last project was to supervise the conversion of Fort Wood, a fort in New York Harbor, as the foundation for the Statue of Liberty and to erect the pedestal on which the statue was to be placed. Crucial to the erection of the symbolic monument were the structural supports to hold the memorial together in the face of the wind currents in the harbor—wind currents that were unkind memories of the time Stone was incarcerated at the harbor twenty-two years earlier.

The scapegoat of Ball's Bluff died on January 24, 1887, after falling ill following the dedication ceremony of the statue the previous October, a victim of the weather in the harbor that day. Stone, unjustly characterized by many of his contemporaries as the Benedict Arnold of the Civil War, was buried at West Point.

PART 4

UNEXPECTED EVENTS

12

FIRST BULL RUN

THE BEGINNING OF A WAR

THERE WAS SO MUCH excitement about the first major battle of the Civil War that hundreds of civilians from Washington rode out to the battlefield on Saturday, July 20, 1861, to see the "contest" that would determine the outcome of the war. In addition to the politicians and curiosity seekers, many women joined their men and brought picnic baskets with them. They found the Union army in camps near Centreville, awaiting orders as Irvin McDowell was forced yet again to revise his battle plans. Off in the distance, they could hear the train traffic around Manassas Junction. Most thought it signaled Confederate reserves coming up from Richmond to join the Rebel ranks; little did they know that much more was involved in the coming and going of the overworked locomotives.

Very few of the Union commanders had wanted to fight this battle. All knew that their volunteer soldiers were not trained sufficiently to perform well under combat conditions. The seventy-five-year-old general in chief, Winfield Scott, had said as much in every war planning meeting to which he was invited.

Instead of seeking a single winner-take-all battle, such as many were talking about at the time, in the weeks following the loss of Fort Sumter, Scott ruminated on a plan to blockade Southern ports and launch a single campaign down the length of the Mississippi River. He estimated that eighty thousand soldiers, a dozen training camps, and four months would be needed before the effort could be launched. Time, however, was more his adversary than the South. Both politicians and the public clamored for action.

In general, the reaction to Scott's plan was that he was too old and too passive for the task at hand. Conventional wisdom also dismissed his idea as too elaborate, because the war wasn't going to last that long. Strategically, Scott's scheme was solid, and in time it would be implemented in full and would achieve the Northern victory. In 1861, however, the country was too impatient for the war planners to consider a long-range strategy.

Scott's plan was ridiculed in the press and called both the "Boa Constrictor" plan (coined by George B. McClellan when the two discussed strategy in the early weeks of the war) and the "Anaconda" plan. Both referred to a passive approach of weakening the South through blockade and isolation. Instead the public was whipped into a frenzy by newspaper editors who urged the military

Irwin McDowell (left) and Winfield Scott (right)

BOTH IMAGES: LIBRARY OF CONGRESS

to exploit the militia troops at hand and seize Richmond before the Confederate Congress was scheduled to first meet in the city on July 20.

Almost no one other than Scott counseled patience in Washington, but aside from devising war plans, it was also clear to him that a younger man was needed to lead the army in the field. All could see that the three-hundred-pound Scott was physically unable to ride a horse, much less prowl a battlefield. There were few candidates for the job after the defection to the South of almost a third of the officers in the army. The lot fell almost immediately to Irvin McDowell more by chance than ability.

McDowell had served during the war against Mexico, but he had been a desk soldier ever since. His candidacy stood out because of his work with Secretary of the Treasury Salmon P. Chase in supervising the early steps in securing Washington and overseeing the defense of the city when the secession crisis bloomed into war.

Scott preferred another man, Col. Joseph Mansfield, whose age handicapped the likelihood of his command.

There was little time to dicker over either man's qualifications or connections. Lincoln was intent on taking an aggressive step because more than thirty-five thousand Federal troops were camped in northern Virginia at Alexandria and near Harpers Ferry (the prewar strength of the U.S. Army was only about seventeen thousand men). Most of these men in the camps were committed to ninety-day enlistments, and the clock had started running in late April.

At a cabinet meeting on June 29, McDowell surprisingly joined Scott in asking for more time. The men, he argued, needed some rudimentary training in order to execute his orders in the field.

Time, however, was not within Lincoln's power to grant. Word had come to Washington of thirty thousand Confederates clustered near the crossroads of Manassas Junction, only forty miles away. The president ordered McDowell to attack.

Scott and McDowell ceased to argue with the politicians and produced a plan of attack they had been preparing in recent weeks. McDowell would lead the army from Washington to hit P. G. T. Beauregard's army at Manassas, and the Federal troops near Harpers Ferry would occupy and otherwise prevent Joseph E. Johnston's army in western Virginia from joining Beauregard. This second body of Union troops was led by Maj. Gen. Robert Patterson, a peer of Scott and also somewhat limited by his age.

McDowell's army of thirty-five thousand, fewer than one thousand of which were regulars of the U.S. Army, began to move across the Potomac from the camps around Washington on July 8. By the time McDowell was ready to lead his men toward Manassas on July 16, his was the largest army ever assembled on the North American continent.

Scott considered accompanying the troops in a buggy so that he could lend his expertise to McDowell on the battlefield. In the end, he settled for waiting in his office for regular news of the upcoming action.

Beauregard was anxious. The Northern newspapers were full of stories that detailed McDowell's preparations. Their reporting was almost as reliable as the loose network of spies that kept the Southern commander informed on the comings and goings and deliberations of the Federal troops and commanders. Beauregard got a little carried away with himself and considered launching an attack on Washington. Jefferson Davis and Robert E. Lee quashed such plans and counseled the commander to wait for the opportunities that might come with the Federal advance. Beauregard considered himself a disciple of Napoleonic tactics, and he contented himself to pattern his plans for the upcoming attack after the battle of Austerlitz. He constantly surveyed and wandered around the Manassas area, absorbing the lay of the land. Four towers were erected for signalmen.

The Confederate line was formed along the stream know as Bull Run. Its five-foot-high banks presented a significant barrier for the Federals. Only one bridge would accommodate a moving army, but there were seven fords that the Federals could also use to cross the small waterway. Beauregard allocated his troops to defend the fords most likely to be used by McDowell's men, but he chose not to protect the northernmost ford, Sudley Ford, because the roads leading to it were little known and too winding. He decided that McDowell would probably avoid the Stone Bridge crossing of the Warrenton turnpike because it was the most obvious approach. Instead he believed that the Union army would try to cross the run at Mitchell's Ford, because the crossing was in a direct line between Centreville and Manassas. The other fords were ruled out because they were surrounded by dense woods, a tremendous impediment to a large body of marching men.

Half of Beauregard's army was positioned at Mitchell's Ford and reinforced downstream at Blackburn's Ford. The rest were parceled out to the other fords according to the likelihood of McDowell's using them. The resulting line was five miles long, from Union Mills to the south to the Stone Bridge to the north. More than 70 percent of the Confederate force occupied the right half of the line. Beauregard kept his options open for using this mass of men to attack across Bull Run and isolate McDowell's army, preventing the Federals from falling back to Washington.

The latest word from one of his most reliable spies, Washington socialite Rose O'Neal Greenhow, was that McDowell's offensive would commence on July 16. Her information was correct.

McDowell's army left Arlington Heights in three columns, each with a slightly different route to Manassas. No one seemed to be in a hurry to get there. Progress was hampered by heat, narrow roads, little discipline, and poor judgment. Word of the Federal advance came in time for many Confederate outposts to withdraw in order and without panic. Communication between the columns and McDowell was also hampered by the lumbering pace of the three columns.

On July 18 McDowell issued orders for a quick thrust toward Manassas through Centreville to see if the latter village had been

Pierre Gustave Toutant Beauregard (left) and Joseph E. Johnston (right)

The attack began at 9:30 A.M. on July 21, a Sunday morning. McDowell tried to outflank the Confederates, but he did so with an exhausted, untrained army.

abandoned. Then he set out to find the column that was to cross Bull Run at Union Mills. En route he saw for himself that the terrain was too rough to accommodate the planned crossing. Such discoveries were the price paid for the absence of good maps. McDowell found the column and ordered it to Centreville.

In the meantime, the probe toward Centreville had gone way too far. Finding the village all but abandoned, the column commander, Brig. Gen. David Hunter, pushed on to Bull Run to see the Confederate deployment there. From a position overlooking Blackburn's and Mitchell's Fords, Hunter glimpsed Manassas in the distance. The sight proved to be too much of a temptation, and a short skirmish ensued. James Longstreet commanded the Southerners defending Mitchell's Ford, and his numbers were too great for the few companies of Federal troops that advanced on his position. Hunter called off the attack just as a furious McDowell arrived to chastise him for exceeding his orders. The Union force pulled back to Centreville.

For two days McDowell considered his options and finally decided to try to outflank the left side of the Confederate line. A diversion would occupy the Southerners at the Stone Bridge while the main body crossed at Sudley Ford—the only position that Beauregard had left undefended.

Action was slated to begin on July 20, but supplies were delayed in reaching him. Picnickers from Washington showed up instead. And train whistles echoed from Manassas Junction.

Hunter's blundering attempt to take Mitchell's Ford led Beauregard to call for reinforcements and specifically for Joseph E. Johnston's army near Harpers Ferry. The movement of these troops began on July 19 across the rickety railroad between Piedmont Station and Manassas. Among the first troops to arrive was the brigade of Brig. Gen. Thomas J. Jackson. His men were quickly joined by those of Col. Francis S. Bartow, Brig. Gen. Barnard E. Bee, and Edmund Kirby Smith.

Johnston himself arrived on July 20. Despite outranking Beauregard, he did not take command, reasoning that Beauregard was more familiar with the field on which the fighting would take place. None of the arriving troops were sent to shore up the left side of the Confederate line, however.

In McDowell's headquarters orders were issued for the crossing at Sudley Ford. At the time the Union commander believed that Johnston's army would eventually get to Manassas, but he hoped to have dispatched Beauregard before Johnston could arrive. McDowell's army was to be prepared to march at 2 A.M.

Nothing went right at the appointed hour. McDowell was sick that night and slept a little longer, hoping to find his troops in position and ready for the attack at 6 A.M. Everyone, however, took longer than expected to get into position. The column sent north to Sudley Ford became lost and did not arrive at the crossing until 9 A.M., but the attack at the Stone Bridge had commenced on time, roughly three hours earlier.

The small force of Confederate defenders at the bridge was commanded by Col. Nathan Evans. As soon as the fighting began, he called for reinforcements but engaged the Federals in piecemeal fashion, masking his numbers. When the Union attackers made no effort to take the bridge, Evans suspected another attack would come from a different direction. When pickets and signalmen reported the Federals crossing at Sudley Ford, he left four companies to keep the bridge attackers occupied and moved the rest of his men toward

Sudley Ford to attack. He found a good position on Matthews Hill, a mile south of the ford. He was in position by 9 A.M. The Federals appeared at 9:15.

Evans caught them by surprise. The Federal column was comprised of David Hunter's and Samuel Heintzelman's commands. Hunter was seriously wounded in the early fighting. He turned command over to Ambrose E. Burnside, whose horse was shot out from under him. Although the Union men far outnumbered the Confederates, they hunkered down and the Southerners charged. It was a foolish maneuver, and Evans pulled back.

Meanwhile, rushing toward the fighting were Bee's and Bartow's brigades. They formed a new line with Evans on the far left.

Burnside's men massed in front of them and beyond the left side of the Confederate line. In the face of the growing presence of the enemy, Evans, Bee, and Bartow did the only thing they could think to do— they charged. For that they paid a heavy price before pulling back.

As he withdrew, Bee saw troops coming from the direction of the Stone Bridge and believed them to be reinforcements. The unit proved to be from Wisconsin and its commander was William T. Sherman. He had forded Bull Run just above the bridge, and another Yankee brigade was just behind him. A devastating fire ripped through the Southerners.

The Confederates fell back below the Warrenton turnpike and reformed on Henry Hill. In the meantime, the Union units united on Matthews Hill. With them was McDowell, and he rode down the length of the line and proclaimed, "Victory! Victory! The day is ours!"

From Mitchell's Ford, Beauregard and Johnston had heard the clamor to the northwest. They had dispatched Bee, Bartow, and Jackson to the fighting there but did little else. Finally, shortly before noon, Johnston announced that he was going to the area because that was where the fight was. His pronouncement seemed to stir something within Beauregard, who ordered Theophilus H. Holmes, Jubal Early, and Milledge Bonham to join Johnston. At the same time, he sent troops across Bull Run to try to develop a position behind the Federals. After a while, he took to horse and rode to the northwest after Johnston.

The fighting between Matthews and Henry Hills exacted a terrible toll from the three Confederate brigades that tried to hold off two divisions of the Union army. Wade Hampton's legion of South Carolinians attempted to reinforce Evans, Bee, and Bartow, but they soon found themselves alone in the fight as the others fell back. Hampton was not long in pulling back himself.

McDowell's troops took time to reform along the Warrenton turnpike. They too had paid a steep price up to this moment, mostly for the tactical manner in which their commanders sent them regiment by regiment against the Confederates rather than attacking in force. Sherman's brigades and others arrived on the scene to solidify the line, which was also buttressed by twenty-four field pieces. Some eleven thousand men awaited orders to sweep the Southerners from Henry Hill.

While Bee, Bartow, and Evans fought for their lives, Jackson's five regiments took a defensive position just shy of the crest of Henry Hill. Thirteen cannon were also positioned on the slope shy of the summit. The artillery gave some assistance to the struggling Southerners in the fight, but Jackson waited and had his men lie down.

Bee was on horseback and rode up to Jackson. After a brief exchange, Bee returned to his men, that is, what was left of them. While rallying them, he allegedly said, "There is Jackson standing like a stone wall. Let us determine to die here, and we will conquer. Follow me."

What he meant by that comment has become something of a mystery. Jackson's detractors have suggested that Bee was frustrated

BATTLES AND LEADERS

For the first time in war, trains shuttled troops from one front to another. When the Federal army began to move against Manassas Junction, Confederate troops from Edmund Kirby Smith's army in the Shenandoah Valley were shifted to swell the ranks of Beauregard's army positioned to protect the vital railroad junction.

This map illustrates the battle lines that formed around Henry Hill late in the afternoon of July 21, 1861, after Beauregard and Johnston had moved up to respond to the Federal approach from Sudley Ford.

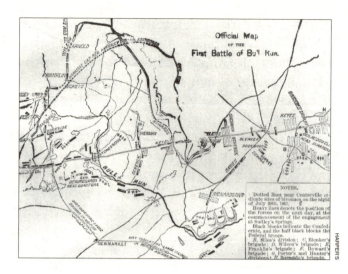

that Jackson did not fling his men into the fighting and allowed Bee's men to be mauled. Others have interpreted the comment to mean that Jackson's brigade had solidified the position for a counterattack. Whatever Bee meant, he did not survive the battle to explain it. Whether the comment was directed in praise or criticism, it dubbed Jackson as "Stonewall" for eternity. Shortly after Bee's rally, he was mortal wounded.

Soon after Bee's wounding, Johnston and Beauregard arrived on the scene. Johnston re-formed the scrambled remnants of Bee's, Bartow's, and Evans's commands and led them back into the line, shoring up the right side. Beauregard directed his energies to the men on the left. Jackson held the center.

Johnston then withdrew from the front line so he could direct reinforcing units now rushing to this sector of the battlefield. Beauregard commanded the scene of the action by detailing the newcomers to positions in the line as the fighting progressed.

The right side of the Confederate line was anchored by Hampton's men near the Warrenton turnpike. Beauregard extended the left side of the line almost to Sudley Road, positioning Jeb Stuart's cavalry in the woods there. By 2 P.M. he had almost sixty-five hundred men and thirteen cannon in position.

McDowell was anxious to end it all. He had taught tactics at West Point, and he decided to move up half of his artillery to blow a hole through the middle of the Confederate line. It was a very Napoleonic maneuver, but McDowell's men faced rifles with far greater range than the muskets encountered by the French emperor's artillerymen.

The guns were brought up without infantry support, which one of the battery commanders, Capt. Charles Griffin immediately protested. The Union guns were moved to within three hundred yards of the Confederates. Infantry support was eventually dispatched to protect the guns, but these Federals stumbled into some of Jackson's men. Some fought back. The vast majority of the Union men withdrew behind the batteries.

Suddenly Stuart's horsemen burst onto the scene and rode through the Federal units sent to support the guns. The Northerners stood their ground but eventually refused to move forward toward the advance batteries. Artillery without infantry support invited disaster.

Griffin moved two of his guns to cover the right side of his position and to fire down the length of the Confederate line. One of Jackson's commanders reacted by seizing the moment and moving out to attack the Federal gunners. Allegedly his blue-uniformed men confused the Union artillerists, who held their fire until it was too late. The Southerners marched to within seventy yards then decimated the gunners with heavy volleys. The Federals pulled back, abandoning their guns on the slope of Henry Hill. A panic erupted in the Union ranks. Many ran back through the line and toward Sudley Ford, where their fear generated a wariness in the units being brought up as reinforcements.

Jackson sized up the situation and ordered his men to charge. The ground was occupied for the next two hours with charges and countercharges. The abandoned Federal field guns became something of a trophy for both sides, but neither held them long enough to either pull them into their lines or turn them against the other side.

McDowell became too occupied with the fighting to call up his reserves. Copying the error of the morning, he sent his men into combat unit by unit.

Commanders were confused by the variety of uniforms worn by the various militias that formed so much of both armies. Some failed to recognize the Confederate banner as distinct from the Stars and Stripes. As a result many units either mistakenly held their fire or fired on comrades. The heat also exacted a toll, especially on men who fought with full field packs and all their equipment. Many fumbled at firing their weapons; they were not sufficiently trained to execute the complicated loading-and-firing procedure while under fire.

The Federals exhausted the units coming into the line, and they fell back in a panic. Whereas McDowell failed to funnel all his men toward the fighting, Beauregard and Johnston summoned the vast majority of their men into this part of the battlefield. Confederate units rushed to the scene included the newly arrived command of Brig. Gen. Edmund Kirby Smith. His men were sent to the left side of the line, where they fell on the last of McDowell's jittery men to join the fighting. The blow shattered the right side of the Union line.

While panic swept through the Federal ranks, Beauregard ordered the Confederate line to advance. McDowell's line fell apart at 4:30 P.M.

The Union commander witnessed firsthand his dispirited troops in flight. He ordered his army regulars to hold as much of the line as they could while the others fled. During the desperate departure from the field, the Federals abandoned twenty-eight artillery pieces, five thousand muskets, twenty-six wagons, and untold amounts of camp equipment and clothing.

The Southerners were hindered in exploiting the panic because their ranks quickly became occupied with huge numbers of prisoners. Few pressed the matter beyond Centreville. Fearful of a counterattack on the right side of his original position along Bull Run, Beauregard held back. He terminated the pursuit of the Federal retreat at 7 P.M.

Both sides were exhausted by the day-long fighting, but the fatigued Federals had many miles to go to return to the safety of their camps in Alexandria and around Washington. Many would not halt until the Potomac River was behind them.

A heavy rain began to fall that night, making quagmires of the roads. At least the Confederates would not be pressing the defeated Northerners any more.

At daybreak the residents of the Federal capital awoke to find the streets infested with the ragged remnants of McDowell's demoralized army. These men were nothing like the proud patriots who had so recently marched on these same streets.

The battle had been the first combat for the vast majority of men on the plains around Manassas Junction. McDowell's army suffered three thousand casualties, including 470 dead. Beauregard had two thousand casualties, with 387 dead.

Confederate heroes were found in the fighting, notably Jackson, Evans, Beauregard, and Johnston. Jackson thanked an almighty God for the victory. Evans and Beauregard patted themselves on the back. Johnston felt ignored and resented Beauregard. Nevertheless, several brigade and regimental commanders distinguished themselves and would continue to do so in upcoming engagements.

In Washington, Lincoln was more than disappointed. He was also under fire himself, for it is the practice of the side to lose such battles to obsess with blaming someone for the defeat. Part of that burden fell on McDowell as commander of the army, and a small part fell on Winfield Scott as the chief military commander, but the lion's share of the blame fell on Lincoln. This was true especially after it was reported that, in the presence of cabinet and congressional members, Scott had exclaimed to Lincoln: "I am the greatest coward in America! I will prove it. I have fought this battle, sir, against my judgment; I think [you] should remove me for doing it."

Although the buzz on Capitol Hill was that Lincoln had prodded McDowell to act before the army was ready, Lincoln did not dwell on

As the fighting progressed on the afternoon of July 21, Johnston took a position not that far from the front so he could direct repositioning units into place to counter the Union attack.

When the Union lines collapsed and the army ran back to Washington, many of the citizen soldiers had tales to tell of what had happened. Their confidence was left on the battlefield, but they shortly found a new discipline in their camps, brought by a new commander, George B. McClellan, who would turn them into an army.

HARPER'S PICTORIAL HISTORY OF THE CIVIL WAR

the issue of blame. The president did not remove his general in chief—yet. He looked instead for a new commander for his army, one who was not as passive as Scott or as deskbound as McDowell. The war that lay ahead was going to be far more difficult than anyone had imagined. This war would be more than a contest of competing virtues; it was going to be a dirty, filthy, costly conflict that could be paid for only with blood.

It is strange that the battle that both sides expected to decide the war became instead the beginning of the costliest war in American history. This first engagement claimed roughly nine hundred men, but by the end of the war more than six hundred thousand would die. Strange indeed was the fact that both armies would return to this same ground almost thirteen months later to fight again, only this time the Southerners would be attacking from the direction of Sudley Ford and the Northerners would have their backs to Henry Hill. That one ended in another Federal rout, too.

13

MISSIONARY RIDGE

A SUICIDAL ATTACK WITHOUT ORDERS

MISSIONARY RIDGE HAS NO close parallel among the many battles of the Civil War. This one-and-only status stems in part from the fact that no other city in the United States has a topography quite like that of Chattanooga, Tennessee.

Chattanooga stands on the south bank of the Tennessee River just east of a radical bend in the waterway known as Moccasin Point. Four railroads passed through the city—the Nashville and Chattanooga, the Trenton, the Chattanooga and Cleveland, and the Western and Atlantic. The last of these linked the city with Atlanta. South of the city was the promontory known as Lookout Mountain. To the east and extending from well above Chattanooga to well below the city lay Missionary Ridge.

Since September 22, 1863, the city had sheltered William S. Rosecrans and the thirty-five thousand men of his army that had survived the battle of Chickamauga. Although encamped here, these men were not safe, for the heights of Lookout Mountain and Missionary Ridge were occupied by Braxton Bragg's Army of Tennessee.

The Southerners controlled all access to the city, and Bragg chose to wait out Rosecrans. His cavalry harassed and destroyed wagon trains of supplies, and his artillery and sharpshooters controlled the usual approaches to the city.

Rosecrans was in a muddle of confusion amid the chaos created by the deprivations caused to his army and the city inhabitants. The War Department responded by dispatching Joseph Hooker and twenty thousand men to protect the railroad leading to Chattanooga. Also summoned to the region was William T. Sherman and seventeen thousand men.

Meanwhile, Bragg took time to purge his army of two generals who had not performed well at Chickamauga—Thomas C. Hindman and Leonidas Polk. At the same time, his general officers petitioned Jefferson Davis to remove Bragg from command. This Davis would not do, both out of a sense of friendship with the man and because he could not think of anyone to whom he could transfer command. The president traveled to Chattanooga in early October for a meeting with all the officers and Bragg. Afterward the malcontents were reassigned.

In mid-October Lincoln created the Military Division of the Mississippi and placed Maj. Gen. Ulysses S. Grant in command. Grant was informed of this in a meeting with Edwin M. Stanton, the secretary of war, in Louisville on October 16. At about the same time, news arrived that Rosecrans was on the verge of abandoning Chattanooga. Grant telegraphed orders to Chattanooga in which Rosecrans was relieved and George H. Thomas, the only Yankee hero of the battle of Chickamauga, was given command as well as the directive to hold the city at all costs.

Grant rushed to Chattanooga and encountered the returning Rosecrans, who apprised him of the situation and made several suggestions, which Grant found compelling and wondered why he had not implemented them. Grant's route was the same as the supply line that kept the Union army barely functioning in Chattanooga, so he was able to see the transportation problem firsthand. He arrived at Thomas's headquarters on October 23. Thomas was already entertaining a plan to end Bragg's siege.

This plan was put into motion on October 27, and a two-pronged attack was laid on the Confederates at the crossing point on the river known as Brown's Ferry. By midafternoon the objective had been

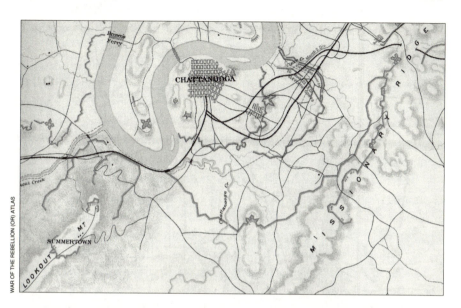

WAR OF THE REBELLION (OR) ATLAS

With Braxton Bragg's army in possession of Lookout Mountain to the southwest and Missionary Ridge to the east, William S. Rosecrans's army was trapped at Chattanooga.

secured, and Hooker's men, formerly encamped to protect the supply line, were on the march toward Chattanooga.

Bragg took his time in reacting to this incursion, not realizing what had been gained for the Northerners. Only by viewing Hooker's advance was he finally moved to act, and he ordered James Longstreet to retake Brown's Ferry. Longstreet initiated a night action at the Federal encampment at Wauhatchie, three miles south of Brown's Ferry. The fighting began shortly after midnight on October 29. Hooker responded with reinforcements from the ferry, and the conflict was over by 3:30 A.M. The sustained Federal presence here ended the siege.

Sherman arrived on November 14, and Grant immediately turned his eyes to the Confederate camps on Lookout Mountain and along Missionary Ridge. Ten days later he sent Hooker and ten thousand men toward the mountain. The eminence was not his goal, however. Hooker was to march past it and clear the valley between the mountain and Missionary Ridge of Confederates and threaten Bragg's army from the rear. If he saw an opportunity to take the heights, Hooker had authorization from Grant to pursue it.

The arrival of Sherman's troops, however, had led Bragg to shift men from the mountain to the ridge. So no more than seven thousand

Confederates were on the twenty-four-hundred-foot-high mass of rock when Hooker's men advanced.

Fog shrouded the Federals. They were on the Southerners before they knew it. A brisk skirmish began at 10 A.M. and escalated throughout the day as both sides threw more men into action. Most of the fighting was enveloped in fog and mist so that few on the ground could see what was happening on the heights. The struggle degenerated into brief skirmishes as night darkened the mountain.

In the morning the Union commanders discovered that the Confederates had abandoned Lookout Mountain during the night. Bragg pulled his men back and repositioned them on Missionary Ridge because he feared losing the troops on the mountain almost as much as he feared an imminent attack by Sherman along the ridge.

Federal control of the mountain removed the last element of the siege that had obstructed the flow of supplies to the Union army. Trains and steamers now returned to the city without hindrance.

Missionary Ridge was all that remained of Bragg's line around Chattanooga. Because Lookout Mountain had been taken fairly easily, many thought that since the ridge was not quite a third as tall as the mountain, the task ahead would be similar or easier than that which had just concluded. The ridge had little timber on its western slope and was deeply scored by gullies, which meant that many of the approaches consisted of nearly vertical bare rock.

At the base of the ridge, the Rebels had dug a heavy line of rifle pits and breastworks. A second line was erected behind the first, about three hundred or more feet higher. This second line was not as strong as the first and seemed to have been built as a refuge for use in the event that any men were forced to abandon the base.

Sherman began to move against Missionary Ridge as soon as the sun shone on November 25. Twenty-six thousand Federals faced ten thousand Confederates at the far right side of Bragg's line, near Tunnel Hill. This line, however, was formidable, made up of log-and-earth breastworks atop a steep slope. A half-mile of fairly open field separated the two armies.

The attack began at 10 A.M., but it was not to be a repeat of the previous day's success. Opposing Sherman was Patrick Cleburne, a man often compared favorably to Stonewall Jackson and perhaps Bragg's ablest general. Cleburne was tenacious in the face of the relentless assaults hurled against his men. When Confederate efforts seemed to fade at midafternoon, Cleburne ordered a bayonet charge that halted the Union attack in its tracks.

Sherman was frustrated by the futile fighting and messaged Grant that he believed the men could do no more that day. Grant replied tersely, "Attack again." Sherman sent a token force against the Confederates. It was turned back easily, ending the day's combat for Sherman.

In the meantime, Hooker's force moved toward Rossville Gap to threaten the Confederate rear. In contrast to Sherman's stalled assault, Hooker made significant gains, including a portion of the far left slopes of Missionary Ridge, mostly because troops from this area had been shifted to support Cleburne's defense of Tunnel Hill. Grant had hoped to break through the Confederate flank, but he expected it to be Sherman's doing, not Hooker's.

Grant and his staff moved forward to Orchard Knob, a small hill in front of Missionary Ridge, to monitor the action. From this position the commanding Union general had a clear view of Bragg's headquarters atop the ridge. As Sherman's attack was stalling, Grant decided to send Thomas's men against the center of the Confederate line. Being somewhat cautious and more than a little unsure of Thomas, Grant ordered him to take only the front line of rifle pits at the foot of the ridge and then await orders.

William S. Rosecrans (left) and George H. Thomas (right)

Joseph Hooker (third from the right) and his staff were photographed on the day of the battle for Lookout Mountain with the mountain in the background.

The three-mile-long line of works looked imposing to the Federal commanders, but Bragg had also thinned the ranks here to support Cleburne. Of the sixteen thousand men left in the area, he sent half to man the breastworks in front of the ridge and ordered them, if attacked, to fire only one volley and fall back. Further weakening his line was the fact that the second line of breastworks was not situated to cover all the ground in front of the ridge.

Grant's attack order stalled when one of Thomas's corps commanders, Gordon Granger, elected to manage the action of one of his batteries rather than act on the order. After an hour's delay, his error was corrected, and the Army of the Cumberland quickly moved forward.

Granger's repetition of Grant's order to advance on the rifle pits and halt caused some confusion among the generals of the Army of the Cumberland. Some doubted the accuracy of the order because they knew their men would never be more vulnerable than when they stood directly below the crest of the ridge and a counterattack was likely. Others were unsure of which of the two lines of rifle pits they were being ordered to seize. Before any could receive clarification, a six-gun volley from the batteries on Orchard Knob at 3:40 P.M. signaled the beginning of the attack.

Many of the men felt Grant's eyes upon them and knew of his disdain for their performance at Chickamauga. Thus there were no more motivated men on the field that day for the work ahead, regardless of how their officers interpreted their confused orders. Thomas, however, believed that his twenty-three thousand men were about to be sacrificed to atone for the failure of Sherman.

The bird's-eye view afforded the Confederates of the advancing Yankees was unnerving. When the Rebel batteries opened on the approaching columns, the valley reverberated with the echo. Some said that the firing was so rapid it sounded like the rattle of rifles. Little damage, however, was inflicted on the Federals, as most of the Southern shells overshot the Union ranks.

As soon as the rifle pits came into view—a yellowish gash in the earth in front of them—the Federals loosed a cheer, and many fairly sprinted toward the breastworks. The open ground was enough stimulus for them to do so, because no officer recalled issuing the order. No doubt these soldiers in blue were electrified by the sight of the chaos within the ranks of the Southerners as they withdrew from the first line of rifle pits and clambered up the ridge toward the second line. Many of the Confederates were caught in the open, abandoning their position on orders from Bragg, who chose to shift troops just as the Federals broke into the open and sprinted toward the rifle pits.

The feeble resistance of the Confederates momentarily confused and thrilled the attacking Union men. Adding to the chaos among the Southerners was the demoralizing effect of the withdrawing Rebels, whose panicked exhaustion disheartened their comrades in the second line of entrenchments. Their only relief was that many of the Northerners were equally exhausted as they claimed the first line of breastworks. The Federals, however, could not linger here for very long, regardless of Grant's orders, for the Confederate guns above opened up, both artillery and rifles, on the congregated Yankee units below.

Col. Frederick Knefler of the Seventy-ninth Indiana was among the first to realize that the rate of Rebel fire from above was increasing rapidly. He recalled: "Nothing could live in or about the captured line of field works. A few minutes of such terrific, telling fire would quickly convert the rifle pits into hideous slaughter pens. There was no time or opportunity for consultation or deliberation. Something drastic must be done—and it must be done very quickly."

Several historians have pointed out that this moment of crisis was one of the most critical moments in the careers of Grant, Thomas, and Bragg. Yet these generals had absolutely no influence on what followed next. Some say that the outcome was the result of chance or accident; others attribute it to Providence.

The soldiers in the pits had no time to ponder orders or await instructions. Many officers pushed their men on up the heights since they had originally understood the orders to direct them to seize the second line of entrenchments. Others sought the refuge of the various outcroppings along the ridge. No one wanted to wait for the aim of the Southerners to improve, so at 4:10 P.M. they started up—orders or no orders or misunderstood orders.

As the Federals began the ascent, a messenger arrived from Orchard Knob with instructions that the troops go no farther. By that time some of the regimental colors showed that their units were approaching the crest. A recall was out of the question.

Several officers with Grant on Orchard Knob witnessed Thomas's command inching its way to the top of the ridge. "Thomas," Grant bellowed, "who ordered those men up the ridge?"

"I don't know; I did not," Thomas answered.

Grant turned to Granger. "Did you order them up?"

"No," Granger replied. "They started without orders. When those fellows get started all hell can't stop them."

Grant turned back to the ridge. "Well, somebody will suffer if they don't stay there."

Granger ordered his chief of staff, Joseph Fullerton, to find the division commanders—Richard Johnson, Philip H. Sheridan, Absalom Baird, and Thomas J. Wood—and ask who ordered the advance and then order them, if possible, to push on to the crest.

Halfway up the slope, word came that the attackers had been ordered to withdraw. A few units in Sheridan's division attempted to pull back, but those that did fled into the open and provided a ripe harvest for the Confederate gunners to reap. Many of the men who made it back to the first line of rifle pits collided with a second wave of advancing Federals. In the minds of many of these men, honor required that they return and climb and take the ridge.

When Sheridan saw that the other divisions were not withdrawing, a fire exploded within him and he called for all in his command to advance and not retreat. "Boys, when I say go," he called out to the men in the pits, "will you go?" A resounding yes echoed from his troops. They mounted the heights eager to catch up with Wood's division.

While all four divisions moved up, there was no order to their advance. In addition to the confusion surrounding the order to ascend, the craggy slope scattered the regiments. The men, one Ohio soldier recalled, joined together and fought under the orders of the closest officer. A sense of competition impelled each man to be the first to reach the crest, but each was also prone to protect himself as much as possible by utilizing the outcroppings of rock that comprised the slope. A Kentuckian remembered that there was no line of men, but rather triangular formations following their banners and creating the impression of arrowheads moving toward the summit of the ridge.

Col. Benjamin Scribner noted that the assault on the crest had become a soldier's battle. "This was their fight; their officers had nothing to do with the advance." Yet he was not optimistic of the outcome and bade farewell to his men under his breath as he progressed upward.

Defenders atop the ridge were nevertheless having a tough time of their work. The layout of their line did not afford them a clear field of fire, and frequently what field of fire they did have was obstructed by the comrades returning to their ranks from the first line of breastworks. In many instances, only fifty yards separated these men from the advancing Yankees. The Confederates' view of the enemy was also

During the battle for Lookout Mountain, the summit was occasionally obscured by mist and low clouds, leading some to dub the engagement "the battle above the clouds."

obscured by drifting powder smoke, which forced them to fire blindly. They further found that their guns could not be depressed sufficiently to bear on the attackers. Desperately, Rebel gunners began lighting the fuses of shells and rolling them down the slope, and other Southerners hurled rocks.

The Union color-bearers paid a steep price for the honor. They fell by the dozens. Their colleagues, however, continued to press onward, pulling themselves up as quickly as their courage and caution would allow them. Occasionally they paused, but they never stopped. One of Bragg's staff officers concluded that only drunken men would attempt such an assault, and their lurching advance seemed to bear him out.

By 5 P.M., as the sun was setting, some of the Indiana, Ohio, and Kentucky units closed to within fifty yards of the top of the ridge. Their presence was masked by the configuration of the ground. Pausing for a moment to catch their breath, they quickly flung themselves up and into the Confederate breastworks before the Mississippians positioned here realized the Federals were there. The breakthrough reached within almost a quarter of a mile of Bragg's line.

The stiffest resistance occurred at the northern sector of Missionary Ridge, where Patrick Cleburne's division clashed with William T. Sherman's corps and held out longer than any other Confederate force.

Once the line was broken, there was little the Confederates could do but flee or surrender. The top of the ridge was extremely narrow and gave no room for the Southerners to put some distance between them and the Yankees and counterattack. Panic swept through the Rebel ranks. Almost as many ran as those who turned to surrender.

The regimental banners of numerous Federal units were planted along the crest, all claiming to be the first to do so. An eighteen-year-old adjutant of the Twenty-fourth Wisconsin, Lt. Arthur MacArthur Jr., was twenty-seven years later awarded the Medal of Honor for taking the regimental colors from his unit's third color-bearer to fall during the ascent. His yells of "On, Wisconsin!" caught his commander's attention and allegedly that of Sheridan, too. As the story was recounted by MacArthur's son, Douglas, the divisional commander approached the young man, embraced him, and announced to the surrounding troops that the eighteen-year-old had just won the Medal of Honor. It was a good story and probably helped MacArthur to receive the award long after the war and well into a long military career. Dozens of other men on Missionary Ridge performed similarly with no less gallantry.

Bragg reacted to the approaching rout by calling for reserves, but there were none. What troops were available were far from the breakthroughs now opening along the line, and very few men were willing to fling themselves on the approaching Federals. Tennesseans, Georgians, Alabamians, and Floridians all began to flee to the rear. Some units fled without recalling any men who had been sent down to meet the Federal advance.

Several gun crews abandoned their weapons, among them two new pieces from the Atlanta foundry that had the names "Lady Breckinridge" and "Lady Buckner" painted on them. As the Union soldiers swept onto the crest, Col. Charles G. Harker, one of Sheridan's brigade commanders, leaped from his horse and straddled one of the guns. He did not linger. The barrel was hot from firing.

Harker's men almost captured Bragg. The Confederate commander rode into the melee in an effort to rally his fleeing men. The sight of him astride his horse and holding a large flag was not sufficient incentive for the Southern soldiers who now despised him. Stories told later claimed that the forlorn Bragg dismounted and waded amid his retreating ranks, but as historian Peter Cozzens observed,

"Bragg was no Napoleon and his soldiers were no Old Guard." Supposedly one of the men offered the general his mule. Whatever else may have happened, Bragg returned to his horse and left the field.

As the ridge filled with victorious Federal soldiers, the men clustered and cheered, feeling as if they had atoned for the embarrassment of the defeat weeks earlier at Chickamauga. Indeed several had, for many who were under threat of some judgment for their behavior in September were allowed to redeem themselves in November.

By 5:15 P.M. it was all over on the ridge except for a pocket of resistance still in place at the south end and Cleburne's men to the north. The Confederates to the south withdrew only after they saw that there were no comrades to support their right flank. Only Union soldiers occupied the center of the ridge by 5:30. The later gains came more from the exertion to reach than heights than having to fight to gain it.

To the southwest, Hooker's command moved toward Rossville. Bragg had sent John C. Breckinridge to oversee the defense there, but by the time the former U.S. vice president arrived, there was little he could do. The Union commander had three divisions to his five regiments. Only because Breckinridge spread his forces out and Hooker encountered them in pockets did the fighting drag out until 6 P.M. The Confederates abandoned the contest. Fatigue forced many to surrender to the relentless Federals.

Cleburne's men watched the fighting to their left, and his commanders formed a defensive line to hold off the advancing Union forces. Darkness quelled the fighting that erupted here, but Sheridan tried to press on, hoping to reach Chickamauga and isolate Cleburne's command. Since he was unsupported by the other divisional commanders, the feisty Irishman relented.

In the night Bragg's order to withdraw reached those elements of his command still on Missionary Ridge. Cleburne later reported that all but the dead and a handful of stragglers were below Chickamauga Creek by 9 P.M. In the flickering fire of a Confederate camp, one soldier described Bragg as "scared . . . hacked and whipped and mortified and chagrined." He determined to retreat to Ringgold and Dalton.

The Federals encamped on Missionary Ridge on the night of November 25 were joined by Grant and Thomas, who rode up from Orchard Knob in time to draw a volley from some retreating South-

Federal troops stormed the summit of Missionary Ridge due in large part to the improper placement of the Confederate line, because the majority of the guns here could not be depressed sufficiently to fire on the approaching lines of Union troops.

erners. They could do little but congratulate the celebrating army on the heights. By 7 P.M. the commanders departed for Chattanooga.

Sheridan could find no other divisional commander who would join him. Most retired early that night. Finally, Sheridan moved his people forward just after midnight, halting two hours later at Chickamauga Creek. He could go no farther in the dark without the other divisions. His men were ordered to fire, staging a fight that the other commanders would hear so they would rush to the scene. The ruse was transparent, and all but Sheridan's men stayed on the ridge to await the next day.

Surprisingly, the normally aggressive Grant did not push his men that night. Bragg was on the verge of annihilation, and suddenly Grant was deluged with worried communications from Washington concerning Ambrose E. Burnside at Knoxville, Tennessee, whose command was under attack by James Longstreet. In reply to both the opportunity to destroy Bragg and prevent the same from happening to Burnside, Grant ordered Granger's Fourth Corps to support Burnside; Sherman and Thomas were to pursue Bragg. Interestingly, Burnside was not in as dire straits as Washington supposed.

When the sun rose on November 26, news of the Union victory at Missionary Ridge reached Lincoln, who was sick in bed. He was more than a little encouraged on this first observation of Thanksgiving to hear that Grant had ordered a pursuit of Bragg. This man was not like George B. McClellan, who had stayed in his camps after the battle of Antietam, nor was he like George Gordon Meade, who had not pursued Robert E. Lee after the battle of Gettysburg.

The pursuit ended with a valiant rear-guard action on November 27 by Cleburne at Ringgold, about fifteen miles south of Chattanooga. The pass through the mountains here was only wide enough to accommodate a railroad track, a wagon road, and a stream. Hooker caught up with Cleburne here, but he could not push through. Cleburne fell back, and Hooker occupied Ringgold, but his supply lines were extended and there were not enough supplies to keep him going. Grant called off the pursuit.

The Union commander returned to Chattanooga to find that the relief force had not yet left for Knoxville, because Granger did not believe it was a good move. Grant sent the Army of Tennessee instead, with Sherman in command rather than Thomas. Granger was reassigned. Grant also saw to it that his plans were well known, anticipating that Longstreet would abandon the effort if he knew of Sherman's approach. Longstreet did just that.

On November 28 Bragg telegraphed his resignation to Richmond. Command of the Army of Tennessee fell to William J. Hardee, but the gateway to the South—Atlanta—was open.

Bragg had been poised to destroy the Army of the Cumberland, but he decided to starve it into submission rather than defeat it. He was too confident of success to consider his tactical needs. Had he not run off Longstreet, he would have had the necessary reserves to likely throw back any attempt to break his line.

As the Southerners retreated into Georgia, one of them observed that the defeat was "the death knell of the Confederacy." He added, "If we cannot cope with those fellows with the advantages we had on this line, there is not a line between here and the Atlantic Ocean where we can stop them." Within the span of ten days Bragg's fortunes had turned to dust.

14

CHEAT MOUNTAIN

LEE'S FIRST CAMPAIGN

MANY KNOW THAT George B. McClellan and Robert E. Lee led opposing armies against each other on the outskirts of Richmond in late May and early June 1862. McClellan was a cautious commander in the field at that time. Lee was aggressive and, over the course of seven days of fighting, intimidated his opponent into withdrawing. That confrontation staggered the confident Union commander, and the world watched in wonder as Lee seized the initiative and repulsed three Union armies from the Virginia theater in less than three months.

The two commanders met again in combat in mid-September, fighting to a tactical stalemate, but Lee withdrew only after McClellan chose not to attack again. For failing to act, McClellan was removed from command. Lee, however, went on to greater victories before stumbling at Gettysburg in July 1863.

By the end of the war, Lee was respected as both a field commander and as a noble figure of the lost cause, but McClellan wore no similar laurels in the popular mind. These fortunes were somewhat reversed from what they had been in the summer and fall of 1861, after the powder smoke had cleared from Charleston Harbor and a call for seventy-five thousand volunteers had been issued from the Lincoln White House.

There was a difference of nineteen years between McClellan and Lee. Both men had ranked second in their class at West Point, Lee in 1829 and McClellan in 1846. Both were assigned to the army's engineer company and later appointed to cavalry commands. Both served in Mexico on the staff of Winfield Scott. Both returned to West Point, McClellan as an instructor in 1848 and Lee as superintendent in 1851. In 1855 McClellan was chosen as one of three officers to observe the Crimean War and study the latest European military developments. At the same time Lee was assigned a field command with the Second Cavalry in Texas.

McClellan resigned from the army shortly after he returned from Europe. Lee requested a leave of absence in 1857 to settle the estate of his father-in-law. He was still managing that task when he was called to Washington in 1858 and ordered to quell a disturbance at Harpers Ferry. This was Lee's first command under fire. The assault that ensued lasted three minutes. When the smoke cleared, a radical named John Brown was in Lee's custody.

Lee returned to his command in Texas in 1860 but was called back to Washington in February 1861, ostensibly to offer him command of the Union army. Sensing that Virginia might follow the states of the Deep South and secede, Lee instead submitted his resignation on April 20. Later that same day he was summoned to Richmond and offered command of the Virginia militia, which he accepted.

The Virginia that Lee was to defend was vulnerable to invasion from four principal routes: from Washington to Manassas to Richmond, through the Shenandoah Valley, from Hampton Roads and up the Virginia Peninsula to Richmond, and from the Ohio Valley into the mountainous western precincts of the Kanawha Valley. As Lee took command, only two of these avenues were under Virginia's control. Militia occupied Harpers Ferry and sealed off the Shenandoah Valley, and Southern troops were massing around Richmond to offset the anticipated Federal buildup near Washington. The peninsula was vulnerable because Union troops still held massive Fort Monroe at Point Comfort, opposite Norfolk, and western Virginia was wide open.

LESLIE'S

After Federal advances in western Virginia at Philippi (depicted above) and Rich Mountain in the summer of 1861, Jefferson Davis dispatched Robert E. Lee to the area to stem any further losses.

In this last region, Lee allocated five militia regiments. As events played out, it soon became apparent that he made two critical mistakes in his assumptions concerning the western precincts. First, he did not believe that the North would threaten this area so early in the conflict. Second, he relied on local commanders to recruit and train men to defend the region. While Lee could do little to alter his first presumption, he failed in the second to recognize that not all Virginians felt as he did toward his state. Common borders with Ohio and Pennsylvania and a sense of isolation from the Tidewater did much to link the people of western Virginia with their neighbors, instilling a strong Unionist sentiment here. Strategically, Lee failed to see the virtue in appointing an overall commander for the region.

Beyond the Virginia borders, McClellan was being considered by New York, Ohio, and Pennsylvania to command their respective state militias. By happenstance he accepted the offer of the Ohio governor, William Dennison, and was commissioned a major general of volunteers on April 23. On the same day Lee accepted command of the Virginia militia in Richmond.

Within a few days of his commission, McClellan proposed a war plan to general in chief Winfield Scott based on a thrust through western Virginia and toward Richmond. He also suggested that all forces in his area be placed under a single commander. Scott acted on both ideas, refining the first into his later maligned and ultimately implemented Anaconda Plan and accepting the second by creating the Department of the Ohio and naming McClellan as overall commander. All that restrained McClellan from acting—which is somewhat ironic considering his later propensity for inaction (until he was ready)—was an order from Washington that no forces encroach on Virginia until the state had seceded officially.

Shortly after Lee called for troops from across the state, the situation in western Virginia began to get out of hand. While other regions responded with eager men, Unionists in western Virginia raised five companies for the other side. Steps were also taken to stymie secession, including separation of the counties from the Old Dominion.

Lee sought to assuage this sectionalism within the state by holding back troops from the Tidewater, believing that a surge of soldiers from anywhere other than western Virginia would energize the agitators and escalate the chaos in the west. While both parties raised troops and jockeyed for position, Lee focused on the Union army massing around Washington and set up a defensive line near Manassas Junction. In prioritizing the threats against which he needed to respond, western Virginia appeared to be the least of Lee's problems.

When Virginia seceded on May 23, the Union army in Washington moved across the Potomac and occupied Alexandria and Arlington.

At the beginning of the war, when he left Arlington for Richmond to take command of Virginia's state troops, Lee had allowed his beard to grow out, but he still looked much as he did in this 1850 image. After his experience in western Virginia, however, he returned to Richmond much grayer than when he had left.

Opposite the western counties, McClellan's Ohio regiments were anxious for action. This was motivated not just by Virginia's secession but also the possible secession of Kentucky, which would place all of Ohio's southern border on a hostile status. In response to some bridge burnings along the Baltimore and Ohio Railroad, McClellan moved men into western Virginia allegedly to protect Unionists in the area until they could protect themselves. Federal soldiers advanced along two routes to secure the two primary transportation centers in the region, Grafton and Gauley Bridge.

The regional commander of Confederate troops at Grafton, Col. George A. Porterfield, was alerted to McClellan's advance by a Southern sympathizing telegrapher. Porterfield withdrew his men to Philippi. When McClellan's forces moved to attack him on June 3, Porterfield withdrew under fire, this time to Beverly. Although the Confederates had been surprised, the Federals had not been in position to seal off a clear avenue of escape to the south. Thus the affair was quickly branded the Philippi Races for the alacrity with which the Southerners fled the scene.

Despite the timely withdrawal of the Confederates, Porterfield was replaced by Brig. Gen. Robert S. Garnett, Lee's adjutant. The action also drew the attention of Richmond away from Washington for a while, but little fighting followed other than a handful of skirmishes. Union occupation of Grafton, however, left the North in control of the railroads in western Virginia, and McClellan made good use of them to bring in more troops faster than Lee could send reinforcements.

These Federal successes also encouraged the Unionists in the region to pursue separation from Virginia. On June 19 a convention in Wheeling founded the Reorganized Government of Virginia, which vacated the earlier plebiscite that had approved secession. Within days the Reorganized Government entertained legislation to withdraw the western counties as a separate state from Virginia. The matter was to be examined later, in November.

Garnett arrived in the west at about the same time that Jefferson Davis, whose government was now in residence in Richmond, authorized former governor Henry Wise to raise a legion (infantry, cavalry, and artillery) and assigned him to the Kanawha Valley. Confusing the situation, Davis also appointed the former U.S. secretary of war,

John B. Floyd, as a brigadier and charged him to raise troops in the Shenandoah and move them into the western counties. All of this was done without consulting Lee or taking into account that Wise and Floyd had a long history as political rivals. Rather than consolidate these troops under a central command, all three were allowed to stand as independent commands.

At the same time, the Virginia militia began receiving orders from both Lee and the Confederate War Department. As troops arrived in Richmond, the War Department assigned some to Lee, who was supposed to be in command of all Southern forces in Virginia, but the majority of the men were directed to other commanders without informing Lee of their disposition.

Eventually the state forces were transferred to the government, and Lee was made a military adviser to Davis as a kind of assistant secretary of war. With regard to the western Virginia situation, Lee continued to command Garnett, and Davis issued orders to Wise. The latter remained in the Kanawha Valley, and Garnett centered his defenses around the mountains on the western edge of the Alleghenies—Laurel and Rich Mountains.

McClellan joined his twenty thousand men near Grafton. As he prepared to move against Beverly, he ordered troops still in Ohio to move into the Kanawha Valley. Turning back to Garnett, McClellan arrayed a small force opposite his position on Laurel Mountain to keep the Confederates in place while Union forces moved on Rich Mountain. McClellan hoped that he would gain more by maneuvering rather than fighting.

Garnett called up additional troops to join his forty-six hundred men and reported to Lee that the animosity of the locals prevented him from gathering good intelligence on McClellan's movements. He also asked that Wise be moved up to threaten the rear of the advancing Federals. Lee submitted Garnett's request to Wise, but by the time the latter responded with numerous reasons as to why he should not move to support Garnett, McClellan's men had shut off any possibility of anyone's assisting the Confederates on Rich Mountain.

The lack of a central command proved the undoing of Southern efforts in the west, not the lack of generalship, particularly on Lee's part. Throughout McClellan's campaign in western Virginia, Lee was held accountable, but he was not authorized to command. Further

John B. Floyd had been secretary of war under James Buchanan. He had been sent to raise troops in western Virginia and commanded a brigade at the time Lee arrived on the scene. Serving in the same region, supposedly in concert with Buchanan, was Henry A. Wise, a former governor of Virginia, but both men squabbled and wrangled with each other with far more energy than they exerted against the Federal army.

eroding his effectiveness was the fact that Lee consistently chose not to confront the commanders around him but rather to ameliorate and to suggest. He hoped to make his point on the strength of his counsel, but for that to succeed, his colleagues had to perceive that his suggestions were militarily sound. Most of them lacked the experience for such perceptions.

McClellan's hand was forced on July 10 by an overeager subordinate, and he had to move quickly against Garnett's defenders at Rich Mountain. The only impediments to his advance were reports from a few prisoners who exaggerated the size of the Southern force before the Federals.

When a local resident informed McClellan of a way to circle behind the Confederate position without being observed, the general ordered the maneuver on July 11. Once in position, he planned to strike the Southerners from the front and the rear. A drenching rain impeded the advance of the troops marching to the rear of Rich Mountain, and the Confederates became aware of what was happening. They abandoned the position to link up with their comrades on Laurel Mountain but surrendered to McClellan after marching in the rain most of the night and getting lost.

On Laurel Mountain, Garnett knew nothing of what had transpired at Rich Mountain until the evening of July 11. The loss of Rich Mountain made his position untenable, and he abandoned the position and marched to Staunton. For his part, McClellan did not pursue the fleeing Confederates with any sense of urgency.

Garnett was killed during a rear-guard action at Corrick's Ford. He was the first general officer on either side to be killed in action.

McClellan set up his headquarters at Huttonsville and found himself in a less polarized region of Virginia. Here Unionists and Secessionists were almost evenly numbered.

Confederate Gen. Henry Wise had raised his legion here and doggedly resisted all efforts to merge his men with those of John B. Floyd. To do so would require him to relinquish command to Floyd, which Wise could not stomach. Politically both men had found favor in the western counties during separate terms as governor of Virginia, and both were appointed to their present tasks by Davis, who hoped that their regional popularity would encourage support for the Confederacy. Once elevated to their command positions, however, neither man had received specific orders from Richmond regarding what to do. So each considered his own course of action. Floyd wanted to confront the oncoming Federals; Wise was in favor of a guerrilla campaign.

While Wise and Floyd argued strategy, McClellan moved men into the Kanawha Valley as far as the junction of the Kanawha and Gauley Rivers. On July 10 Floyd was ordered into the Kanawha Valley to reinforce Wise. By July 16 Wise's scouts skirmished with

LIBRARY OF CONGRESS

Preceding Lee into western Virginia was Brig. Gen. William W. Loring. He had outranked Lee in the prewar army and was not open to taking suggestions from him now; after all, Davis had not placed Lee in command but had defined Lee's role as that of consultant. Since the ambiguity of the situation was not lost on either man, Lee chose not to remain at Loring's headquarters but worked as best he could with the volatile partnership of Floyd and Wise.

the advancing Federals. There the two armies stalemated. Within days, however, the Federals lost their confidence, and Confederate pride was buoyed with news of the Southern victory at Manassas on July 21.

In the days just prior to the battle at Bull Run, McClellan released glowing reports of his victories at Rich Mountain and Corrick's Ford, which made an indelible impression on the people of the North. The instant adulation he received did more to halt his progress than any resistance put up by the Confederates. Shortly after one of his field commanders encountered difficulty with a force of Southerners near Scary Creek, McClellan telegraphed "abandon the pursuit to avoid the possibility of disaster. . . . [A]t least save me the disgrace of a detachment of my Army being routed." Having earned the accolades of the nation, McClellan wanted nothing to sully his newfound fame.

Lee reacted to the news of McClellan's victory and Garnett's death by urging Floyd to link up with Wise; he also sent Brig. Gen. William W. Loring to join the two feuding politicians. Davis prevented Lee's going to the western counties because the Federals were just then closing on Manassas. Lee played a powerful role in orchestrating the Confederate victory there, but because he was not on the field, the praise went to P. G. T. Beauregard and Joseph E. Johnston.

Washington responded to the defeat at Bull Run by summoning the man who claimed that his work was finished in western Virginia. On July 26 McClellan assumed command of the Union army that had fled from Virginia and found refuge in the Federal capital.

Richmond responded by offering Johnston command of its uncoordinated units in western Virginia. He declined. Davis turned next to Lee. He accepted. Unfortunately, the Confederate president did not specifically give Lee command of these forces. The commanders already there retained their independence.

With McClellan departing and Lee arriving, the two sides reversed themselves in western Virginia. Command of the Union forces was given to William S. Rosecrans, and he began by reorganizing his army. The Federal defeat at Bull Run also influenced him to be cautious and to shift from aggressor to defender. Southern strategy took courage from the victory at Manassas and assumed an offensive posture focused on expelling the Northerners from the western counties. Their first objective was the Union stronghold on Cheat Mountain.

Then the weather turned against the Southerners. One Confederate soldier facetiously claimed that it rained for thirty-two days that August. Lee's letters home confirm the dismal situation. On the Federal side, several ninety-day regiments were approaching the end of their term of enlistment, and several veterans of the previous victories departed for their homes in Ohio and Indiana.

Lee arrived in the area on July 28. He was appalled by the demoralized and sickly troops he encountered. When he met with Loring at Huntersville, the latter had no difficulty in expressing his displeasure at being supervised. Lee responded by deferring to Loring, which was all he could do in the role cast for him by Davis.

In the meantime, a convention in Wheeling entertained the creation of a new state to be known as Kanawha, which would remain loyal to the Union. A referendum was scheduled for October 24.

In addition to the rain, the weather turned unseasonably cold. It snowed on August 14. Morale declined. The one positive element in the Confederate column was that Rosecrans assumed that Lee's presence implied that the Confederates were planning a coordinated offensive.

Perhaps the greatest negative for the Southerners was the ongoing feud between Wise and Floyd. Wise was convinced that western Virginia was a lost cause; Floyd blamed Wise for the situation. They met on August 6 to argue strategy. On August 11 Floyd was given command of all Confederate forces in the western counties, but Wise continued to do all he could to ignore any orders Floyd directed toward him. Occasionally the two recognized that the Federals were the enemy.

On August 19 they moved in concert to outflank a Union force at Gauley Bridge. Even then the two political rivals managed to annoy each other.

Floyd and Wise decided that Wise would advance on Carnifex Ferry while Floyd would secure Wise's supply lines. Wise's men marched through seventeen miles of ankle-deep mud. Floyd, however, learned that the Union position at Cross Lanes had been abandoned. He found an abandoned Union ferry, crossed the Gauley River, and advanced on Carnifex Ferry ahead of Wise. Somewhat disgusted with this turn of events, Wise was ordered back to the point at which he had begun his march. It was not the last time his men would have to retrace their steps in following Floyd's orders.

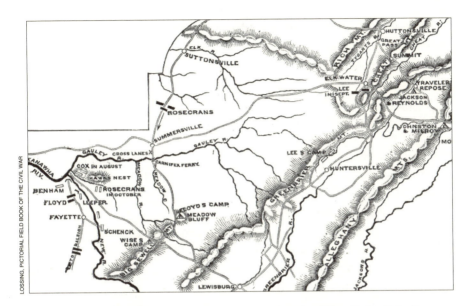

Lee wanted Floyd and Wise to move into the Kanawha Valley. When Union Brig. Gen. William S. Rosecrans moved against Floyd, Lee attempted to seize Cheat Mountain.

For the remainder of the month of August and into early September the two wrangled away and Floyd issued and countermanded his own orders. On occasion the two generals would meet and agree on a course of action, but as soon as Wise returned to his command to carry out his responsibilities, Floyd would send word of a change in plans. By mid-September, Wise was fully frustrated with Floyd, and reports from prominent citizens were reaching Davis of just how bad the "partnership" was going.

While these two Confederate commanders bickered, Rosecrans solidified the gains made by McClellan in the early campaigning, and the Unionists were gaining support for the idea of separation. The residents of the western counties were disappointed that Richmond appeared to be doing nothing to expel the invaders; they only saw Floyd and Wise giving up ground. Loring was content to watch the Federals entrench at Cheat Mountain, and Lee was unable to generate a consensus among any of these commanders. Davis failed to grasp the need to empower Lee to command, so little good came of his being there.

Since Floyd and Wise seemingly squandered any chance of success in the Kanawha Valley, Lee focused on evicting the Federals from Cheat Mountain so as to create an opportunity to seize the initiative and push Rosecrans out of Virginia. Yet Loring was occupied with the logistics of preparing for a long campaign and resisted Lee's efforts to coax him into action.

Finally Lee reverted to what he had done best during the Mexican War, scouting out the enemy position for weaknesses, and he did so for most of the month of August. This was not the role for one who should be planning the overall strategy of a campaign. It was a necessary exercise for one trying to assess the tactical situation. This is a critical observation for those who seem inclined to pillory Lee for the outcome of the campaign.

What Lee lost in not being entrusted with the overall responsibility was made up for in what he learned about leading men in the field. His constant presence among Loring's soldiers had a great effect in endearing him to them, but the never-ending rain also bred malaria, typhoid fever, and measles, which incapacitated more than a third of the army.

On August 31 Lee received news that he had been promoted to full general. Rank was something that Loring had to respect, and he slowly became Lee's subordinate and allowed Lee to take control of the campaign. After almost a month of personal scouting, Lee also found not one but two ways to get behind Cheat Mountain. Now that he had discovered the means to attack, Lee examined how to go about doing it.

His force was divided and spread between two camps, but the Federals had a similar problem. Coordination would be a problem, but Lee also realized that his forces were further reduced by almost half due to illness and disease, and he lacked the resources for a prolonged campaign. If he did not attack, he would have to withdraw. He decided to attack.

Battle plans were prepared on September 8 for an assault on September 12. They were complex, possibly too complex for the raw recruits that filled the Confederate ranks, men who had never been in battle before. In a nutshell, Lee's six brigades were to move out in five columns from two separate camps against two separate enemy positions and simultaneously launch a surprise attack against a force of unknown size. The plan would have had a good chance for success had the orders been issued to battle-hardened troops under experienced officers. Such, however, was not the case in the fall of 1861.

Perhaps Lee's greatest mistake in issuing these orders was that the most crucial element was entrusted to the least-experienced commander, Col. Albert Rust, who had helped to scout out one of the routes around the Federal position. Rust was to initiate the attack on the flank of the Union line at Cheat Mountain.

Two columns were focused on Cheat Mountain, two were to assail the Federals at nearby Elkwater, and the fifth was to be ready to isolate the rear of either Federal position. The attack would commence as soon as Rust was in position at daylight on September 12. As the final orders were issued, the rain ceased and the sun shone. When the columns began to march to their destinations, the rain began again.

Somehow all five columns were in position and undetected at daybreak, per Lee's plan. Everyone waited for Rust to begin the attack.

Elements of Rust's command surprised some Federal pickets. When they were interrogated, they exaggerated the number of their comrades and Rust believed them. He surveyed the Union position again, which now seemed much larger to him than it had before. Morning bugles startled him, and he surmised that he had been discovered. After consulting with his officers, he ordered a hasty retreat without firing a shot.

As the morning progressed, the other four columns grew anxious at not hearing anything from Rust. Lee was with the column near Elkwater. At 10 A.M. he ordered an attack, but the exertions of the previous night of marching caught up with the Confederates, and they could offer only a lackluster fight. With no clear communication with the other columns, each commander acted independently. Lee hoped that he might be able to take at least one Federal position and scouted for ways to salvage something from the failed attack on Cheat Mountain. The loss of the element of surprise and a lack of supplies, however, induced him to fall back.

Lee had been in the area for six weeks, and Confederate fortunes were unchanged. He decided that his next best opportunity lay in motivating Floyd and Wise in the Kanawha Valley. He set out for their camps on September 20; Loring followed a few days later.

Floyd was camped at Meadow Bluff, and Wise was centered at Sewell Mountain. The two now feuded over which of them occupied the stronger position. After Lee inspected both positions, he noted that Wise possessed the better site but the condition of Wise's command disturbed him. Again he chose only to suggest to Floyd that he might unite his men with Wise's at Sewell Mountain.

It was not long before Rosecrans probed both Confederate positions, and Wise and Floyd probed his. On September 23 it looked as if Sewell Mountain might be attacked. Loring was coming up, Wise called for reinforcements from Floyd, and skirmishers collided with Union skirmishers. A Confederate soldier recalled, "It was nothing but an Indian fight—Virginians behind trees fighting Ohioans behind trees." Lee hoped that the common enemy might influence the two recalcitrant generals to cooperate, but during the fighting Floyd forwarded a dispatch from Richmond to Lee that ordered Wise to relinquish his command to Floyd. Wise had disobeyed earlier orders, but he asked Lee for his advice and the general counseled him to do as he was ordered.

Fighting continued sporadically for several days. Loring arrived on September 29. Rain, however, dampened more than the men's spirits on both sides. Flooding threatened Federal supply lines and posed a significant barrier between the Confederates on Sewell Mountain and Meadow Bluff. Rosecrans elected to withdraw.

Before Lee could pursue Rosecrans, the Federals on Cheat Mountain initiated a short-lived offensive of their own. It stalled, and the Union commanders went back on the defensive. After two

Lee's bold attack against the Federal camp at Cheat Mountain had tremendous potential. The primary role, however, was entrusted to Col. Albert Rust, who had never experienced combat before but had helped to find a protected path to the top of the mountain. His attack would signal four other columns to attack, but at the last moment Rust feared that his force had been discovered and he withdrew.

weeks of searching for alternatives, Lee fell back to defensive positions to seal off the eastern approaches. Suddenly Floyd turned combative. Lee allowed him to act as he saw fit, and Floyd surprised Rosecrans so that the latter remained on the defensive. Lee was summoned back to Richmond, and he turned command of the "campaign" over to Floyd on October 30.

In early November the Federals tried to assume the offensive to dislodge Floyd from Cotton Hill, where he had been able to harass their supply lines for a short while. Just as Rosecrans prepared to attack him, Floyd withdrew, fearful that his capture would be the ultimate embarrassment following his ignoble departure from the Buchanan administration.

The end result as winter curtailed any further campaigning was that the Union army controlled all of western Virginia, but it did not yet have access to the Shenandoah Valley. The Alleghenies served as a natural barrier between the two, and the two sides assumed defensive positions along these mountains.

For Lee this first campaign of the war was a disappointment to him and to his government. Ranked as the third-highest general of the Confederacy, many policymakers were writing him off as a disappointment. Southern newspaper editors were extremely harsh in their pronouncements and judgments. He was criticized for his "dilly-dally, dirt digging, scientific warfare" and dubbed "Granny Lee," the "Great Entrencher," and the "king of Spades." One Confederate veteran recalled, "Those old enough to remember the time will recall the obloquy and reproaches heaped upon him by the press and people; but, so far as I am aware, no word of protest or explanation came from him."

Lee did not speak publicly about the campaign. He did not enunciate Loring's jealousy, Floyd and Wise's pettiness, or Rust's error at Cheat Mountain. Nevertheless, Davis required some explanation from Lee, which the general gave with the understanding that his report would not be published. Afterward Davis dispatched him to South Carolina, Georgia, and Florida to assess the coastal defenses in the wake of several Federal successes.

This time Lee had clear orders from Davis that named him as commander of a military department. Once on the scene, Lee instituted a program that was later emulated in all Southern coastal regions to thwart the relative ease with which Union combined forces had seized Hatteras, Port Royal, and Roanoke.

This first campaign was far from the success that McClellan had experienced (or at least claimed). Whereas McClellan now had a reputation to protect and he sought to do so at all costs, Lee had a reputation to redeem. The strange battle of Cheat Mountain, a battle that never happened, did more to school Lee on how to be a field commander than any engagement he had ever been involved in before.

15

IUKA

THE SILENT BATTLE

T HE SPRING OF 1862 was not going well for the Confederacy. In the East, George B. McClellan's Peninsula campaign was rolling up Joseph E. Johnston's army to the outskirts of Richmond. In the West, Albert Sidney Johnston's army had failed to dislodge Ulysses S. Grant's army from its Tennessee camps near a little church known as Shiloh. As a result, the Southerners were impelled to abandon the important railroad junction at Corinth, Mississippi, and command of the Confederate army passed from P. G. T. Beauregard (who had replaced Johnston after the latter had been killed during the first day of fighting at Shiloh) to Braxton Bragg. As the Confederates regrouped, Bragg concocted a strategy to win back the lost territory and extend his influence into Kentucky.

In Mississippi, occupied Corinth was transformed into a base for the huge army assembled by Henry W. Halleck, who had replaced Grant following the embarrassment of the unexpected attack at Shiloh. While Union fortunes were somewhat brighter than those of the South, the Federal campaign in the West nevertheless stalled.

Disease was rampant in the Union camps, and Halleck was himself incapacitated. When McClellan's Virginia campaign collapsed, Halleck was called to Washington as general in chief. Grant was given command again, but Union forces were divided between him and Don Carlos Buell.

Halleck dictated that Buell's command would operate in eastern Kentucky and Tennessee and Grant's in the western districts of the same two states. Buell targeted Chattanooga while Grant focused on Vicksburg, but Halleck had little faith in Grant. He continually bled men from his command to reinforce Buell.

Grant's efforts in northern Mississippi bogged down, and his army endured a miserable summer as the drought continued and the temperature remained above one hundred degrees. Water was scarce, and disease remained prolific. Approximately 35 percent of the army was sick.

Most of the men left to Grant were occupied with a construction project begun by Halleck to supplement the earthworks erected by Johnston and Beauregard when the Confederate army had been headquartered at Corinth. Grant himself was not enthusiastic about the project, commenting that the works were "on a scale to indicate that this one point must be held if it took the whole National army to do it. They were laid out on a scale that would have required 100,000 men to fully man them."

Noting the lethargy in Federal affairs, Braxton Bragg glimpsed an opportunity to seize the initiative and gain a foothold on Kentucky. He envisioned a two-pronged advance into the Bluegrass State, with his army entering from the south and Edmund Kirby Smith's army approaching from the southeast, through the Cumberland Gap. His first step would be to threaten Buell's supply lines and force him to abandon his operation against Chattanooga. If that proved successful, Bragg's and Kirby Smith's armies would join forces and defeat Buell before Grant could reinforce him. To accomplish this, however, Grant had to be engaged in Mississippi. For that purpose, Bragg had at his disposal two small Confederate armies in Mississippi: Sterling Price's Army of the West and Earl Van Dorn's Army of West Tennessee.

Grant's army, minus those units involved in the construction of the fieldworks around Corinth, was mostly scattered across northern Mississippi tasked with the duties of guarding railroads from guerrilla bands and Confederate cavalry and restringing downed tele-graph lines. William T. Sherman oversaw his divisions from Memphis, and William S. Rosecrans administered his from Corinth. Rosecrans and Grant often dined together, and after a while he convinced Grant that a better defensive system than Halleck's line of earthworks could be achieved by a system of five redoubts designed to protect the railroad depot. Grant agreed, and the work was begun. Time would prove that this was a far better idea than either general imagined.

Bragg, meanwhile, was ready to move against Buell. Since Price and Van Dorn were operating independently at the time but subordinate to Bragg, orders were issued sending Price's twelve thousand men toward Corinth to block Rosecrans should his divisions be dispatched to support Buell. If Rosecrans were to retreat into Tennessee, which Bragg estimated he would, then Price could move to join Bragg in Middle Tennessee.

Grant was alerted to the shifting of Southern troops toward Corinth at about the same time that Halleck again ordered him to send more men to support Buell. Grant quickly moved to gather his scattered forces, ordering Rosecrans to concentrate his divisions at Corinth. To protect his flank and rear, Rosecrans pulled Col. Robert Murphy's brigade out of Tuscumbia, Alabama, and charged him

Sterling Price (left) and Earl Van Dorn (right)

with protecting one of the army's supply depots at Iuka, Mississippi, about twenty miles from Corinth.

Iuka was at a crossroads and well known for its mineral springs. In 1860 the population was almost fifteen hundred. To a Wisconsin soldier, the town was "the first place we had seen in the South that looked anything like a business town. Wealth, affluence, and southern grandeur were plainly visible. Homes built in the most improved style. Gardens beautifully arranged and blooming. It seemed a pity to see such a beautiful village become the prey of contending armies."

Murphy's men had not been there long when Price's cavalry brigade attacked at 8 A.M. on September 13. The Federals fended off three attacks, but Murphy abandoned the depot when he saw that the main body of Price's army would be there the next day.

Union cavalry stayed behind to torch the supplies, but they botched the job and fled at the first sight of the Confederates. A Texan later recalled, "It was a sight to gladden the heart of a poor soldier, whose only diet had been unsalted beef and white leather hoecake, the stacks of cheese, crackers, preserves, mackerel, coffee, and other good things." The Southern commanders had no choice but to allow their men to indulge themselves.

While his army feasted on the abundant stores, Price learned that Rosecrans had two divisions at Corinth. He decided that the only way he could prevent Rosecrans from joining Buell was to attack him, and he sent word to Van Dorn that they should join forces to do so.

Twenty miles away, however, Rosecrans and Grant now knew where Price was. Rosecrans relieved Murphy of command, reassigned the brigade to Joseph A. Mower, and sent the unit back to ascertain Price's next movement.

Grant surmised that Price was in Iuka as a first step toward an attack on Corinth and reported his suspicions to Halleck in Washington. Halleck dismissed any idea that either Price or Van Dorn or both were capable of attacking Corinth successfully. "There can be no very large force to attack you," he replied to Grant. "Attack the enemy if you can reach him with advantage." The words were eerily similar to Halleck's messages to Grant prior to the embarrassment of Shiloh.

Mower's column encountered Confederate cavalry and skirmished continually until he came upon the main Confederate line about two miles from Iuka. Darkness scotched any thought of immediate attack, and Mower decided to hold off until morning. When he saw that Price was preparing to attack him with his full strength, Mower pulled back to Burnsville, about eight miles from Iuka, and reported the situation to Rosecrans.

In Corinth, Grant clearly grasped that Price was operating apart from Van Dorn, and he decided to attack him, estimating that Van Dorn was at least four days away. Working with Rosecrans, he devised a risky pincer movement against Price. Rosecrans would take two divisions, about nine thousand men, and approach Iuka by two roads from the south. Gen. Edward O. C. Ord would bring his three divisions, about six thousand men, down on Iuka from the northwest. They would hit Price from three directions simultaneously. Although Grant's fifteen thousand outnumbered Price's twelve thousand, the Confederates would outnumber the individual attacking groups. Coordination, therefore, was essential to success.

There was, however, a possibility that Price might evade Rosecrans and Ord and move against Corinth. On that basis, Grant did not commit all his resources to the march on Iuka but kept some units in positions from which they could quickly move to Corinth's defense should Price execute such a threat or should Van Dorn appear unexpectedly. Ord's divisions were moved in part along the Memphis and Charleston Railroad and could be hustled back to Corinth by train if necessary.

Ord's column departed Corinth by rail on September 18, pausing at Burnsville so that Grant could establish his headquarters there. Two regiments remained with him and saw that the road was open to Rosecrans's line of march to the south. Ord continued his advance to within six miles of Iuka, establishing contact with Price's army and pushing back skirmishers.

In Burnsville, Grant received exaggerated and inaccurate reports of the battle of Antietam, noting correctly that Robert E. Lee's army had withdrawn from Maryland back to Virginia, but also claiming: "[James] Longstreet and his entire division prisoners. General [A. P.] Hill killed. Entire rebel army of Virginia destroyed." The Union commander reasoned that if the report were true then the war was all but over. Thus there would be no need to engage Price.

During the early morning hours of September 19, Grant had Ord convey the Antietam information to Price and offer the Confederates

HARPER'S PICTORIAL HISTORY OF THE GREAT REBELLION

Iuka is roughly halfway between Corinth and Tuscumbia, just west of the Alabama border.

a chance to surrender. Price, however, disputed the claims and reasoned that if Lee had been destroyed, such a development "would only move him and his soldiers to greater exertions in behalf of their country." This response was not, however, immediate; Ord received Price's reply around midafternoon. Consequently, by the terms of the truce under which the commanders exchanged messages, Ord was immobilized.

Although the Antietam information did not induce the Southerners to surrender, the news lifted the sagging spirits of Grant's men. Then word arrived that Van Dorn might be threatening Corinth. While Ord could do nothing against Price, Grant charged him with investigating the situation behind them at Corinth. Thus Ord was absent from the Iuka front from 9 A.M. to 3 P.M. as he verified the situation at Corinth.

By having access to the railroad, Ord's movement toward Iuka was easier than Rosecrans's. The latter had to march over indirect roads, and his progress was impeded by a sudden rainstorm. After the first day's advance, he was halfway to Iuka but still twenty-two miles west of his goal. Nevertheless he communicated to Grant that he would be in position by 2 P.M. the next afternoon.

At his headquarters, Grant seemingly interpreted the message to say that Rosecrans would not be in position until after dark the next day. Apparently he dismissed the possibility of any action at that time, but he sent word to Ord to advance to within two miles of Price's position and to be ready to attack when he heard the sound of Rosecrans's guns from the south or southwest. "Do not be too rapid in your advance this morning," he cautioned, "unless it should be found that the enemy are evacuating." Inexplicably, Ord did not push on but stayed six miles to Price's front.

Meanwhile, Price's army began preparations to withdraw and link up with Van Dorn. Given Ord's presence, Price sent a message to his colleague: "I will move my army as quickly as I can in the direction proposed by you. I am, however, expecting an attack today, as it seems, from the most reliable information which I can procure, that they are concentrating their forces against me." Price's planned route of evacuation was on a collision course with Rosecrans's column.

Sometime during the morning of September 19 couriers from Van Dorn arrived. The gist of their message, however, did not address Price's immediate threat but announced that Richmond had named Van Dorn the area commander and that Price was subordinate to him.

Rosecrans had begun his second day of march at 2 A.M. After making three miles of headway he began fending off skirmishers and pickets. News of the Federal column to the south quickly reached Price, who saw now that he was between two large Union forces.

By noon Rosecrans had reached Barnett's Crossroads, about five miles southwest of Iuka. According to the original plan, he paused for two hours to listen for Ord's guns. Finally riders appeared with the news that Ord was awaiting Rosecrans's opening salvo. At the time, there was hardly a single Confederate soldier between Rosecrans and Iuka; Price's army still faced Ord. By midafternoon, however, Price knew that Rosecrans was advancing toward him and sent a quarter of his army, Louis Hébert's division, to block him.

As he continued to implement the battle plan, Rosecrans discovered that his maps were in error. The two roads he had planned to use to reach Iuka were not just over a mile apart from each other but five miles apart. If he were to separate his men, neither column would be able to support the other if the need arose. He elected to use only the westernmost thoroughfare, known as the Jacinto road, which left the other roadway open should Price choose to withdraw.

His lead elements began encountering Southern pickets and pockets of cavalry. Gradually the opposition became heavier until by 4 P.M. it appeared that his column had come upon Price's main force. The wide, level field was marked by a two-story farmhouse on its western edge and a log meetinghouse about four hundred yards north of the farmhouse.

The surrounding ground, composed of steep slopes and heavy timber, favored the Confederates. These contours would prevent Rosecrans from bringing the full weight of his force to bear on the outnumbered Southerners.

One of the first Confederate units to arrive on the scene was a two-gun section. It entered the field without infantry support and opened fire on the forming Union line, which took shape around a full artillery battery that was brought up quickly. Contrary to the normal rules of deployment, the Federal gunners took a position at the front of the Union line, which made them highly vulnerable to Confederate infantry. As the battle played out, most of the fighting centered here on the Eleventh Ohio Artillery and on the infantry regiments, the Forty-eighth Indiana and the Fifth Iowa, that were placed alongside the battery.

Union commanders took their time placing their regiments on the field. Confederate gunners fired for almost thirty minutes before the Federals—awaiting orders—responded. "Why they did not move forward and attack us at once is not understood. Their delay, which enabled us to form the nearest three regiments in line of battle . . . was our salvation," recalled the division commander, Charles S. Hamilton, whose men were engaged. Rosecrans himself appeared shortly after the first shots were fired. He personally directed reinforcing units into position to bolster the flanks that his mostly inexperienced officers had overlooked.

By the time the Federals were satisfied that they were ready to fight, the Southern infantry had advanced almost up to the guns. When the order was given to fire, the Confederates were so close that the Union battery opened with canister. "The effect . . . was terribly increased because of the rebel method of charging in masses," noted Lt. Henry Neil from his vantage point amid the gunners.

Sgt. W. P. Helm, one of the Texans on the receiving end of the Union guns, recalled, "I can never forget that moment—it came like lightning from a clear sky. The roaring artillery, the rattle of musketry, the hailstorm of grape and ball were mowing us down like grain before we could locate from whence it came. We were trapped; there could be no retreat, and certain death was in our advance." At

BOTH IMAGES: LIBRARY OF CONGRESS

Edward O. C. Ord (left) and William S. Rosecrans (right)

one point Helm fell to the ground then looked up to see his company commander lose his head to a cannonball. Another officer stopped one of the Texans from retreating, and Helm saw them both cut in two by canister. "Our ranks were shattered in the twinkling of an eye," he summarized.

Price arrived on the scene shortly after the shooting erupted. "The fight began," he observed, "and was waged with a severity I have never seen surpassed." Quickly he realized that his one brigade could not stop Rosecrans. He called for a second division, massing at least half of his men for this battle.

In the meantime, farther north, Ord waited six miles from Iuka. His men remained in position for the rest of the afternoon, poised for an attack that was never made. Afterward he claimed that he did not hear the sounds of battle. Grant also said that he heard nothing. "The wind was still blowing hard and in the wrong direction to transmit sound toward either Ord or me," he reported to Halleck afterward. "Neither he nor I nor anyone in either command heard a gun that was fired in the battle-field."

The phenomenon was not unknown. It was called an acoustic shadow.

At Grant's headquarters the commanding general remarked to Ord that Rosecrans "was from last accounts from him too far from

Iuka for us to attack on our front until further information was received as to his whereabouts." He nonetheless ordered Ord to advance to within four miles of Iuka and listen for any sounds that might indicate that Rosecrans had launched his attack. Ord did not move up, however.

To the south, Price's second brigade, commanded by John D. Martin, divided to form on the left and right flanks of Hébert's brigade. The arriving units on the right, however, advanced too far and were caught in a crossfire between their comrades and Union soldiers and pulled back.

After an hour's combat, the sky darkened significantly as the sun began to set. Powder smoke filtered out what little light remained.

The Confederates had their greatest success against the inexperienced Forty-eighth Indiana. After an exchange of volleys, the Indianans collapsed and fled to the rear. The onrushing Confederates intermingled with them as they approached the Sixteenth Iowa, which was placed to support the Indiana regiment. Despite orders not to fire on the approaching mass of men for fear of killing their fellow soldiers, many in the Sixteenth unleashed a volley. More Indianans fell than Southerners.

Partially exposed now, the Eleventh Ohio battery was almost swept away. Within the battery, Lt. Henry Neil observed, "The guns were worked with greater speed and smaller crews. Cannoneers were falling. Other cannoneers coolly took their place and performed double duty. Drivers left their dead horses and took the place of dead and wounded comrades, only to be struck down in turn."

After several attempts to take the guns, the remnants of the Third Texas Cavalry (Dismounted) were caught between the Ohio battery and the main body of Hébert's brigade. The Texans decided to try one last time. "Seeing certain death between friend and foe," one of them recalled, "the order was given: 'Boys, if we are to die, let it be by Yankee bullets, not by our friends.'"

The left side of the Union battery was overrun, but the Sixteenth Iowa came charging up and pushed the Texans back. Three more Union companies came up in support, but their numbers were not sufficient to hold on to the guns. The battery commander, Lt. Cyrus Sears, was wounded, and command passed to Neil, who tried to enlist a nearby Missouri regiment's help in withdrawing the guns.

One of the Missourians, Capt. De Witt Brown, noted, "A terrible fire was poured into the battery from the left and the front, and the horses harnessed to the fore carriages of the guns, brought up from the ravine to haul them off, were wounded unto death, and rearing, bleeding, and charging, came like an avalanche down on my right, wounding my men, . . . and lunging forward, one horse over another, in the pains of madness of death, and massing themselves on a caisson in one awful pile of wounded and dying horses, dead men, and broken gun carriages."

Fresh Federal units rushed forward to reform the line and recapture their battery. At twilight they counterattacked, forcing the Confederates back. Control of the ridge seesawed back and forth.

Finally the Union infantry had to withdraw. The fight for the guns was over by 6:30. Of 97 men in the Ohio battery, 18 were dead and 39 were wounded. Of 54 cannoneers—those who worked the guns—46 were injured. Of 80 horses, 3 survived. A few artillerists were captured while swinging rammers and sponges. Chivalrously, the Southerners spared their lives and later released them. "Those battery boys," a Confederate explained, "had so much spunk that we took pity on the few who were left."

To the north Ord received a message at around 6 P.M. from his front division, written two hours earlier: "For the last twenty minutes there has been a dense smoke arising from the direction of Iuka. I conclude that the enemy are evacuating and destroying the stores."

Ord moved his column forward cautiously, but hearing nothing, he halted again and waited. No reconnaissance was initiated.

The fighting to the south continued until "it was so dark that friends could not be distinguished from foes," Charles S. Hamilton reported. Both sides continued to struggle anyway. Gradually the firing became sporadic until it finally sputtered out at 8 P.M.

Darkness claimed the battlefield with the Rebels in possession of the ridge on which most of the fighting transpired. Four of the five Union regiments placed here had been routed, and the Ohio battery had been captured. After seventy-five minutes of combat, the fighting stopped. The Southerners had suffered heavy casualties, but one fatality came close to undoing all that had been accomplished.

As the sky darkened, Price sensed victory within his grasp and met with his senior officers. A stray bullet passed beneath his arm

During the years before the war, Iuka, Mississippi, had a reputation as a resort. Its military value lay in its proximity to the Memphis and Charleston Railroad.

and struck his divisional commander, Henry Little, killing him instantly. Price was grief-stricken.

During the night the Southerners worked to consolidate their position. Price was intent on renewing the fight the next morning. After he went to bed, his generals began arriving to report on the condition of their troops. Talking among themselves, they concluded that they could not press the issue in the morning. Ord was still to the north and might attack. Many wondered why he had not already done so.

The issue was forced when one of Van Dorn's staff officers arrived. Price was awakened and confronted with the argument that his army was in no condition to take on both Rosecrans and Ord. The Confederate commander relented and consented to withdraw.

Rosecrans's troops could hear the noise coming from the Southerners' camp and wondered if it meant that they were evacuating the area or preparing to renew the fight. The Union commander noted, "They made great noise of establishing batteries in the woods during the night and massing troops. It excited my suspicions. I watched the movement all night, but could do nothing until daylight, when skirmishers going out reported [the] enemy retreating."

When the Confederate officers roused their men at 3 A.M., many were astonished to hear that they were evacuating. Price's army withdrew by the southeastern road left open by Rosecrans.

As the sun rose there was scarcely a living creature between Rosecrans and Iuka. The contested ridge of the previous day was covered with dead men and animals. The sights were horrible. By 8:30 there was no doubt that Price had moved on. A pursuit was launched but only minor skirmishing followed. Rosecrans's column advanced, fired on Iuka, and received the town's surrender. After surveying the dead and wounded, Rosecrans's casualties were estimated at eight hundred. Price lost as many as fifteen hundred, most of whom were lost during the fierce contest for the Ohio battery.

Rosecrans was still puzzled that he had heard nothing from either Grant or Ord. He had sent three messages to Grant, but his first report did not reach Grant until 3:30 A.M. on September 20. Immediately Grant issued orders for Ord to attack "as early as possible." By all accounts Ord began his advance before dawn, but he proceeded cautiously and halted at intervals to listen for the sounds of fighting.

Sometime around 10 A.M., while inspecting an area west of the town, Rosecrans encountered Ord's column as it came marching down the road in step with the cadence of the company drummers. He demanded an explanation, but Ord silently passed a slip of paper to him. It was Grant's order from the previous day ordering him to postpone the attack. A similar order was to have been delivered to Rosecrans, but he never received it.

After Price linked up with Van Dorn, their joint force marched on Corinth. Following two days of fighting, October 3 and 4, they were repulsed with heavy casualties. The key to the Federal victory was the inner ring of redoubts that Rosecrans had advocated to Grant.

Buell received the reinforcements he needed to thwart Bragg's plans to gain Kentucky. At the battle of Perryville on October 8—which had its own instance of acoustic shadowing—Buell defeated Bragg. It was the last time a significant Confederate army operated within the borders of the Bluegrass State.

Rosecrans never accepted Ord's and Grant's explanation that they had not heard the fighting below Iuka. Col. John Fuller, one of Rosecrans's brigade commanders, noted, "This miscarriage was the beginning of a misunderstanding which grew into positive dislike between Grant and Rosecrans—a breach that was never healed."

Grant and Ord were not alone, however, in claiming such deafness. Letters from soldiers with Ord and Grant confirm that nothing was heard. Out of the nine thousand men along this line above Iuka, only a handful reported that they thought they heard something.

The veterans of Iuka refused to accept these answers. Camp rumors spread that Grant had been incapacitated by his fondness for the bottle, since that seemed to be the only plausible explanation. Commenting on the allegation, a captain of the Eleventh Missouri asserted, "General Grant was dead drunk and couldn't bring up his army. I was so mad when I first learned the facts that I could have shot Grant if I would have been hung for it the next minute."

For his part, Grant never contested or criticized anything that Rosecrans did at Iuka. He was nothing but complimentary of his general in his report to the War Department and confirmed the correctness of Rosecrans's decision not to occupy the road by which Price escaped. After riding over the ground in question, he saw for himself that Rosecrans did not have sufficient men to cover the road and engage the enemy.

At the same time, Grant began to question Rosecrans's ability and leadership, especially as he watched his general prepare for the coming engagement at Corinth, which Rosecrans viewed as a personal contest between himself and Van Dorn, who had been his classmate at West Point, albeit at the opposite end of their class rankings.

Acoustic shadowing was not uncommon. In addition to the two situations at Iuka and Perryville, instances were also noted at the June 27, 1862, battle of Gaines's Mill and during an engagement near a Rappahannock River bridge on November 6, 1863. Thus it is highly possibly that Rosecrans fell victim to the phenomenon at Iuka, where the rolling ground may have dissipated the strong winds experienced by Ord but not by Rosecrans, and damp air may have played a role in deadening the sounds of battle. Had the circumstances been otherwise and Ord and Rosecrans executed their battle plan, Price's army would most likely have been destroyed.

16

HONEY HILL

On November 30, 1864, a force of less than two thousand men—including about twelve hundred Georgia militia, a squadron of the Third South Carolina Cavalry, two hundred men of the Forty-seventh Georgia and some South Carolina artillerists—stubbornly held on to a small ridge known as Honey Hill against repeated assaults by more than fifty-five hundred Federals. The Union soldiers were attempting to advance on Grahamville, South Carolina, to cut the rail lines between Charleston and Savannah.

In mid-November 1864, William T. Sherman abandoned and torched Atlanta as he began the famous March to the Sea. By November 23 his men made a feint toward Macon and took the towns of Gordon and Milledgeville, the latter being the capital of Georgia at the time. The area covered by Sherman's troops in this movement was so large that the Confederates could not discern what his primary objective was; however, they suspected his ultimate goal might be either Savannah or Charleston.

Whatever available troops Georgia had were used to find, harass, and defend the interior of the state against Sherman. The commander of the Georgia militia, Maj. Gen. Gustavus W. Smith, arrived at Savannah with a body of troops on the evening of November 29. There he received orders from Lt. Gen. William J. Hardee to move at once to Grahamville, thirty-five miles away by rail, to contest an expected attempt to cut the railroad line there. The men of the Georgia militia, however, were charged with protecting Georgia, not South Carolina. Mild protests were made by some of the troops. Eventually all were made to see that by protecting the railroad they were also defending Savannah, for without the railroad there would be no way of rapidly bringing in additional forces and no last resort of escaping Sherman.

Smith, a native of Kentucky, was an 1842 graduate of West Point. He had served in the Mexican War and then taught civil engineering at the military academy prior to pursuing civilian pursuits and becoming the street commissioner of New York City. With the outbreak of war, he demonstrated his loyalty to the South and accepted a commission as a major general in the Confederate army.

In 1863 Smith was disgusted at having been passed over for promotion and resigned his army commission. Subsequently Georgia Gov. Joseph E. Brown offered him command of the state militia and the rank of major general. Smith accepted the post.

As Sherman was marching across Georgia and making the state howl, Federal planners proposed a raid against Grahamville to cut the rail and communication lines. Troops were gathered around the Union base at Port Royal, and the small command was entrusted to Maj. Gen. John G. Foster.

During the evening of November 28, 1864, this force of five thousand soldiers and five hundred sailors filed onto transports at Hilton Head Island. At 2:30 A.M. the flagship signaled the transports to set sail. Fog, however, dispersed the small flotilla, and several transports lost their way, some grounding on bogs and others venturing up the wrong river. By morning a small number of the vessels entered Broad River, where the troops disembarked at Boyd's Neck—seven miles east of Grahamville.

The only Confederate force in the area was a small element of the Third South Carolina Cavalry. It took the night and part of the next day for the Federal expedition to complete the landing. Upon their arrival, Foster turned over command of the operation to Brig. Gen. John P. Hatch.

Hatch was a seasoned professional soldier. A New Yorker, he was a member of the West Point Class of 1845 and had served with distinction in the Mexican War and subsequently on the frontier. His participation in the battle of South Mountain in September 1862 later earned him the Medal of Honor.

Sometime during the evening of November 29 the grounded troops began marching toward Grahamville. Since the Federal commanders were unsure of the route, they enlisted the aid of a slave from nearby Boyd plantation. The guide was fearful of these men who had taken him unwillingly from his home. He led them down the wrong road, a mistake that was not realized until midnight, after the soldiers had hacked their way through four miles of underbrush and swamp. There was no choice but to retrace their steps and bivouac at Bolan Church for whatever remained of the night.

Early in the morning of November 30, Confederate Col. Charles Colcock, the district commander, arrived at Grahamville just ahead of the train bearing Smith, most of his men, and his chief of artillery, a colonel named Gonzales. Smith asked Colcock, who was preparing to approach the enemy, to find a position for his leading brigade, which would be sent up as soon as it arrived. In the meantime, Smith would wait at the depot for the rest of his troops and the

Maj. Gen. Gustavus W. Smith led Georgia militia into South Carolina to block the progress of William T. Sherman's army as it marched from Savannah into South Carolina.

LIBRARY OF CONGRESS

Forty-seventh Georgia. Their numbers would bring the Confederate force to fourteen hundred men. Since the telegraph line was intact, communication with Savannah and Charleston was still possible.

Between Boyd's Landing and Grahamville, roughly two miles east of the latter, the Confederates had erected earthworks and emplaced artillery on a fifteen- to twenty-foot rise known as Honey Hill. But Colcock was not content to wait here for the Federals. He took the available horse soldiers under Maj. John Jenkins and a few pieces of light artillery to meet the approaching Federals.

Roughly a half-mile in front of Honey Hill, he set the artillery across the road. The cavalrymen dismounted and formed a skirmish line across a large field to the right of the road. The field was covered with tall, dry grass, and ditches offered some semblance of protection. The left side of the road was impassable swamp land.

Around 10 A.M. the forward line of the Federals came into range, and the Southern gunners began their deadly work. Union soldiers quickly abandoned the road and began advancing through the open field. The guns could be flanked, but before that was accomplished, Colcock ordered the grass torched. The wind was blowing toward the men in blue, so the flames caused a rapid but orderly retreat. Colcock pulled back to the breastworks on Honey Hill, joining the rest of the troops there.

Brig. Gen. John P. Hatch (left) and Maj. Gen. John G. Foster

BOTH IMAGES: LIBRARY OF CONGRESS

The Federals regrouped and resumed their advance. Near the hill they were stopped in their tracks by heavy firing from the Confederate position. Smith wired Hardee in Savannah, "The enemy have extended both their wings, and are evidently in force. Fight still progressing. The troops have not yet arrived. We shall need reenforcements." Hardee was already sending all the men he could by rail to Grahamville.

In charge of the Federal assault, Hatch reported:

At 11 A.M. the head of the column came unexpectedly on the main body of the enemy in position. At this point the road bends to the left. The advance following it found themselves in front of an enclosed work pierced for four guns. The redoubt, situated on the crest of a small ridge, was the center of the enemy's line. It is said to have been built two years since, although until now unknown to us. Following the crest of the hill on either side of the redoubt, the enemy had thrown up a line of rifle pits, and within these waited with seven pieces of artillery our attack. In front of the enemy's line ran a small creek, bounded by a marsh covered with dense undergrowth. This was not impassable, but presented a serious obstacle to our advance, being completely commanded by the enemy's fire.

One of the Federal soldiers involved in the action, John J. Abercrombie, recounted his experience at Honey Hill. Given his description of the closeness of the railroad, he was on the extreme left side of the Union line.

We pushed on, however, until we finally arrived at a large rice plantation crossed by narrow dykes, which offered quite a serious obstacle to our farther advance. Just beyond this we could see Grahamville and nearer by the railroad, in front of which rifle pits had been thrown up. Advancing across the rice fields, waist-deep in water and mud, we could see fresh troops disembarking from a train evidently just arrived, and before we could reach the thither side they too had taken their place in the opposing line, joining in a rattling fire of musketry. The main road crossing the plantation was so narrow that we could bring into action but two guns of the 3d New York Battery, which opened vigorously. This brought speedy response from a heretofore unnoticed earthwork mounted with 34-pound seacoast howitzers, which had been part of Fort Moultrie's armament at the outbreak of the war. Then a field battery opened from opposite our left center, all resulting in a crossfire of shell and case shot in addition to the singeing musketry fire from the infantry who had now gotten our range. From this converging fire our men could secure no protection, the muddy water being too deep to permit them to lie down; and, furthermore, as the wounded began to fall, they were in danger of drowning, thus necessitating the dropping out from the firing line of two additional men each time to carry them off the field. This so speedily decreased our force that we were compelled finally to fall back to the edge of the woods from where we had begun our charge less than an hour before.

Some of the Georgia militiamen were mere boys. Two were observed taking turns shooting in a most unusual manner. Since both were too short to see anything from their rifle pit, they alternated between standing on each other's shoulders to aim and fire.

Repeated attempts were made to advance on or flank the earthworks, but all such attempts were in vain, according to Hatch:

> The left of [Gen. E. E.] Potter's brigade—re-enforced by two companies of the Fifty-fourth Massachusetts Volunteers and part of Fifty-fifth Massachusetts Volunteers, which had by mistake taken position on the left of the road—made two desperate attacks on the main work of the enemy, led by Col. A. S. Hartwell, commanding Second Brigade. They were repulsed with severe loss. The Fifty-fifth Massachusetts Volunteers were rallied, and, with the Marine Battalion, sent to the support of the right wing of the line of battle, with orders to turn the left flank of the enemy. They advanced gallantly, but were unable to carry the intrenchments.

By late afternoon the Federals were running low on ammunition. It was obvious that the hill could not be taken without more artillery. Throwing more men at it resulted only in higher casualties. Accordingly, Hatch ordered his men to fall back, thus ending the battle of Honey Hill.

A small Confederate force, consisting mostly of men and boys from the Georgia militia and fighting on "foreign soil," successfully

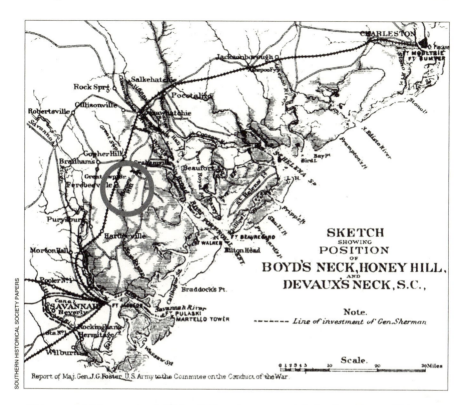

SKETCH
SHOWING
POSITION
OF
BOYD'S NECK, HONEY HILL,
AND
DEVAUX'S NECK, S.C.,

Note.
------- *Line of investment of Gen. Sherman*

Scale.

Report of Maj. Gen. J. G. Foster, U.S. Army to the Committee on the Conduct of the War.

This map, which accompanied John G. Foster's account of the battle at Honey Hill, shows the position of Honey Hill (highlighted about halfway down in the left third of the map) in relation to the railroad connecting Savannah and Charleston.

repelled a Union force almost four times its size. Southern casualties were reported to be 8 killed and 42 wounded. Federal losses were fifteen times that number, officially totaling 746.

Reinforcements for Smith arrived in the afternoon and during the morning of December 1 at Grahamville, guaranteeing the safety of the railroad there and ending the possibility that the Federals might make another attempt to take the depot. The Georgia militia was released and returned home.

The strange little battle of Honey Hill was a Southern victory because the Union force sent to raid Grahamville became lost in the night. Had it been able to advance directly on the depot, it would have accomplished its mission long before the Georgians arrived and added their weight to the small but formidable redoubt on Honey Hill. The delay was the price of victory that day.

Although the Federals had been successfully repulsed at Honey Hill, the Confederates evacuated Savannah three weeks later, and the city fell into Sherman's hands without bloodshed or destruction. In a telegram to Abraham Lincoln, Sherman announced the successful conclusion of his march across the Peach State and presented Savannah to the president as a Christmas gift.

PART 5

MAJOR BLUNDERS

17

BETHEL CHURCH

T HE SITUATION AT THE beginning of the war was, to say the least, confused. Nowhere was this more true than in Virginia and the District of Columbia. Federal property within the Old Dominion included the state-of-the-art facilities at the Gosport Navy Yard in Norfolk and the Harpers Ferry Armory in western Virginia that had been the focus of the 1859 John Brown incident. Also in question was the largest military facility in the country, Fort Monroe, situated at the tip of the Virginia Peninsula. Meanwhile, the seat of the Union government in Washington, D.C., was virtually defenseless at the time of the attack on Fort Sumter and Abraham Lincoln's subsequent call for seventy-five thousand men to save the Union. Many nervous days passed before the first troops arrived and made their camps in various government buildings.

Also in question was whether or not Maryland would secede. Lincoln, of course, did all that he could to prevent that, and in so doing he ignored due process and several other Constitutional guarantees.

At risk strategically, however, was the primary avenue by which troops could reach Washington.

Thus there was no small relief in the Federal capital when a Massachusetts politician and a brigadier of the Bay State militia, Benjamin F. Butler, led his men to occupy Baltimore to protect the railroads from sabotage and other mischief. Lincoln was appreciative, but his general in chief, Winfield Scott, reprimanded the amateur general and removed him from command. Such censure, though, was brief.

Butler was one of the most colorful men of the war. He was a Democrat and had voted for Jefferson Davis during the 1860 Democratic convention that eventually dissolved with no candidate. When Southern Democrats held a subsequent convention in Baltimore, Butler supported the candidacy of John C. Breckinridge, James Buchanan's vice president. Nevertheless, when Sumter was fired upon, Butler responded on behalf of the Union, despite the fact that the men whom he had championed for the presidency had become president of the Confederacy and a general in the Southern army.

Although Butler had occupied Baltimore without orders, he had found favor with the public and the administration for his decisive and bold action. Plus there was something to be gained for the new Republican power brokers by having a Democrat so obviously in the forefront of the effort to restore the Union. Butler was named head of the Department of Virginia and North Carolina, which was headquartered at Fort Monroe in Virginia.

While other Federal facilities in Virginia had been confiscated by Virginia, Fort Monroe remained in Union hands throughout the war. The hexagonal structure was the largest such edifice ever built in North America, but at the time of the war it held a garrison of only four hundred men. In a matter of weeks, however, this number was increased to six thousand. Since the facility could be resupplied from the sea, the position was fairly impregnable.

Fort Monroe's location at Point Comfort, at the tip of the Peninsula, controlled access from the sea for Hampton Roads and thus monitored Confederate shipping around Norfolk and Newport News and on the James and York Rivers. The fort also marked one of the shortest attack routes to Richmond, but in 1861 that virtue was not yet in the forefront of anyone's mind. In the spring of 1861 the

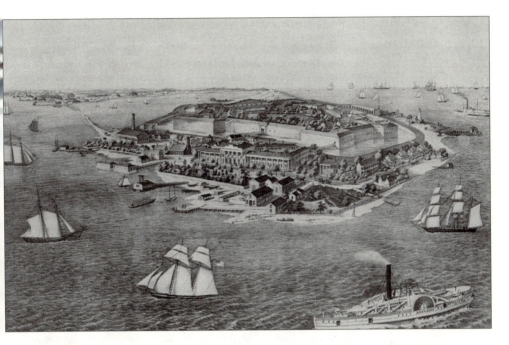

Impressive Fort Monroe occupied Old Port Comfort at the farthest extreme of the Virginia Peninsula. The Federal installation remained in Union hands throughout the war.

bastion was an isolated outpost in not-yet-hostile territory; no shots had as yet been exchanged between Union and Virginia forces.

That does not mean that nothing happened here during the early weeks of the war. In mid-May 1861 reports reached Richmond that two companies from the fort had taken possession of an area around a bridge on Mill Creek, about a mile from the fort. This was justified on the grounds that the fort's commander, Col. Justin Dimick, wanted to secure a freshwater source above the creek, which would be needed for the incoming troops who could not be housed within the fort. Apparently this was not the only incursion. Following a meeting between Dimick and Virginia Lt. Col. Benjamin S. Ewell, both regional commanders agreed to avoid future confrontations by keeping their men well apart from one another.

Nevertheless, Federal patrols ventured as far as Hampton, Newport News, and allegedly Big Bethel. One Confederate report noted that a party of three hundred Union soldiers briefly occupied the church at Big Bethel and left graffiti proclaiming "Down with the Rebels" and "Death to Traitors."

On May 22, 1861, Butler arrived to take command of the fort. In sending him off, Winfield Scott said, "You are fortunate in being assigned duty at Fortress Monroe. This is just the season for soft shell crabs, and the hogfish have just come in. They are the most delicious food you'll ever eat." Whether Scott spoke as a connoisseur whose girth attested to his knowledge of such delicacies or as a commander who had little regard for political generals, his posting of Butler to Fort Monroe essentially transformed the ambitious Massachusetts politician into an isolated caretaker, a figurehead.

Scott's orders, however, gave Butler license to act as he saw fit. Noting that the fort would eventually support some seventy-five hundred men and that only fifteen hundred would be needed to protect the facility, the general in chief stated, "[Y]ou will consider the remainder of the force under your command disposable for aggressive purposes, and employ it accordingly." Four "aggressive" priorities were also dictated: (1) prevent the construction of any Confederate batteries that might be used against the fort; (2) seize any batteries within a half-day's march ("or which may be reached by land"); (3) seize any batteries "at or above Craney Island"; and (4) capture the Gosport Navy Yard long enough to complete its destruction. In essence, Butler's orders were to maintain the status quo.

Charged with these responsibilities, Butler was motivated to act largely because he did not know any better. Scott, however, warned

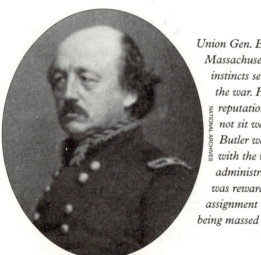

Union Gen. Benjamin F. Butler was a Massachusetts politician whose leadership instincts served him well at the beginning of the war. His lack of military discipline and reputation of heavy-handed patronage did not sit well with the high command. Yet Butler was a Democrat who aligned himself with the war aims of the Lincoln administration, and this political bravery was rewarded with a seemingly plum assignment to command the volunteer troops being massed at Fort Monroe.

NATIONAL ARCHIVES

his new general: "Boldness in execution is nearly always necessary, but in planning and fitting out expeditions or detachments great circumspection is a virtue." As if that were not sufficient warning, the general in chief added: "Where time clearly permits, be sure to submit your plans and ask instructions from higher authority. Communicate with me often and fully on all matters important to the service."

The day after Butler arrived, he encountered the defining moment of his command. This time the incident came to him as three runaway slaves sought sanctuary within the Union lines. When the owner of the slaves, Confederate Col. Charles Mallory, appeared and demanded the return of his property under the terms of the Fugitive Slave Act, Butler refused, justifying his position on two fronts. First, he claimed that domestic laws applied only within the boundaries of the United States, of which Virginia no longer claimed to be a part. Second, he noted that the slaves were being used to construct Rebel earthworks, and thus they were now contraband of war. The term was thereafter applied to all escaped slaves who sought freedom in Federal territory. Again Butler received support for his actions from the Lincoln administration.

Also on the day after Butler arrived, Virginia's voters ratified the April 17 ordinance of secession. The North responded on May 24 by sending eleven regiments across the Potomac and onto Virginia soil, occupying a buffer zone from Arlington to Alexandria. This first invasion of the South was almost bloodless, in part due to an unofficial truce that allowed the Confederate troops in the area to withdraw just prior to the arrival of the Union men. Two casualties, however, occurred when the regimental commander of a New York Zouave unit personally removed a Confederate flag from the roof of an Alexandria inn. Union Col. Elmer Ellsworth was killed by James W. Jackson, the owner of the inn, and Jackson was killed almost immediately by a soldier in the flag-removal party. Ellsworth came to be regarded as the first Union casualty of the war.

Interestingly, up to this point, more than a month after the bombardment and surrender of Fort Sumter, no real fighting had erupted between the two sides. Such are the fortunes of war when hostilities explode between two parties clamoring for action yet who are unprepared to act when the moment of truth is thrust upon them.

On the Peninsula, the growing garrison at Fort Monroe had noted that there was little or no Confederate military presence in the area. As more and more men arrived, the Federals needed additional territory for camps and for a little distance between the fort's personnel and the surrounding communities. Numerous Union patrols showed the flag at Hampton and Newport News and other points along the lower Peninsula.

Shortly after Butler's arrival, he moved on Newport News and, meeting little resistance—as per the agreement between Dimick and Ewell—he decided to occupy the town. In Washington, Scott was not pleased to receive the news and ordered Butler not to act on anything unless he had orders to do so.

Both sides slowly began to realize the strategic value of the Peninsula as one of the four principle approaches to Richmond, the newly named capital of the fledgling Confederacy. The Virginia government responded by allocating resources toward these perceived threats, and the man responsible for overseeing the disposition of the state's military assets was Robert E. Lee. Among the men at hand for these critical assignments was John Bankhead Magruder, recently commander of the defenses of Washington. Magruder was first assigned to organize artillery batteries around the Confederate capital then given command of all Richmond defenses and then dispatched to the Peninsula "in command of troops and military operations on the line to Hampton."

On May 24 Magruder established his headquarters at Yorktown. Lee's orders charged him to "take measures for the safety of the batteries at Jamestown Island and York River, and urge forward the construction of the defenses between College and Queens Creeks, in advance of Williamsburg." This ground was drenched with two and a half centuries of exceptional history for it included the site of the Jamestown colony, the colonial capital of Williamsburg, and the Yorktown battlefield. Magruder's ultimate responsibility, however, was to bottle up the Federals at Fort Monroe and keep them there.

For the next two weeks Magruder roamed his territory, estimating the numbers of Union soldiers both at the fort and in its outlying camps and gauging his own need for additional troops. A defensive line was already under construction along the Warwick River from Mulberry Island to Yorktown. The new area commander reviewed and approved this work, as required by Lee's orders, and began laying out plans for a second line, which was to be just east of

Williamsburg, spanning the width of the Peninsula as did the War-wick line.

While the work progressed, Magruder observed, "I felt so com-posed to dispose my feeble forces in such manner as to accomplish these objects with the least risk possible." In fulfilling this goal, he found that the land itself was his greatest ally, because much of the area was swamp and bog. There were only so many roads over which an armed force could advance. From Richmond, Lee telegraphed, "I take pleasure in expressing my gratification at the movements that you have made, and hope that you might be able to restrict the advance of the enemy and securely maintain your own position."

Of course much of the work involved in the erection of the War-wick line was not performed by Magruder's men but rather by hun-dreds of slaves impressed from the plantations on the Peninsula. The number fluctuated because several fled the work zones for the Fed-eral lines, a precedent now already established for their safety by the commander of Fort Monroe. Usually the former slaves were there-after employed in erecting fieldworks for the Union army.

Noteworthy among the men serving under Magruder were D. H. Hill and John Bell Hood. All three were West Point graduates, and Magruder and Hill were veterans of the war with Mexico. Hill com-manded the First North Carolina, and Hood was in charge of the

Col. John Bankhead Magruder (left) and Col. D. H. Hill (right)

cavalry. All the regiments were composed of fairly raw recruits, so much time was devoted to training and drilling. With regard to the cavalry, Lee ordered a "judicious disposition of the pickets and vedettes." In response, Hood's men began probing the Federal positions near Hampton, Newport News, and Fort Monroe.

Eighteen miles separated Yorktown and Fort Monroe, but the buffer between the two headquarters was about to shrink. On June 7 Hill led fourteen hundred of Magruder's twenty-five hundred troops to a small crossroads on the primary road between the two strongholds. The position was only eight miles from the fort. Near a church known as Big Bethel, which distinguished it from a nearby black congregation called Little Bethel, Hill's men cleared trees and formed earthworks on the western bank of a creek off the Back River. An outerwork was laid out on the opposite bank.

Marshy ground was to the left of Hill's position, but it was open field, so he positioned sharpshooters to cover it. To his right, on some higher ground overlooking the few buildings in the area, Hill placed one of his guns and two hundred men. Within the primary

This map of the Virginia Peninsula shows the position of Fort Monroe at the far right and the close proximities of Little Bethel and Big Bethel. Magruder was charged with developing two defensive lines across the span of the Peninsula, north to south, at Yorktown and Williamsburg.

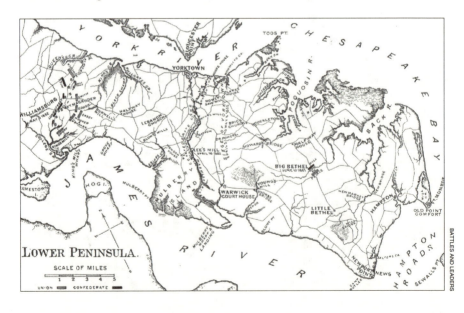

defensive compound he installed the remaining four cannon. He noticed a ford just east of the small bridge that spanned the creek and positioned men there as well. All of this was accomplished in roughly two days.

Needless to say, Hill's work did not go unnoticed. Butler surveyed the military scene and determined that eight miles was not as comfortable a buffer as eighteen. In his account of the action that followed, he recalled, "There was a point nine miles [actually eight miles] from the fort . . . which I learned the rebels intended to entrench and hold. . . . After the most careful and thorough preparation and . . . reconnaissance of the lay of the land . . . , I came to the conclusion to attempt to take this post."

Butler, however, was not the only commander in the field to feel an urge to act. Magruder's interpretation of developments was that the Federals were on the verge of occupying Hampton in force. Then he received reports from Hill that Union cavalry was probing the position at Big Bethel. Two "marauding bands" had come within a mile of the Confederate works and had been chased away by Hood's horsemen. Shortly afterward Magruder came to Big Bethel and took command.

During the early morning hours of June 10, without consulting Scott in Washington, Butler dispatched a force of forty-four hundred men against the Confederate outpost. Two columns, one from Hampton and the other from Newport News, were to converge at Little Bethel and attack Big Bethel at dawn. One column was made up of the First Vermont and Fourth Massachusetts; the other was comprised of the Third and Fifth New York. Two regiments—the First and Second New York—were held in reserve. Butler, however, did not command these troops in the field. That responsibility was given to Brig. Gen. Ebenezer Pierce, a general of Massachusetts militia.

For the purpose of identifying one another during the inevitable fight, the Federals wore white armbands and a watchword was supposedly issued. The precautions proved to be pointless.

This stealthy march went well until the troops were roughly halfway to their target. The two Union columns surprised one another in the dark. "When the troops got out four or five miles to the junction where the regiments were to meet," Butler reported, "it being early dawn and the officers very scared, Colonel [John E.] Bendix mistook the colonel and staff of the other regiment for a body of cavalry, and

LOSSING, PICTORIAL FIELD BOOK OF THE CIVIL WAR

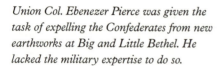

Union Col. Ebenezer Pierce was given the task of expelling the Confederates from new earthworks at Big and Little Bethel. He lacked the military expertise to do so.

fired upon them. The fire was returned; and by that performance we not only lost more men than we lost in the [upcoming] battle, but also ended all chance for a surprise." Twenty-one casualties resulted. The clamor led the foremost elements of the attackers to believe that they were being attacked from the rear, and they fell back.

During those same early morning hours, Hill's First North Carolina had ventured beyond the works at Big Bethel with the goal of surprising the Federals in Hampton. The shooting in the Union ranks, however, had alerted the Confederates to the approaching columns, and Magruder had recalled his men. The forward camp at Little Bethel was also evacuated, which eliminated it as a target for the advancing Union troops.

Out of the chaos that swept the Federal ranks, Pierce called for reinforcements from Butler, which were dispatched in haste. The regimental commanders appealed to Pierce to cancel the attack; their untrained men were unnerved and the Confederates were aware of their presence. Pierce never entertained the idea of withdrawal. He pushed his men back into march and proceeded to Big Bethel.

At 8 A.M. skirmishers caught sight of the Confederate position and were immediately discouraged. When shots were exchanged, many in the Union ranks viewed the Southerners as cowardly for remaining behind the protection of the breastworks and avoiding a "fair" fight. At 9 A.M. a blast from Magruder's artillerists shook them even more, especially since Pierce's guns could not deploy effectively, although they were manned by U.S. regulars. Pierce was as unproven and ill-trained as his men. He arrayed his command for a frontal assault, which suited the defenders quite well. One Southerner recalled that the Northern soldiers "did some pretty scientific dodging" in response to the early shots.

When Pierce found that he could not advance in force against the Southern position, he concentrated his men against the right and center segments of the Confederate line. The Federals, however, lacked coordination and the first attack withered in the face of the Southern artillery. B. M. Hord of North Carolina recalled, "A regiment would come up, fire a volley or two, mostly over our heads and precipitately fall back. . . . It seemed that their principal object was simply to get a sight or a shot at a Rebel, then fall back as quickly as possible."

On the Union right, Col. Abram Duryée led the Fifth New York, a Zouave regiment, in an attempt against the Confederate left, near the York River swamps. Hill's sharpshooters, two hundred of whom were cadets from a Charlotte military academy, drove them back. On the left,

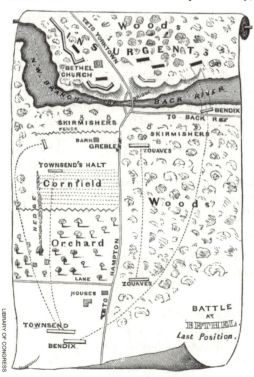

the Third New York tried to break through. Rough terrain caused one company to separate from the regiment. In the confusion, all the other companies fired on the out-of-position unit.

D. H. Hill had assessed the geography well and placed his artillery on the west side of the Back River. Pierce's infantry could not outflank him because of marshy ground to the Federal right and well-emplaced Confederates at the center and to his left. Confederate losses were one man; Union dead at the two Bethels totaled eighteen.

BATTLES AND LEADERS

Big Bethel remained a Confederate outpost throughout 1861 and into 1862. Hill's earthworks can be seen here on both sides of the river, pretty much as they existed for the battle.

The unit commander believed the Confederates were on the verge of turning his flank and ordered his men to fall back.

Pierce called for the Vermont and Massachusetts men to attack on the left. They successfully forded the creek and, according to one account, placed their white armbands on their caps as if to call for a truce while they consolidated their position near the angle of Hill's fieldworks. Apparently the Federals believed the works were open at the rear, which was not the case. The North Carolinians laid a heavy fire on these men for more than twenty minutes, and Hill's artillerists incinerated the few buildings there, which were the only shelter the Union soldiers could find. This phase of the attack ended when Maj. Theodore Winthrop, one of Butler's staff officers, was struck in the chest while trying to encourage his men forward. Afterward, in his report to Richmond, Magruder stated that Winthrop "was the only one of the enemy who exhibited even an approximation of courage the whole day."

All Union organization broke down, and Pierce reluctantly ordered his men to retreat. After the war a Confederate veteran with many battles to his credit observed that the fighting at Bethel "reminded me more of a lot of boys fighting a bumblebee nest than a real battle. One would rush up for the nest of bees a time or two with his switches, get stung, run back, and another would take his place."

Hood's cavalry chased the withdrawing Federals for five miles, more than halfway to Fort Monroe. The Southern horsemen broke off the pursuit when they came to a destroyed bridge over the Back River. In the meantime, Magruder's men buried the ten Union corpses left on the field—including Lt. John T. Greble, the first West Pointer to be killed in action during the Civil War—and brought their wounded as well as those of the enemy back to Yorktown for treatment.

On the battlefield, the lone Confederate loss was Pvt. Henry L. Wyatt of Company B of the First North Carolina. According to Edward Porter Alexander, Wyatt was one of four men who volunteered "to go out & burn a house between the lines." He was the first Confederate casualty in the first land battle of the Civil War.

In his reports to Richmond, Magruder was effusive in his praise of his subordinates, especially Hill and his artillerist, George W. Randolph, a grandson of Thomas Jefferson. Despite downplaying his own role in the fighting, Magruder was promoted to brigadier general on June 17, and throughout the South he was perceived as the man of the hour.

This perception remained unchecked for more than ten months, during which time little happened on the Peninsula. Magruder exercised his troops in entrenching and fortifying his lines, which now included the second line of redoubts about twelve miles west of Yorktown, near Williamsburg. When men and weapons soon proved to be scarce, he took advantage of the low terrain, exploiting the boggy ground by erecting dams at the five fords across the Warwick River and creating water barriers as needed. Magruder's star reached its zenith the following spring when he managed to stall George B. McClellan's Peninsula campaign outside of Yorktown for more than a month with little more than bluff and deception.

In the meantime, the road from Fort Monroe to Yorktown—and toward Richmond—had been effectively blocked by the Confederate success at Big Bethel. Butler was severely criticized for the embarrassing defeat, and his report of the affair admitted that the matter had been badly managed. He claimed, "This attack was not intended to enable us to hold Big Bethel as a post, because it was not seriously in our way on any proposed road to Yorktown, and therefore there was never any intention to maintain it even if captured." In the end he found that Pierce had waged the battle poorly. Pierce resigned and later reenlisted in the Union army as a private. Southerners, however, focused their scorn on Butler, which prompted this little ditty sung to the tune of "Yankee Doodle":

> Butler and I went out from camp
> At Bethel to make battle,
> Then the Southerners swept us back
> Just like a drove of cattle.

> Come throw your sword and muskets down,
> You do not find them handy;
> Although the Yankees cannot fight,
> At running they are dandy.

> Old Butler stays at Fort Monroe
> And listens to the firing,
> And when his men have met defeat
> He then goes out inquiring.

For weeks the South was enamored of the victory at Big Bethel and exulted in it. Much was made of the fact that only one Confederate and ten Federals had been killed, which seemed to support the prewar assertion that one Southerner was worth ten Yankees. Not only did Confederate newspapers revel in telling soldiers' stories of the fighting, but pro-Southern publications in the Border States also played up this battlefield success. It was better news than the fighting in western Virginia, where George B. McClellan was beginning to make a name for himself.

In the U.S. Senate, Butler's confirmation as a major general passed by only two votes. Had he been a professional soldier rather than a political general, his career would have most likely ended quietly. Perhaps all that saved Butler from censure was that his defeat at Big Bethel was soon overshadowed by the Federal defeat at Bull Run (Manassas). Nevertheless, the Massachusetts general was removed from command on August 17 and his energies directed toward recruiting Democrats in his home state. Things, however, did not slow down at Fort Monroe. Throughout the summer additional men and supplies continued to arrive. The fort became the staging area for the upcoming spring campaign, which came within miles of capturing Richmond.

In comparison to the battles of the next four years, the fight at Big Bethel was later viewed by historians of the war as "an aimless contest" fought by a handful of inexperienced men. Such an assessment casually dismisses the fact that fourteen hundred Southerners turned back twenty-five hundred Northerners in a near rout. The difference between victory and defeat lay in the leaders in the field. As was mentioned earlier, many of the Confederate commanders were trained at West Point and veterans of the Mexican War. The majority of the Union commanders, however, held their rank by virtue of their political connections within the militias of Vermont, Massachusetts, and New York. These men proved incapable of executing a successful assault against this entrenched position.

To be sure, Northern soldiers were not devoid of pride. After the battle, one reflected, "I have seen enough to satisfy me first, that war ain't play, and second, that our regiment ain't got no cowards in it." That sentiment stayed with the Union army in the East for most of the war. Addressing the lack of leadership at Big Bethel, another

During the early stages of the Peninsula campaign, the Union Army of the Potomac marched through Big Bethel, and for a while George B. McClellan's headquarters was here.

LESLIE'S

Union soldier suggested, "We earnestly hope it may be the means of removing our New York troops at least from Massachusetts generals, who have been fledged in the foul nest of party politics, without the least military merit." It would take some time to weed out the ineffective commanders, but eventually better leaders rose to command.

There was nothing strategic about the battle for Big Bethel. The South was in no position to exploit it as a launching point for an assault against Fort Monroe. At best it was an observation post, an early warning position for the Warwick line headquartered at Yorktown. To the North the area was little more than a viable roadway from Old Point Comfort to Yorktown. After the battle the area became more important to the Federal army because it represented a blot on the Union escutcheon that could only be rectified by occupation.

It would take several months for the Federals to return to Big Bethel, but they did in January 1862. A reconnaissance from Camp Hamilton proved to be of sufficient strength to threaten the undeveloped fieldworks and compel the small force of Confederates there to temporarily abandon the area and flee to Yorktown. In the ensuing months the site was manned only sparingly, and during the opening days of the Peninsula campaign it was abandoned altogether. In early April, McClellan established his headquarters there. After the army moved on, Big Bethel passed into a kind of oblivion. Today most of the site of the battle is submerged under a reservoir—a not unlikely ending to a strange little battle that had more propaganda value than strategic worth.

18

STREIGHT'S RAID

NEVER SEND A MULE TO DO A HORSE'S JOB

In April 1863 the two largest Federal forces in the western theater were those of Ulysses S. Grant, poised near the Confederate stronghold at Vicksburg, Mississippi, and William S. Rosecrans, whose army occupied most of Middle Tennessee in opposition to the Southern command headed by Braxton Bragg and encamped at Tullahoma. Rosecrans had blunted Bragg's earlier attempt to expel the invaders from the Volunteer State in an engagement at Stones River that spanned the last hours of 1862 and the first two days of 1863.

Action between these armies, however, was not limited to major clashes. For most of 1862, Confederate cavalry raids had kept things lively for the Union troops in Tennessee. In the forefront of these activities were Nathan Bedford Forrest, John Hunt Morgan, and Earl Van Dorn, all of whom had done what they could to contain Rosecrans and also hamper Grant's enterprise in Mississippi. While such raids did hinder these Federal efforts to some degree, the lessons in raiding were not wasted on the Union army commanders.

211

Independently of each other in early 1863, both Federal commands shaped plans for bold long-range raids behind Confederate lines. Both targeted railroads. When the Union leaders learned of each other's plans, a decision was made to coordinate them so as to frustrate the Southern commands in northern Mississippi, northern Alabama, and western Georgia.

In preparation for the raids, on April 15, 1863, Federal troops moved from Corinth, Mississippi, into the northwestern region of Alabama with the goal of occupying Tuscumbia, which would be a launching point for one of the raids. At the same time, Union infantry also marched out of Memphis and La Grange to engage the enemy in northwest Mississippi.

As part of the latter movement, Col. Benjamin H. Grierson led seventeen hundred horse soldiers into Mississippi on a sixteen-day raid, from April 17 to May 2, that climaxed at Baton Rouge. During that time his men disrupted communications and destroyed railroad tracks and bridges and other war material. They succeeded because Grierson used a third of his force to distract pursuing Confederate cavalry by moving toward a near railroad target and returning to La Grange. The Southern horsemen followed the smaller force, which allowed Grierson to conduct the rest of his raid with little opposition.

Grierson's primary target was the strategic railroad junction at Newton Station, which he attacked and wrecked on April 24. The raiders then turned toward the Mississippi River and disrupted other targets of opportunity along the way.

From Vicksburg, Confederate Gen. John C. Pemberton directed the effort to contain and capture Grierson's cavalry. The Union horsemen, however, evaded their pursuers and continued to attack railroad targets. By the time the Federal horse soldiers arrived at Baton Rouge, Pemberton's reserves were scattered far and wide. This dispersion allowed Grant to move his army even closer to Vicksburg, because Pemberton's attention was focused farther south.

The second prong of the coordinated Union effort was directly under the guidance of Rosecrans. The Federal commander surmised that if Bragg were driven from his camp at Tullahoma, he would most likely fall back to Chattanooga, which was a strong position that could be held for some time. If Bragg's supply lines through

Georgia were sufficiently threatened, however, the Confederates would have to fall back into Georgia, possibly to Atlanta.

This scenario was much discussed in Rosecrans's headquarters. Finally, Col. Abel D. Streight of the Fifty-first Indiana submitted a plan for a long-range raid with two thousand men on the Confederate arsenal at Rome and the railroad depot at Dalton. The attack route would traverse northern Alabama, a remote area of the state with strong Unionist sympathies and very little telegraph communication. To expedite the raid's passage through the region, two companies composed of area natives who had joined the Federal cavalry were among the units involved in the operation. Streight's proposal went through his brigade commander to Rosecrans's chief of staff, James A. Garfield, the later president, and finally to Rosecrans, who approved the proposal.

From the beginning, Streight's raid did not fare as well as Grierson's. In fact, very little went well with it. For one thing, such raids were usually conducted by cavalry, and this phase of the Federal enterprise was to be executed by mounted infantry—possibly because Streight was a commander of infantry. Yet even this quirk was somewhat more peculiar, because the two thousand raiders were to ride mules. Someone in Nashville convinced the planners that these animals were better suited than horses to the rugged terrain of northern Alabama. Thus was born the Mule Brigade.

Col. Abel D. Streight led a Union raid across northern Alabama that was supposed to strike at targets in Georgia and possibly influence the Confederate army to abandon Chattanooga. There was much merit to the plan, except for one thing . . .

Someone convinced Streight to use mules instead of horses. While it was true that mules could handle rugged terrain better than horses, only a portion of his men were "mounted" at the beginning of the raid, and most of the mules taken from the countryside for the task were sickly. Compounding Streight's problem was that his men had little training in riding and controlling mules, and they were pursued by Confederate cavalry on horseback.

BATTLES AND LEADERS

Time was the greatest enemy of this second deep-penetration raid, and it reared its head throughout the venture. Because the four regiments involved—the Fifty-first and Seventy-third Indiana, Third Ohio, and Eighteenth Illinois—were infantry, more than a day and a half was spent on acquainting the men with the mules. Somewhat complicating the matter was that only eight hundred mules were available in Nashville, and many of these were sickly. To solve this problem, it was decided that the raiders would confiscate animals from the countryside through which they marched toward steamers that would carry them down the Tennessee River, from Fort Henry to Eastport, Mississippi, and a rendezvous with a five-thousand-man force under Brig. Grenville M. Dodge. The flaw in this plan was that the confiscated mules were unshod, which meant that the rigors ahead would take a high toll of the animals.

Streight was late in joining forces with Dodge, and Dodge moved against Tuscumbia without him. Along the way he encountered Confederate cavalry under Col. P. D. Roddey. Although Roddey was outnumbered almost three to one, he seized the initiative and forced Dodge to fall back and call for more troops. On April 19, as twenty-five hundred reinforcements marched out from Corinth to join Dodge, Streight arrived at Eastport. While he went to meet with Dodge, his men erected a camp and fashioned a makeshift corral for the mules. That night a number of Roddey's soldiers invaded the corral, selected some of the finer animals, and stampeded the rest. For two days Streight's soldiers rounded up the strays, but they recovered only about half of the four hundred mules. More would have to be culled from the countryside as the command moved out.

With reinforcements and Streight's men added to his own, Dodge led the nearly ten thousand men into Tuscumbia on April 24. This advance did not go unchallenged, however. Roddey skirmished with the Federals almost continually, and his actions allowed Nathan Bedford Forrest to bring his command to Tuscumbia from Spring Hill, Tennessee. Upon arrival, Forrest would command the opposition to Dodge's incursion.

At Tuscumbia, Streight streamlined his command to roughly fourteen hundred men. He separated from Dodge's command on April 26 and set off across northern Alabama for his targets in Georgia, a fact that some locals noted and reported to Forrest. The Confederate commander grasped the significance of the news and separated his force, with one element focusing on Dodge and the other inserting itself in between the two Federal forces, preventing them from rejoining. Roddey would threaten Dodge; Forrest would pursue Streight.

Rain and mud limited the progress of everyone. Streight pushed his men onward, but not too quickly. He was unaware that Forrest was roughly twelve hours behind him and coming on fast. Around midnight on April 30 Forrest's scouts reported that the Federals were camped below Sand Mountain. The Confederate commander allowed his twelve hundred men to rest in anticipation of overtaking his prey the next day.

A Unionist civilian rode into Streight's camp to offer his services. He was appalled by what he saw and shortly afterward jotted down the only known description of the Mule Brigade: "Some of his [Streight's] men were on foot, some were on bare-backed boney beasts that moved with difficulty, while others strove to maintain their seats on capricious creatures that reared and ran, then halted and moved sideways and backwards without regard to spur or rein."

At daylight Streight's column was on the march and scattered across the rugged trail up the mountain. When the Federal commander arrived at the summit, he received word that his rear guard was under attack and heard the thunder of cannon. Streight's Alabama scouts brought word that Confederate cavalry was also trying to flank him.

The sound of gunfire aided the Federal commander in getting his men to close ranks, but Forrest's men pressed so hard that Streight had to find a position from which to make a stand. He positioned his men across the ridge of the hill, known as Day's Gap, anchoring the ends with a ravine on the right and a marsh on the left. Two howitzers were positioned in the middle. As soon as the Federal rear guard passed into the line, the rest opened fired on the advancing Confederates.

Forrest's brother, William, was wounded in the first volley. When Bedford Forrest arrived, he formed a line of dismounted troopers with mounted men on both flanks. Many of the soldiers on horseback rode in advance of their comrades on foot, paying a steep price for the act and causing no little confusion in the Southern line. Streight saw this and ordered a charge into the Confederate ranks, taking several prisoners and capturing two of Forrest's guns. While the Southerners paused to regroup, the Federals resumed their advance. Streight gained an hour on Forrest, but the ensuing pursuit would be relentless.

Forrest dispatched some riders to check on the situation with Dodge and sent one of his regiments to parallel Streight's column. One hundred handpicked men were charged with maintaining a close pursuit of the Federal rear guard. The remaining cavalrymen were ordered back into motion with orders to "shoot at anything in blue and keep up the scare."

Streight devised an ambush nine miles later. Under bright moonlight, he positioned his men, now unmounted, in the shadows provided by a thicket of pine trees.

Forrest suspected such a trap and halted his men before blundering into it. He called for volunteers to pinpoint the Yankee position, and the men came forward to draw fire while two of the Confederate commander's guns were stealthily positioned and shotted with canister. The first gun opened on the Federals and drew a hornet's nest of return fire.

As soon as the second gun opened up, Streight's men fell back, but Forrest advanced some troopers to block their withdrawal. He then led several charges and had one horse shot out from under him and two others wounded. The Federals eventually were able to pull back, but Forrest retrieved the two guns he had lost earlier, although they were now spiked and worthless to him.

In Forrest's estimation, Streight had no choice but to press on to Rome, so the Confederate cavalry leader allowed his men and their mounts to rest and eat. Meanwhile, the Mule Brigade entered

Blountsville on May 1 and confiscated all the food and mounts Streight's men could find, but they had no time to rest.

Near Gadsden, Alabama, the Federals crossed Black Creek and torched the only bridge for miles around. Streight posted his rear guard here along with two field pieces. Forrest would have to take some time to find a way across the waterway, giving Streight a little breathing room.

Forrest arrived on the scene while the bridge was still burning. He saw a young girl, Emma Sansom, nearby and asked if there was another crossing. She said that the nearest bridge was more than two miles distant but that a cattle ford was not that far. Emma offered to saddle a horse and show him, but the Confederate commander had no time to waste. He hefted her onto his horse, and she directed him, under fire now from the Yankee soldiers on the other side, to the spot. Forrest left her with a note of his thanks, a rare item considering the general's near illiteracy, and requested a lock of her hair. Then he brought up his guns to silence the Federals on the opposite bank and crossed his men.

Quickly the pursuit resumed. Streight had not gained as much time as he had hoped.

The Union column had paused at Gadsden, some four miles from Black Creek, but quickly departed when Forrest's advance troops arrived. Streight anticipated another all-night march and saw

Whereas a previous raid had succeeded because Southern horsemen were decoyed away from the main body of the raiders, when Streight employed the tactic, only a portion of the pursuing Confederate cavalry was drawn off his trail. Worse news for the Union commander was that he was being tracked by one of the premiere cavalry leaders in the South, Nathan Bedford Forrest (right). As Streight found out, if Forrest was anything, he was tenacious.

that his best hope lay in getting his men across the Oostanaula River and firing that bridge. He chose two hundred men to rush to Rome to capture and hold the bridge for him.

Forrest too saw that such would be his opponent's best bet and sent a rider to Rome to arouse the citizens. They should defend the bridge or destroy it if needs be, so that Streight could not escape.

When the two hundred Federals approached Rome, they saw that home guards defended the bridge. Capt. Milton Russell, the advance group's commander, decided not to attack and sent word of the situation to Streight.

The Mule Brigade had advanced fifteen miles and paused at Blount's plantation to secure forage for the animals. Forrest's men had maintained a steady contact with the Federal rear guard, nipping constantly at the Northerners. So here Streight formed his men in a line of battle, and Forrest brought up his main body while skirmishers and sharpshooters pecked at the Yankee troops. A sharpshooter's bullet killed Streight's second in command, Col. Gilbert Hathaway, and all but destroyed any morale still in the Federal ranks.

Again Streight withdrew, this time to a place opposite Cedar Bluff, which had at one time been a ferry across the Coosa River. Undaunted, the Federal commander led his men to a bridge several miles upstream. Because the men and animals were exhausted, many moved in their sleep.

Along the way the Federals encountered an old coal chopping, described by Streight as "where timber had been cut and hauled off for charcoal [for Rome's iron foundries], leaving innumerable wagon roads running in every direction." The several roads were disorienting to the sleep-walking mule soldiers. The Union commander noted, "The command became separated and scattered into several squads, traveling in different directions." When they did find the bridge, the crossing took hours. Once they were across, that bridge was torched, too.

On May 3 the Federals arrived at Lawrence. What few men were still awake fell asleep quickly. Here Streight received Russell's report on the situation at Rome as well as word that a Confederate force was closer to the city than was he. Almost immediately gunfire was heard coming from the rear guard. Strangely, several Union soldiers fell asleep while under fire.

Forrest had only six hundred men with him when he undertook the assault, but he stretched them out, giving the impression that he had many more. Streight and his officers could not rouse all their men, so they entertained the idea of surrender when Forrest offered a truce to discuss terms. The Federal commander was far more pugnacious than his subordinates, but he consented to discuss options with Forrest.

The two men met, and Forrest requested Streight's surrender, "your men to be prisoners of war, officers to retain sidearms and personal property." The Confederate commander added that reinforcements were en route to Rome and that he had sufficient men on hand to overrun Streight's position.

To underscore his point, Forrest engaged in some more battlefield theatrics, and brought up one of his two guns. Streight protested this repositioning of weapons during a truce, and Forrest ordered the gun pulled back. The gun was withdrawn, moved to another spot, brought forward again, and pulled back several times.

Finally, Streight asked, "Name of God, General Forrest, how many guns have you got?! I have already counted fifteen."

Forrest offhandedly replied, "I reckon that's all that has kept up."

Streight returned to his officers and polled them. Against his better judgment, he surrendered 1,466 men along with their equipment and two guns.

When the Southerners' ruse was revealed, Streight demanded that his men and weapons be returned.

Forrest refused, saying, "Ah, Colonel, all's fair in love and war."

Streight and his men were taken to Rome—as prisoners—and departed aboard the rolling stock of the Western and Atlantic Railroad over track they were supposed to have disrupted or destroyed. The officers were consigned to Richmond's infamous Libby Prison; the enlisted men were dispersed among several other prisons and soon exchanged.

That would have ended the saga of the commander of the Civil War's only Mule Brigade had not POW Streight learned that a daring escape from Libby was being planned. On the night of February 9, 1864, 109 Union officers crawled to freedom through a tiny tunnel. Although 48 of the escapees were eventually recaptured, Streight was among those who safely reached Union lines.

LIBRARY OF CONGRESS

Streight and his officers ended up in Richmond's Libby Prison. Some eight months later, Streight was one of the men to escape successfully from the prison. He encountered Forrest again, but in November 1864 he managed not to surrender.

In May 1863 Forrest received the Thanks of the Confederate Congress among other profuse praises. His dogged pursuit of the Mule Brigade did much to redeem the honor of the South that had been besmirched by the Grierson raid. Had Streight been able to execute his raid with the impunity enjoyed by Grierson, there is no telling the profound effects these successes would have had on subsequent raids.

Streight and Forrest did face each other later in the war. After returning to Washington and a short leave, Abel D. Streight was promoted to brigadier general and assigned a command in the Army of the Cumberland, which was then stationed near Nashville. Following the November 15–16, 1864, battle for the city, Streight's men took up the pursuit of the Confederate rear guard, which was commanded by Nathan Bedford Forrest. Forrest and the remnants of the Southern army were able to escape.

19

SHILOH

A REVERSAL OF FORTUNE

MOST STUDIES OF THE Civil War focus on the front line in Virginia where the great men of the conflict engaged one another in the tug-of-war for victory. The names of Lee, Jackson, and Longstreet dominate the literature just as do those of Grant, Sherman, and Sheridan, albeit for their achievements in the last year of the fighting. This emphasis on the East continually captivates most students of the war, but one of the longstanding assessments of the war's progress is that victory was defined very early in the conflict in the western theater. Indeed the West was the incubator for the greatness that eventually came to Grant, Sherman, and Sheridan.

Confederate efforts in the West were botched from the beginning. This is usually attributed to the fact that many of the men chosen to command here were woefully poor choices for the task that faced them. Most of them were friends and acquaintances of Jefferson Davis, who based his decisions more on his memories of these men from his days as a cadet at West Point than on his more recent experiences as

Franklin Pierce's secretary of war. Unfortunately the majority of these reminiscences were clouded with a first-year cadet's tendency to hero-worship upperclassmen. Thus Leonidas Polk, an Episcopal bishop who had never served a day in uniform after his graduation from the military academy, was entrusted with the department charged with defending the strategic gateway to the Southern heartland in the area around the Mississippi River.

At the time, the state of Kentucky was in between aligning itself with either side, but Polk polarized the parties by marching his army into the Bluegrass State. In response, Ulysses S. Grant moved his men into Paducah, and he was followed by other Union commanders. Polk was vastly outnumbered, but Davis had earlier named Albert Sidney Johnston to command this wide-ranging "department," and Johnston arrived in Nashville on September 14, 1861, eleven days after Polk had invaded Kentucky. Johnston and Polk had been roommates at West Point and upperclassmen to Davis, and Johnston had the reputation of being the best commander in the regular army in the years prior to the war.

Johnston took his army into Kentucky and occupied Bowling Green; his presence alone seemed to intimidate his opponents. Over the next three months he developed a line from Columbus to Bowling Green to Cumberland Ford, stretching his resources to the maximum to protect the Tennessee border, but it would not withstand any aggressive Union action. So Johnston called on Richmond for more troops, claiming, "All the resources of the Confederacy are now needed for the defense of Tennessee." Before the Davis administration could respond, Grant struck at Forts Henry and Donelson, beginning operations to seize the Mississippi, and split the South in two. Johnston's line was compromised, and he pulled back, abandoning Kentucky and regrouping at Murfreesboro, forty miles south of Nashville.

By March 1862 three Union armies stood ready to exploit this opportunity. John Pope's twenty-five thousand men were based near Columbus, Kentucky, in position to advance along the Mississippi River. Grant's thirty-five thousand men were moving along the Tennessee River toward a critical railroad junction at Corinth, Mississippi. And Don Carlos Buell's fifty thousand men were encamped in Nashville and poised to join Grant. Also scattered across the area were three Confederate armies, including Johnston's and Polk's, but these totaled only thirty thousand men.

Acting on the advice of Braxton Bragg and P. G. T. Beauregard—who was now in Tennessee mostly because Davis was exasperated with the hero of Sumter and Manassas and wanted to get him out of Virginia—Davis approved a plan that gathered several Southern commands to defend the Mississippi Valley and moved men from New Orleans and Mobile into the area to accomplish that goal. They were to congregate at Corinth, and their goal was to strike at Grant before Buell could join him. Johnston called the plan a "hazardous experiment," because there was a risk that the armies being shifted in this massive undertaking might be intercepted and destroyed before joining with the others.

While the Southerners reallocated these resources, the Union position was greatly weakened when Grant's departmental commander, Henry W. Halleck, relieved him of command and brought him up on charges of neglect and inefficiency. Grant's men continued to move south, however, and William T. Sherman's division was ordered to forge ahead and destroy a segment of railroad. Heavy rains and rising water, however, fouled the mission, so Sherman sought high ground and encamped his men at Pittsburg Landing. His headquarters was set up near a one-room log Methodist church that had

Albert Sidney Johnston (left) and P. G. T. Beauregard (right)

seen better days. The meetinghouse was known as Shiloh, a biblical name meaning "place of peace."

News of Grant's removal was not received well in the White House, where the general was perceived as a field commander who gained positive results. Abraham Lincoln intervened on his behalf by requesting a copy of the specifications against the general. In truth, Halleck's allegations against Grant were more personal than professional, and the departmental commander quickly grasped that to pursue the matter would not be in his own best interest. The charges were dropped, and Grant returned to his command.

Grant chose to encamp all of his men at Pittsburg Landing. After pondering their performance at Henry and Donelson, he elected to take a short time to drill and train his troops and wait for Buell to join him for the push into Mississippi.

The land around Sherman's camp lent itself to those purposes, and Sherman estimated that the area could easily accommodate as many as one hundred thousand men. Within a three-week span the camp became enormous, and the days were occupied with inspections and drills. Morale was high as regiments engaged in friendly competitions. One Indiana soldier wrote home, "To a civilian the scene would have been quite imposing, but to us it was only a 'little grand.'" Many spoke of the next battle as the last of the war.

Ulysses S. Grant (left) and Henry W. Halleck (right)

Since there was no perceived immediate threat in the area, the Union divisions laid out their camps on the basis of comfort, particularly the availability of drinking water and firewood, rather than defense. No breastworks were erected, supposedly because the commanders did not want to give the men the idea that they were vulnerable. The camp was triangular in shape, with one side formed along the Tennessee River and another bounded to the west by a smaller river and a creek. The remaining side was open to the south—in more ways than one.

Twenty-three miles separated Grant from the congregation of Confederates at Corinth. A quick reorganization established the Army of the Mississippi, with Johnston as commander, Beauregard as second-in-command, and Bragg as chief of staff. Johnston, however, did not want the command, because he had been severely criticized for the collapse of Confederate efforts in Kentucky and the abandonment of Nashville and believed that he lacked the confidence of his men. Beauregard refused to accept command, because he claimed that he had been sent to assist Johnston, not replace him. He was also suffering from a two-month bout with laryngitis, a bronchial infection, and a recurring fever. According to Col. Edward Munford, the Louisiana general graciously declined command with the words, "I could not think of commanding on a field where Sidney Johnston was present." In the end, however, Beauregard functioned as commander in that he issued orders, devised the organization of the army, and directed operations in Johnston's name. Johnston essentially endorsed everything Beauregard did.

Diversity amid the Southern ranks was subtly illustrated by the array of flags borne by the separate elements. Beauregard tried to standardize the army's banner with the design he had championed in the East, which has come to be known as the Confederate Battle Flag. It was distributed to Bragg's command. Polk used a flag of his own design, eleven stars on a red cross on a blue field. Most of Johnston's troops hoisted the Stars and Bars, but William Hardee's division displayed a white-bordered blue flag with a centered white disk.

On March 31, 1862, Confederate horsemen briefly engaged pickets from Lew Wallace's division near Adamsville. When he heard of the episode, Beauregard decided that the time to attack had come.

LIBRARY OF CONGRESS

By drawing units from across the South together at Corinth, a formidable force was assembled to attack Ulysses S. Grant's advancing army that had already succeeded in taking key positions on the Tennessee River.

With all the pieces in place, the Confederate Army of the Mississippi numbered approximately forty thousand effectives when they marched out of Corinth toward the Union camp, which now totaled close to forty-six thousand men. The attack was scheduled for April 4 and then delayed twenty-four hours. Even then, with the men in position, the order to attack was held back. Beauregard believed Grant was on the verge of discovering them and suggested that the army withdraw, but Johnston was ready for a fight. "I would fight them if they were a million," he told an aide. Referring to the triangular shape of the Union camp, he added, "They can present no greater front between those two creeks than we can."

Beauregard's plan, modeled after Napoleon's battle plans for Waterloo, called for three lines of attack. The first two were five hundred years apart, and the third was eight hundred yards behind the second. Cavalry protected the right and left flanks, and artillery was positioned to take advantage of whatever passable roads existed and also behind the third line. Three brigades were held in reserve. This differed from a battle plan outlined in a telegram from Johnston to Davis that described a three-wing formation, that is, the three corps

Among the Confederate army that Johnston and Beauregard were to lead was the noted Washington Artillery from New Orleans, some of whose members were brought together for this image.

would advance side by side rather than in tandem. For whatever reason, Johnston did not alter Beauregard's blueprints.

The ground in front of the Confederates sloped down to the Tennessee River then dropped off to form a steep bank. Numerous thickets and woods, however, did not allow the Southerners to maintain a linear advance. Further complicating the attack was their approach, which was not straight into the open side of the Federal camp, but angling across it. The impetus of their advance would press Grant's men toward the Tennessee River, from which they could be resupplied and reinforced, not toward the creek and river that framed the right side of the camp, which would have isolated the Federal command.

In placing his army on the road *to* Corinth, Grant had failed to consider that he had also placed it on the road *from* Corinth, giving an approaching army fairly easy access to his camp. As far as the positioning of the various divisions was concerned, his most inexperienced troops were closest to the Southerners. Grant also established his headquarters nine miles away from the landing, in the more comfortable environs of the closest town, Savannah. Yet since he had removed himself from the area, he failed to appoint a camp commander, although Sherman was generally understood to be in control of the bivouac. This would hinder the camp's defense when the battle came.

From the moment that Sherman had landed here with his division, Confederate cavalry had almost continually probed the line around the Union camp. Over time the Federals had become accustomed to the sound of sporadic shooting. Reports of Southerners in the woods had also been rampant and generally discounted. When one of Sherman's units tangled on April 5 with a Confederate picket line, Sherman scolded the colonel and said, "Take your damned regiment [back] to Ohio. There is no enemy nearer than Corinth!" In response to another report of a strong Southern presence, Sherman condescendingly dismissed the information with the observation, "You militia officers get scared too easy."

As Confederate activity increased, one Union regimental commander, Col. Everett Peabody, was not easily discouraged by the rebuke of his divisional commander, Benjamin M. Prentiss. Peabody ordered an early morning reconnaissance for 3 A.M. on Sunday, April 6. At 5 A.M. his men entered a clearing known as the Fraley field and encountered elements of the Third Mississippi. Volleys were exchanged, and wounded Union soldiers returned with word of their encounter. Peabody sent reinforcements, but the Southerners did not attack in force until almost ninety minutes after the first shots were fired.

Even then the Confederates caught the stirring Federals by surprise. When Sherman ventured out to see what was happening, he glimpsed a large force about a half-mile in front of him. Suddenly skirmishers appeared fifty yards away and fired, striking him in the hand and killing one of his orderlies. Sherman took to his horse to coordinate the repulse and told Col. Jesse J. Appler, the elderly commander of the Fifty-third Ohio volunteers and a man recently browbeaten by Sherman as too alarmist, "Hold your position. I will support you." He then dispatched riders to the other divisional commanders to report the attack and organize a defense. Quickly he realized that all the Federal camps were under attack.

The men at this first camp held the Southerners at bay for almost ninety minutes before they were overrun. They were among the first to see the new Confederate Battle Flag, and a private in the Sixty-first Illinois described it as "a gaudy thing." Peabody was killed in the fighting. Appler finally called out to his men, "Retreat and save yourselves!"

Grant reached the battlefield between 8:30 and 9:00, coming by steamboat from Savannah. Uncharacteristically, he wore his full uniform, including a buff sash that made him very conspicuous. Along the way he had alerted all his commanders of the fighting, paused at Crump's Landing to consult briefly with Gen. Lew Wallace and express his concern that the brunt of the Confederate attack might yet be directed at Crump's rather than Pittsburg Landing, and sent word to Buell to join him as soon as possible. When his vessel docked at Pittsburg Landing, he was greeted with the sight of masses of men huddling under the protection of the steep riverbank. Some estimates claim that at least three thousand were seeking safety there when Grant arrived.

Advancing toward the front, Grant encountered W. H. L. Wallace, commander of the Second Division, who described the progress of events as he knew them. Seeing now that the Confederates were

At the outset of the battle, a significant number of Union soldiers ran for the rear and found shelter on the bank of the Tennessee. By the end of the first day of fighting, several thousand men were clustered here.

LESLIE'S

attacking from the south and not threatening Lew Wallace's division to the north, Grant issued orders that Wallace bring his men down from Crump's Landing. He then went in search of Sherman and found him around 10 A.M.

Sherman's hand was wrapped in a handkerchief, and four horses had been shot out from underneath him. He allegedly escaped death many times during the first hours of the fighting. One of his aides, Lt. John T. Taylor, later recalled, "General Sherman's conduct soon instilled . . . a feeling that it was grand to be there with him."

In Grant's opinion, Sherman seemed to be holding up the right side of the line. The center of the line, however, appeared to be the most troublesome. Regiment after regiment was falling back, giving ground to the attackers. About the only good Grant could see in the situation was that there was no lack of Confederate targets in front of him.

The conversation between the two generals was brief. When Grant departed, all Sherman knew was that more ammunition had been ordered to the front and that Lew Wallace was coming.

After falling back to a sunken farm road, many of the frontline Federal units made a stand that became the focal point of the Confederate attack. The area was dubbed the Hornets' Nest.

To Grant it was painfully obvious that his situation was not good, but he expected that this would change once Lew Wallace appeared, and he expected that would happen by early afternoon. Nevertheless, he was anxious that Wallace's division should reinforce Sherman and at 10:30 sent a courier back with the message, "Hurry forward with all possible dispatch."

An aide to Grant, Douglas Putnam, commented on the general's anxiety after his meeting with Sherman, when he saw a column of troops approaching from behind:

> Riding toward the right the general saw a body of troops coming up from the direction of Crumps Landing and exclaimed with great delight and satisfaction, "Now we are all right, all right— there's Wallace." This I think must have been near noon. I mention the occurrence here as evidence to show what his expectations were and upon what he had depended. He was, of course, mistaken, as the troops he saw were not those he so earnestly looked for, and of whose assistance he was beginning to feel the need.

As bad as the situation was for Grant's army, the layout of the Federal encampments, although not arranged to be defensive, contributed nonetheless to a strong line, since there were layers of defenders to support one another as the fighting progressed. The defenders were sheltered by trees; the attackers had to advance across open fields.

Up and down the improvised Union line, Grant's men fought off the attack with a stubborn determination to hold their ground. These early efforts prevented a rout, even though masses of men fled the fighting. One famous anecdote quotes a man making for the rear as calling out to those he encountered, "Give them hell, boys. I gave them hell as long as I could." One of those whom he addressed later commented, "Whether he had really given them any, I cannot say, but assuredly he gave them everything else he possessed, including his gun, cartridge box, coat and hat."

Aside from the general confusion of the battlefield, many of Grant's commanders failed to coordinate their men in combat. Thus regiments tended to fight in isolation and in many cases fell back piecemeal as the Confederates broke their flanks. When these soldiers withdrew, several artillery batteries were exposed and had to pull back or risk being lost. The majority of troops in the center of the line, made up mostly of Prentiss's Sixth Division, fled to the landing when their line broke. Along the way they encountered Stephen Hurlbutt's advancing Fourth Division, which formed a line roughly half a mile behind Prentiss's original position and then retreated after loosing a few volleys into the oncoming Rebels. Hurlbutt's troops, almost all of whom were veterans of the fight for Fort Donelson, fell back another half-mile and took cover near an old wagon road.

Confederate commanders had difficulty in managing the battle, too. As their men traversed the southern perimeter of the Federal camp, the three battle lines extended and became intertangled. While commanders navigated from unit to unit, the length of the line created gaps in supervision, and many regiments were left without orders. To address this, Beauregard dispatched his adjutants, Cols. Thomas Jordan and Jacob Thompson, to roam the field and direct detached units toward the sound of the heaviest fighting. Polk and Bragg saw what was happening and decided among themselves to divide the front into more manageable segments and sent word of their decision to the other corps commanders, Hardee and John C. Breckinridge. By the time they arrived at their designated zones, however, they found their men exhausted and running short of ammunition. Reports of Union reinforcements led Johnston to reallocate some of his men, and he had to pull many of these from the units advancing on the center of the Northerners' line.

In the late morning hours the focus of the fighting began to shift to the three-hundred-yard clearing known as the Duncan field, which fronted the eroded farm lane where Hurlbutt's veterans had taken up position. After glimpsing the Federal line, Johnston called for his reserves, but it would take them almost two hours to reach the battle line. By the end of the day, this ground would be dubbed the Hornets' Nest.

Hurlbutt's position was strengthened during the delay when additional units and remnants of units came up to join him. More than one thousand men from Prentiss's division, rallied by Prentiss and directed back into the line, and three brigades from W. H. L. Wallace's division formed to Hurlbutt's right. In all, eleven thousand Federals and thirty-eight guns occupied this half-mile-wide position.

They were all that stood between the Confederates and Pittsburg Landing. For the rest of the day they held off eighteen thousand Southern soldiers and survived ten to twelve charges, but rarely did they have to face more than four thousand attackers at a time, and none of the charges were supported by artillery until the last.

While Braxton Bragg attempted to wrest the Federals from the center of the Hornets' Nest, Johnston tried to bring up the right elements of his line to engage a portion of Hurlbutt's command occupying the extreme left side of the Hornets' Nest. He planned to shatter the defense here and drive the Union troops inland and away from the landing and the river, cutting off Grant's easiest avenue of reinforcement. The attack was carried out very cautiously, and John C. Breckinridge, the former U.S. vice president, complained to Johnston that his men refused to attack. Finally Johnston rode to the troops to take command of the action. His presence stirred the men, and he led them at least partway in a charge that dislodged the defenders occupying the area of the field known as the Peach Orchard.

It was Johnston's finest hour. It was also his final hour.

Sometime around 2 P.M. Johnston paused to assess the situation. He was exultant in the moment when he was joined by an aide, Tennessee Gov. Isham Harris. The general showed him the sole of his boot, which had been split in two by a bullet, and at least two places

Benjamin M. Prentiss (left) and William T. Sherman (right)

LESLIE'S THE SOLDIER IN OUR CIVIL WAR

Near a peach orchard on the far left side of the Hornets' Nest, Hurlbutt's division repelled charge after charge. Around 2 P.M. Johnston was mortally wounded here. His death was kept quiet lest the news dishearten his army.

on his clothing that had been nicked by fire. He then sent all of his aides with orders to the other commanders in the field. Harris was the first to return to the general's side and found him semiconscious in the saddle. Apparently Johnston had suffered a leg wound but had paid it no mind. The bullet, however, had severed an artery behind his right knee. A simple field tourniquet would have stanched the blood loss, but Johnston continued to focus on the fighting until he slumped in his saddle. He had earlier sent his personal physician to attend to a small cluster of injured men, including many Federals.

Harris inquired if the general was wounded. Johnston replied, "Yes, and I fear seriously."

The governor led the general's horse to better cover, and he and another aide pulled him to the ground, but they could do nothing as Johnston's life slowly ebbed away. The general died from loss of blood. Most likely the mortal wound had been caused by Confederate troops; the bullet had struck his knee from behind. After his death, the body was discreetly removed from the field so as not to unnerve the Southern soldiers.

Johnston's last charge had been effective, however. The left side of the Hornets' Nest rolled back like a swinging door, turning the defenders' line into something of a U shape. The ground was open from the Peach Orchard to Pittsburg Landing, but no Confederate commander seized the initiative.

A lull in the fighting instead allowed some of the defenders of the Hornets' Nest to pull back, but Prentiss and Wallace stubbornly held their men in position. Meanwhile, several Confederate field commanders and their artillery officers decided to form all of the guns they could find into a massive battery and hammer the remaining Union defenders into submission. (Gen. Daniel Ruggles claimed credit for the idea, but several officers also asserted that the plan was of their making.) They mustered between fifty-three and sixty-two guns, depending on which sources one consults, and unleashed a fierce bombardment. One of the officers on the receiving end commented that the shelling "continued so long that it was a relief when the Rebels began to advance upon us." Recently an argument has been made that the barrage had little effect on the situation; the defenders surrendered because their ammunition was exhausted.

At the least, the shelling allowed Southern infantry to approach the weakened position, and gradually the Northern men surrendered. After holding out for seven hours, twenty-two hundred were still in place to surrender. The seven-hour stand that was performed here had likely saved Grant's army from destruction.

For the remainder of the day, Grant's goal was to hold out until reinforcements arrived. His line had been driven back, almost to the river. The center was in tatters, and the left was pretty much open, but the right was still in position. The one thing, however, that kept the Confederates from overrunning the tenuous position at the landing was a battery of 24-pounder siege guns that had been brought up for the action against Corinth. More than four thousand men cobbled from various units protected and manned the weapons. Behind them masses of shell-shocked men huddled on the riverbank.

Buell had arrived in person at about 1 P.M. and met briefly with Grant an hour later. He requested transports for one of his divisions and inquired as to what preparations had been made for a retreat. Grant responded, "I have not yet despaired of whipping them, general." That concluded the meeting, and Buell inspected the area and fumed at everything he saw. By nightfall between ten thousand and fifteen thousand Union soldiers huddled on the riverbank.

The first Union reinforcements appeared at dusk. Lew Wallace's division appeared at 7 P.M. and took a position on the right. William Nelson's division, part of Buell's army, disembarked at the landing at almost the same moment.

Several Confederate commanders sensed that victory was theirs but knew that they had to act before the sun set. Most of their men, however, were worn out by the many charges against the Hornets' Nest, and great numbers of them turned to forage for food in the overrun campsites. Finally, at 5:30 a line of battle was formed to attack the Federal position backed up to the river. It was a highly disorganized affair.

In addition to the Union artillery massed at the landing, two Federal gunboats—*Lexington* and *Tyler*—joined in the defense but fired blindly at the Southerners. Before Confederate reserves could be brought into action, Beauregard, in command following Johnston's death, ordered a halt to the fighting.

Far from the fighting, Beauregard had seen multitudes of wounded returning from the front lines and had received reports that Buell would not be reinforcing Grant and was instead marching into Alabama. He also interrogated captured divisional commander Prentiss and, according to Bragg's recollection of the conversation, learned that Grant had already begun retreating across the river. Thus Beauregard decided to preserve his army and claim victory in the morning.

That night a cold, hard rain fell on the two armies. It became a thunderstorm, and one Yankee soldier noted, "It seemed like the Lord was rubbing it in." Flashes of lightning illuminated bizarre tableaus of death, hogs rooted among the dead, and the moans and cries of the wounded and the dying haunted every soul.

Most of Grant's men lacked everything but the clothes they were wearing and the weapons they carried. Regimental bands attempted to lighten the mood and raise morale.

In the near distance, the Confederates plundered the captured camps. A spirit of victory infused the Southerners, now convinced that they had vanquished the Federals and that the fighting was over. The postwar memoirs of Sam Watkins of Tennessee record, "The sol-

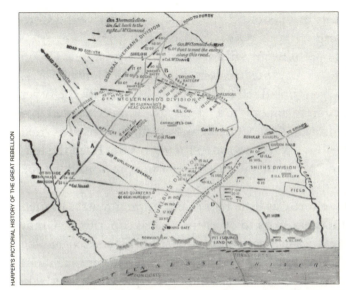

This map of the Shiloh battlefield (north would be to the right) shows the successive lines of defense around Pittsburg Landing. Despite the early Confederate successes, Grant's army held out and began the second day of fighting by seizing the initiative and attacking.

diers had passed through the Yankee camps and saw all the good things that they had to eat . . . it was but a short time before every soldier was rummaging to see what he could find." A Louisiana regimental surgeon noted that, as the night progressed, it seemed that half the army, laden with trophies of the battle, meandered back to Corinth and many were intoxicated on "Cincinnati whiskey" and "Philadelphia claret." In addition to the wide variety of food that was quickly consumed by the hungry and battle-weary Rebels, items such as weapons, uniforms, headgear, overcoats, blankets, and haversacks were confiscated.

Not all Southerners were as confident as the masses of soldiers. Col. Nathan Bedford Forrest sent scouts into the Federal line, and they witnessed the transports arriving with Buell's men. When Forrest tried to report these findings to his superiors, no one could find Beauregard, who had commandeered Sherman's tent but not informed anyone of this. "We will be whipped like hell before ten o'clock tomorrow," Forrest asserted to Gen. James Chalmers.

Grant spent the night in the rain but made no effort to form plans for the next day or to meet with Buell. Meanwhile, Buell supervised the offloading of his men and nursed feelings of contempt for Grant and Grant's army. He made no effort to meet with Grant. The two Union gunboats, following orders from Nelson, fired at irregular intervals throughout the night so as to deprive the Confederates of any rest.

With the infusion of twenty-five thousand troops, a new Union line formed and at 5 A.M. pushed forward into the Confederates. Because neither Grant nor Buell had communicated with the other or planned the action together, the Federal attack was executed in a fractious manner much as the Confederate assault had been carried out the day before. Lew Wallace formed the right side, Buell the left, and what remained of Grant's units engaged the previous day took the center.

Tactically, the effort was little more than hurling masses of men against the Southerners so as to exert numerical superiority. Grant recalled that such tactics had been successful at Fort Donelson, and he was sure that the same strategy would triumph in his current situation.

Buell's men surprised the Rebels, but before pressing the attack, he halted to consolidate his units and allowed the Southerners sufficient time to take up positions that would make this a fierce fight. Beauregard responded by calling for his men and all his reserves to

These formidable 24-pounder Parrotts were to have been used to seize the railroad center at Corinth. Instead they were installed around Pittsburg Landing to protect Grant's army by forming its last line of defense.

march to the sound of the heaviest fighting. After so many had wandered off during the night, he probably had about twenty thousand men still in the field.

The Confederates formed an irregular line with some units assembling at the point of their farthest advance on the previous day while others took positions near the former Federal camps, where they had spent the night. Some units even returned to their starting points of the previous day. Again the shortcomings of a few Confederate commanders weakened the line, notably Polk, who allowed his divisional commanders to form where they wanted while he moved to the rear. Other commanders failed to take advantage of the available Federal munitions, so their men did not replenish their ammunition. Some units were so spread out that they could assemble only a fraction of the previous day's strength.

Southern artillery helped to stave off a rout, and most of the Confederate infantry resumed the fight with a confidence engendered by the action of the previous day and an ignorance that Federal reinforcements had arrived. The fighting was also extended because of the excessive caution exercised by several Union commanders who followed the example of Buell. Furthermore, most of Buell's command had never seen action before and behaved accordingly.

Whatever advantage these factors might have given Beauregard's Army of the Mississippi were quickly offset by the same kind of wrongheaded orders that had prolonged the fight for the Hornets' Nest. The Confederates gradually gave up the ground won less than twenty-four hours earlier. Superior numbers won out. At 3:30 P.M. Beauregard ordered his men to retreat.

As the Southerners withdrew, the Northerners let them go. One Iowa soldier noted, "The two armies are like two tenacious bull dogs. They have grappled and fought until both are exhausted and worn out. One has crawled away to lie down and the other one cannot follow."

These armies were not unlike those that had collided near Manassas Junction in July 1861 in that, with the exception of the veterans of Fort Donelson, the vast majority of men were basically untrained, unorganized, and inexperienced. After Buell's and Wallace's men joined the battle on the second day, roughly one hundred thousand men participated in the fighting, approximately twice as many combatants as those involved at Bull Run. Here, however, the fighting lasted three times as long, casualties were five times greater, and neither army was routed from the field. Total casualties for both sides totaled just less than twenty-five thousand, making Shiloh the bloodiest battle of the Civil War up to that time.

Beauregard returned to Corinth at a leisurely pace. The battle was over and in his own mind he had won, but casualties of 10,699 men plus the loss of Johnston was a high price to pay for some prisoners and munitions. He contended that he left the battlefield on the second day only after eight hours of fighting against superior troops, repulsing every attack and crippling the Federals. The Northern interpretation of the battle was that it was their most brilliant victory.

To Grant's credit, he learned from his mistakes, which was not a common virtue among Civil War commanders. Immediately after the Southerners withdrew, he implemented all the precautions that were lacking from his camps before the battle, including cavalry pickets, breastworks, and clearing the fields so that no approach would be hidden from view.

Nonetheless, Halleck rushed to the scene from Saint Louis to take command of the massing armies and to replace Grant with George H. Thomas. Grant was relegated to the mostly administrative position of second in command and all but shamed out of the service. He compared his new role to being under arrest and considered resignation, a leave of absence, and assignment to the East. In the end, he waited. Within six weeks Halleck eventually led the troops into Corinth, which had been abandoned by Beauregard, and was reassigned to Washington and elevated to chief of staff. Grant was given independent command of the District of West Tennessee.

Many in the army and the Northern public blamed Grant for the attack at Shiloh and the high casualties. The western press in particular was relentless in its criticism. In short order the matter focused around allegations that Grant and Sherman had been surprised. Both men steadfastly denied that they had been negligent.

Sherman was an obvious scapegoat since he was in charge of the organization of the camp at Pittsburg Landing. His reputation was also under something of a cloud because of an earlier experience in Kentucky when his sanity was questioned. Yet the manner in which he led the defense on the first day of fighting did much to garner the esteem of most of those who saw him in action. Grant was profuse in praising his leadership, and that went a long way—despite Grant's own problems—in securing promotion for Sherman as well as cementing his newfound popularity with the public.

Meanwhile, Grant's future was hotly debated from the Tennessee countryside to the White House, where Lincoln heard many call for the general's dismissal. Grant's congressional sponsor, Elihu B. Washburn, spoke eloquently in the general's defense and deflected the matter in the Capitol, but privately Col. J. E. Smith of Galena commented to Washburne that the army "had not been surprised; it was worse, we were astonished."

The president weighed the matter but rebuffed Grant's critics with the words, "I can't spare this man; he fights."

In the weeks that followed the fighting at Shiloh, Beauregard abandoned Western Tennessee and then took a leave of absence because of poor health. Neither went down well with Jefferson Davis, especially when Beauregard took his leave without giving notice or asking permission. Beauregard was relieved and Bragg was given command of the army, which was subsequently renamed the Army of Tennessee.

Bragg's assessment of the failure at Shiloh was that victory had been lost because of a lack of organization and a lack of discipline. The steps he took to address these shortcomings made him one of the most despised commanders in the Confederate army, and his inability to lead made the army one of the most underutilized elements of the Southern military.

The Confederate army had approached Shiloh with more men than any Southern commander had ever massed for battle previously or would again in the West until the battle of Chickamauga in September 1863. The Rebels probably had more to gain by winning at Shiloh than they would ever have again in the western theater, because victory would have presaged a dramatic reversal of fortunes in this arena.

Over time the myth of the "lost opportunity" arose, and Beauregard was blamed for calling off the attack before sunset on the first day. To blame Beauregard, however, is to overlook the role that Sidney Johnston refused to play here. Rather than command the army, Johnston waded into the fighting to play the role of gallant combat leader and redeem something of his reputation. To blame Beauregard is also to overlook the stubbornness of Bragg, who was obsessed with taking the Hornets' Nest and could easily have bypassed it and, before Lew Wallace's division or Nelson's arrived, shattered the remnant of Grant's army that had fallen back to Pittsburg Landing.

The Confederacy had suffered approximately five thousand casualties prior to the battle of Shiloh. Twice as many were lost during this two-day battle. In fact, the combined casualty figure for both armies, close to twenty-five thousand, more than doubled the combined losses of the major actions of the war to date: Manassas, Wilson's Creek, Fort Donelson, and Pea Ridge. The total casualties exceeded all those lost in previous American wars, from the Revolution to the Mexican War.

Despite these appalling casualties, not one inch of ground was gained by either side. The greatest change was in the mood of the two armies. Prior to the battle Grant's army was sure that victory was within its grasp. Johnston's soldiers were equally confident that all the reverses of the past months would end with this battle and the Yankee invaders would be expelled, if not exterminated. Shiloh shocked both armies. The Federals were less cocksure of themselves, and a depression swept over the Southern army.

After Shiloh, a resident of New Orleans commented, the South never smiled again. After Shiloh, the war in the West became a two-front conflict waged largely by the Army of Tennessee and a new army in Mississippi commanded by John C. Pemberton and Earl Van Dorn. Grant would fight both of them, defeat both of them, and move on to find fame in Virginia. Yet whenever he looked back, he was strangely reminded of the lessons of Shiloh.

The literature on the battle of Shiloh is filled with innumerable anecdotes, because so much happened to so many people during these two days of fighting.

20

MALVERN HILL

THE AMBIGUOUS ORDER

For almost three months, beginning in April 1862, George B. McClellan's Army of the Potomac had slowly and steadily marched up the Virginia Peninsula until it was on the outskirts of Richmond, the Confederate capital. Throughout that time, the Union commander had waged war on two fronts, one against the Southern army in retreat before him and the other against the Lincoln administration concerning the manner in which his campaign was to be conducted. Across the lines, the Confederate commander, Joseph E. Johnston, had fallen back until he had no place to go. When McClellan bogged down, his army divided into two wings and separated by the Chickahominy River, Johnston finally attacked. After eleven thousand casualties on both sides, one of the results of two days' fighting at Seven Pines was that the Southern commander was wounded and taken out of action. He was replaced by Robert E. Lee, who spent three weeks preparing to attack McClellan. The Union commander was content to allow Lee all the time he needed. A furious weeklong campaign began on June 25, 1862, pushing the Federals away from Richmond and south to the James River. This thunderclap campaign came to be known as the Seven Days' battles. The last battle—Malvern Hill—was perhaps the most dramatic.

McClellan's army was reeling. The general himself was reeling. Shortly after the battle at Gaines's Mill on June 27, he had decided to withdraw toward the James River, what he termed a "change of base." Supposedly he could renew the assault on Richmond from there; the York River line was more vulnerable than the James. After three days and two more battles, his army occupied Malvern Hill, a narrow plateau one mile north of the river. For the first time during the Seven Days, all elements of the Union army were together on the same field.

There was little doubt that the situation was somewhat desperate. Since the fighting had been renewed, the Confederates had been relentless. Now McClellan's army had its back to the river.

The Malvern Hill plateau was a strong defensive position, about one and a quarter miles wide, running north to south, and about three-quarters of a mile wide. The heights ranged from 100 to about 150 feet above the surrounding countryside. The only approach was from the north, because the west was marked by steep bluffs, the east side fell off to a wooded bank, and the south was little more than marshland. McClellan's chief topographical engineer, Andrew A. Humphreys, noted that it "was a splendid field of battle on the high plateau where the greater part of the troops, artillery, etc. were placed." The high ground was a stark contrast to the sweltering swamps in which the army had fought up to this point.

In command of the army at the time was Fitz John Porter; McClellan had taken to the water to direct a shelling upstream and then to look over Harrison's Landing, the site the navy was recommending as a supportable camp for the army. Porter explained that he placed the army at Malvern Hill "to prevent the enemy from turning our flank and getting in our rear" as well as to protect the artillery and supplies then moving toward Harrison's Landing to the southeast. McClellan's only command was to "hold . . . at any cost."

Porter first arrived at Malvern Hill on June 30 with several officers. Among them was Col. Henry J. Hunt, the commander of the artillery reserve. Hunt was a respected artillerist of the prewar army.

He had served in the war with Mexico and in 1860 had been one of three officers to revise the army's light artillery tactics. The reserve that he commanded amounted to roughly one-third of all the artillery in the Army of the Potomac. This equaled approximately twenty batteries, siege guns, and horse artillery.

After inspecting Malvern Hill, Porter pronounced it the "best adapted for field-artillery of any [site] with which we have so far been favored." Hunt's reserve moved into position later that morning. Thirty-six pieces were placed along the western bluff that faced a wide stretch of open lowland known as the Crew field. Several batteries were also installed at the southern end of Malvern Hill, near Porter's headquarters, a brick home known as the Malvern house.

At around 4 P.M. the first shots of the approaching battle were sounded by five Confederate guns belonging to Gen. Theophilus H. Holmes and placed in the woodline of the Crew field, about one thousand yards away from the Federals. As soon as the first shell landed, the hill was cleared of unnecessary wagons and personnel, "as if by magic," one soldier noted.

Holmes had heard that a Federal wagon train was withdrawing by way of Malvern Hill and had come to investigate. While his guns were unlimbered, he surveyed the surrounding ground and encountered

Union chief of artillery Col. Henry J. Hunt (left) and his counterpart,
Confederate Gen. William Nelson Pendleton (right)

Lee doing the same. What was true of the Federals would also be true of Confederates; the Army of Northern Virginia would be united on this field as well.

Lee decided that the brunt of the attack would fall on the commands of Thomas J. "Stonewall" Jackson, John Bankhead Magruder, and Benjamin Huger, which had not been in action the day before. James Longstreet's and A. P. Hill's divisions would form the reserve, because they had been in combat the previous day. Lee himself was not feeling well and called for Longstreet to ride with him should he need to assume command on the field.

Federal gunners, meanwhile, returned the fire of Holmes's guns with twenty-eight guns, eight of which were powerful and accurate 20-pounder Parrotts. Their shelling was joined from two and a half miles away by the 100-pounder Parrott and 9-inch Dahlgren naval guns of the Union vessels *Galena* and *Aroostock*. After a half-hour's action the Southerners withdrew; Holmes lost seventeen men and fifteen horses.

The surrounding ground was not favorable to the Confederate gunners. One battery's animals stampeded, entangling their limbers in the heavy woods around the open fields. Two guns and six caissons were retrieved later by the Federals that night.

From atop the plateau, Union forces had two clear fields of fire: the Crew field to the west and the Poindexter field to the northeast. These combined in an arc of open land four hundred yards wide. Twenty-five guns were emplaced on the left flank of the Union line, which resembled something like an inverted V. The guns included 10-pounder Parrotts, 3-inch ordnance rifles, and 12-pounder Napoleons. To the south the larger guns were set up, 20- and 30-pounder Parrotts and 4.5-inch Rodmans.

Perhaps the greatest weakness in the Federal line was the narrow northern end of the plateau, which was about twelve hundred yards wide. Only so many men and batteries could be installed here. There was a chance that it could be stormed, much as the Confederates had done at Gaines's Mill some three days earlier. If anything, the realization stirred determination in both the Union defenders and the Confederate attackers.

Confidence soared throughout the Southern ranks. For six days McClellan's army had retreated, abandoning equipment along the way. A final battle was in the offing. Lee's greatest problem, however, had been coordinating his army. Miscues, inadequate communication, and poor timing had prevented the annihilation of the Union army, and such would hinder Lee's efforts at Malvern Hill.

In this instance, the defeat ahead began when Magruder lost three hours in getting to the battlefield after local guides led his troops down the wrong road. Magruder was one of the most capable commanders on the Peninsula, but he fell victim to poor maps and unmarked country roads. Nevertheless, he required far more time than had been allotted for him to arrive on the field to execute his responsibility.

On the morning of July 1, as Jackson's division moved into position on the left side of the Confederate line, a survey of the Union line across from Confederate Gen. W. H. C. Whiting reported that he faced at least thirty guns superior in size to anything to which he had access. The only option Whiting had was to compensate for quality with quantity.

Longstreet scouted this portion of the field and found a low, open ridgeline that he believed could hold as many as sixty guns. Lee found a similar site on the right. Both were almost as high as the Malvern plateau. They decided to mass no fewer than thirty guns on each ridge to pour a converging fire on the Federal position. The necessary batteries were called up, but the orders issued from Lee's headquarters were drafted poorly and delegated the full weight of any upcoming assault to the discretion of a single brigade commander, Lewis Armistead, in the center of the Confederate line.

Much of the battle's outcome depended on the artillery branch of the Army of Northern Virginia, and specifically on its artillery reserve head, William Nelson Pendleton. Throughout the Seven Days, however, the artillery had failed to distinguish itself. Malvern Hill was not to be its redeeming moment.

Although the army's organization was similar to that of the Federal army, Pendleton failed to deploy his reserve with anything like the skill of his counterpart, Henry J. Hunt. Pendleton searched out no positions for his guns and chose to await orders from Lee. As a result, more than eighteen batteries in the artillery reserve saw no action.

One of Pendleton's commanders, Lt. Col. Allen S. Cutts of Georgia, noted, "Although I am sure that more artillery could have been used with advantage in this engagement, and also that my command could have done good service, . . . I received no orders." Thus while the Confederates had far fewer guns than the Federal army, they failed to use all that they had.

Perhaps the most outspoken critic of Pendleton was Edward Porter Alexander, who in later years would establish his own reputation as an effective head of artillery. Alexander claimed that Pendleton was "too old and had been too long out of army life to be thoroughly up to all the opportunities of his position." Moreover he accused Lee's chief of artillery of making himself inaccessible so that no orders could reach him.

Jackson himself arrived on the left side of the Southern line while Whiting's first guns were being positioned. Stonewall called for these first three batteries to be set up instead in the Poindexter field, but Whiting protested, "I understood we were not to enter the field until fifty guns arrived." He also pointed out, "These few guns will not be able to live in the field five minutes." Jackson would not be dissuaded and had the sixteen guns brought onto the field, to a site within a thousand yards of the Union position. He even helped with their placement.

Union gunners opened almost immediately and forced the Confederate cannoneers out of the field after fifteen minutes or so. The other Southern battery had not yet been set up on the Confederate right, which meant that no converging fire was possible. By the end of the day, however, these sixteen guns in the Poindexter field would represent the largest concentration of Southern artillery of the battle, and it did do some damage within the Union position that caused the Federals to pull back.

The Confederate battery being set up on the right side, in the Crew field, performed far less admirably. Only five batteries were even brought up, but each went into action separately and each was pounded by the Union gunners into withdrawal. Some guns were destroyed before they could be unlimbered, and some guns were discharged prematurely by incoming shell fragments. Eventually one of the batteries took to rolling its guns behind a sheltering hill to load then pushing them back into position for firing.

At 10 A.M. the Union guns opened on a line of skirmishers forming across the Crew field to the north. To preserve ammunition, they were ordered to fire slowly and deliberately every few minutes.

Yankee artillery dominated the battle of Malvern Hill, but the gunners did not bear the fight entirely by themselves. Union infantry supported the guns when the Southerners charged into the line, but the attack was launched by mistake and lacked coordination.

Around 11 A.M. two Confederate guns were brought into the Crew field and began an uneven two-hour duel across eleven hundred yards. Four batteries were brought up to support the guns. From Malvern Hill, the Federals threw an assortment of solid shot, case, and shell.

The first serious attempt to break the Union line at the Crew field began around noon. It failed to get far after Federal gunners opened across the front of the Confederate line and also managed an enfilading fire. No Union infantry as yet had entered the combat. Porter explained, "Our desire was to hold the enemy where our artillery would be most destructive, and to reserve our infantry ammunition for close quarters to repel the more determined assaults."

Confederate matters were even more chaotic in the Poindexter field. Rumors of withdrawal led many gunners to leave the area almost as soon as they arrived. No more than six guns were even working at the same time. Meanwhile, across the way, Union gunners worked somewhere between twenty and thirty guns at a time.

An officer in the Fifth New Jersey observed that the Southern artillerists "did not even get their guns unlimbered before our guns drove them like the flock of frightened sheep into the woods."

For a while Confederate gunners were able to bring a converging fire from the Crew and Poindexter fields to bear on the center of the Union line. They managed to work the guns for almost three hours, but the majority of the heavy metal overshot the Federal position. Nevertheless, in one soldier's estimate, the Southern shells "plowed up and tore the earth and trees in all directions."

Greater danger to the Union position came, not from the Confederate guns, but from the 30-pounder Parrotts near Porter's headquarters and from the naval guns of the vessels *Mahaska* and *Galena.* Lacking a clear line of sight to the battlefield, the ships' gunners were dependent on signalmen at the Malvern house. After one of these shots exploded a Federal ammunition chest, Porter dispatched an urgent message to the Union vessels to cease fire. In his report, he asserted, "Not one of their projectiles passed beyond my headquarters." Another officer noted that the ships' guns "threw a few

The guns on Malvern Hill were supported by two Union gunboats on the James River, more than two miles from the scene. Their fire, however, did more damage than good to the Federal effort, and Gen. Fitz John Porter, who was managing the battle, had to call them off.

shell[s] here and there . . . with . . . no beneficial results" and that the men in the ranks "feared them as much as the enemy."

At 3 P.M. Armistead's men mounted a charge against the center of the Union line after they fended off Union skirmishers who had advanced to pick off the Confederate gun crews. They came within 150 yards of the Federal line but were driven back to seek shelter in the ravines around the Crew farmhouse rather than return under fire from both sides.

Magruder's men finally arrived on the field shortly after this episode. Around 4 P.M. they filed into position, extending the right side of the Confederate line. A muddle of orders and confusion over Lee's initial battle orders led him to mount an immediate attack.

In Longstreet's account of the battle, he claimed that this attack had been scheduled for this time, but the Confederate command had since determined that no attack would dislodge the Yankees from Malvern Hill. Lee, however, did not expressly order cancellation of the assault, so Armistead had attempted it alone and Magruder had compounded the error by viewing Armistead's action as the signal to attack.

In his postwar memoirs, Edward Porter Alexander claimed that movements behind the Union line were interpreted by some field commanders as a Federal withdrawal, and this information was paired with other reports that Union skirmishers had been repelled by Armistead's men in the Crew field. All of this, he believed, led Lee to order the advance, hoping to follow up on this perceived success.

Southern gunners opened a spotty barrage around 4:30, but there was little effect. Confederate Gen. D. H. Hill called the firing "farcical."

Magruder commandeered two brigades and launched his attack at 5:30 P.M. with roughly five thousand men, none of whom were from his own command. The field in front of them had been harvested and the wheat gathered into shocks—behind each of which was a Federal sharpshooter from Hiram Berdan's elite regiment. They were not enough to break the onslaught and had to fall back to their lines. In the view of many Union commanders, the Confederates were uncomfortably close, so infantry was sent forward to support the guns and the gunners began firing canister.

Across the field, the ruckus stirred D. H. Hill to join the assault, following Lee's original orders that called for a general attack when the Rebel Yell rose over the sounds of battle. Hill's eighty-two hundred men swarmed into the woods on the Union right and into the open field before realizing they were mostly alone. A North Carolina soldier described the scene in a letter home: "The enemy mowed us down by fifties."

Hill's men fell back and charged again, fell back and charged again. Five times. An officer from Massachusetts wrote, "We murdered them by the hundreds but they again formed & came up to be slaughtered." Union reinforcements were called up in the face of the relentless charges, which forced the Federal troops to exhaust their ammunition.

Hill called for reinforcements but found few. He lost more than seventeen hundred men and gained nothing.

Magruder too called for reinforcements, and his message found Lee with Lafayette McLaws's division. The Confederate commander dispatched McLaws to attack, directed Magruder to shift his attack farther to the right, and sent another brigade to support. Magruder also called up his own three divisions, but rather than mass them, he sent them in piecemeal as they came up. Their fate was the same as Hill's men. Walking wounded, stragglers, and shirkers, however, impeded the progress of other reinforcements being rushed to the front.

McLaws's brigades led a last desperate charge in concert with the ragged remnants of the other units who had been decimated on the field. The Southerners came closest to breaching the line at the center, forcing some Federal gunners to limber their guns and pull back.

A Union account of the incident notes that the advancing Federal infantry preserved the Northern gun positions. The assault could not have been repulsed by the batteries alone, but the guns did some of the deadliest work. One Union gunner said that the sight of his gun's effectiveness made him heartsick.

During a lull in the fighting, Hunt replaced some batteries and shifted others. Lee pondered an assault against the eastern flank of the Federals, but he knew that any such attack would have to be the next day. It would fall on the shoulders of Longstreet and Hill, his reserve, and they would need time to get into position.

On Malvern Hill, howitzers were brought to the fore at dusk. Most of these were worked by German-immigrant soldiers, which created no small confusion in the issuance of commands. These gunners fired into the night, strobing the darkened sky with dull red

Union sharpshooters were placed in the fields in front of the guns. Many found cover in the partially harvested wheat field behind shocks still in place.

BATTLES AND LEADERS

pulses that lent an eerie hue to the powder smoke wreathing the crest of Malvern Hill. The German gunners continued to work their guns even after Hunt issued orders to cease fire. Finally someone was able to translate, and the firing slowed and stopped around 10 P.M.

One effect of the night shelling was that the Confederate lines were in a state of near havoc. The booming of the shells drowned out all other noise. A Southern chaplain observed, "One could easily imagine, while witnessing this bursting storm of human passion, that he was within one step of the council chamber of his Satanic Majesty."

Porter sent word to McClellan around 9 P.M. announcing, "We have driven the enemy beyond the battle field." He also claimed that if Hunt's ammunition chests could be resupplied, "We will hold our own and advance if you wish."

McClellan, however, had already determined to get the army to Harrison's Landing and had issued orders to that effect. Porter executed the withdrawal from Malvern Hill before dawn on July 2.

The casualties for the day were over fifty-six hundred for Lee's army, and just over three thousand for McClellan's. As a percentage of total damage to the enemy, Federal artillery played a bigger role in inflicting casualties here than in any other battle of the Civil War. D. H. Hill summed up the day: "It was not war—it was murder."

Lee had not planned for the battle to be fought in the manner it was. During the night, he went looking for Magruder and asked, "Why did you attack?"

Magruder replied, "In obedience to your orders, twice repeated."

There was no rejoinder. The orders had been issued, but Lee's chief of staff, Robert H. Chilton, had composed the first badly and failed to mark the order with the time at which it was issued.

When Magruder arrived in the late afternoon and received his copy of the order, he acted accordingly, not realizing that the situation had changed dramatically from what it had been three hours earlier when the order was first written. Plus he received verbal orders from Lee in response to the observations regarding the alleged Federal withdrawal and Armistead's advance. Missing from Magruder's aide's recitation of the commanding general's instructions were the qualifying discretions Lee tended to give his commanders. Further complicating the moment was the criticism Magruder had received two days earlier for his lack of aggressiveness at Savage's Station.

He attacked and the rest of the Confederate army could only follow. Lee attempted to make the best of it, but there was nothing to salvage. Nevertheless, victory hung in the air, and better management of his commanders could have allowed Lee to grasp it.

When the fighting died down as darkness fell on the battlefield, Porter was planning to push the opportunity gained by his gunners. McClellan, however, had already issued orders for a withdrawal, which was carried out that night during a thunderstorm.

The Army of Northern Virginia was more than a day behind McClellan's in moving toward Harrison's Landing. When the Confederate commander scouted the new Federal encampment on July 4, he saw a position much like Malvern Hill and elected not to attack. Instead he maintained a watch of McClellan's camp and pulled his army back. To Jefferson Davis, he explained, "As far as I can see there is no way to attack him to advantage." McClellan was content to do nothing further.

Much is made of the Union artillery at Malvern Hill, and conventional wisdom claims that these heavy weapons won the battle for Porter. There is much to buttress this interpretation of the battle. Henry J. Hunt and Charles Griffin managed the placement and performance of the guns throughout the day. Hunt's own assessment, "Not a gun remained unemployed and not one could have been safely spared," encapsulated the action for most who have studied the battle.

At the same time, as well as the Federal gunners performed, much has been made of how poorly their Confederate counterparts functioned. The Southerners were inexperienced and uncoordinated, whereas the Northerners built their artillery branch around a core of well-trained professionals, some of whom had been under fire in Mexico as shave-tail lieutenants fresh from West Point. At Malvern Hill, a majority of Union sergeants and corporals in charge of individual guns averaged five years of military service.

Of the fifteen Confederate battery commanders, only one was trained at West Point, two had been cadets at VMI and the Citadel, and the rest were citizen soldiers with only a few months' experience. Many Southern artillery commanders were hardly versed in the complicated procedure of loading a cannon. Their gunnery skills were raw, and they tended to overshoot their targets.

The Army of the Potomac also possessed a quantity of fine guns. More than half had rifled bores, giving them longer ranges and making them more accurate than smoothbores, of which the Confederates had plenty. Standardized ammunition also kept the Yankee guns working, whereas the Southerners had several calibers of which they had to keep track.

Hunt's and Pendleton's qualifications have been alluded to earlier. Essentially, everything that Hunt did well, Pendleton failed to do. In the end, Lee lost fifteen batteries and at least one hundred gunners.

Without a doubt this was the finest performance of the Federal artillery branch, but the gunners could not have won the battle alone. The action of the Union infantry in rushing to the fore at the height of Magruder's attack did much to preserve both the Union guns and the ultimate victory. They bore the brunt of the battle in concert with the big guns, but neither would have been successful with the other.

Although Malvern Hill was ultimately a defeat for Lee, against the backdrop of the Peninsula campaign, it marked the end of a brilliant campaign. Within the span of a week, he had reversed Confederate fortunes in Virginia from imminent disaster to unlikely victory. The Yankee army was bottled up and would go nowhere for the time being, except to be evacuated. Richmond had been delivered from the hand of the conqueror—for the moment. And Lee weighed his next step in expelling the Northern invader from his state.

McClellan found little glory in the victory at Malvern Hill. While he was on the field in the midafternoon, he left the battle to Porter, and his absence was noted by his men. The Sixty-first New York's Col. Francis Barlow observed, "I think the whole army feel that it was left to take care of itself and was saved only by its own brave fighting."

The Peninsula campaign ended on August 16, 1862, when the last elements of the Union army were evacuated from Harrison's Landing. McClellan was the last man to leave, and his final act was to walk to the farthest point of his encampment and to shake his fist toward Richmond.

21

THE CRATER

A TRAGEDY OF ERRORS

OR MORE THAN TWO years the Army of Northern Virginia and the Army of the Potomac battled one another off and on in Virginia, Maryland, and Pennsylvania. In the spring of 1864, however, the two armies were locked in almost constant combat, suffering massive casualties, until they dug in around Petersburg, Virginia. There approximately two hundred thousand men entrenched and bided their time, plotting and taking potshots at each other. One of the schemes played out sadly for both sides.

It all began with Lt. Col. Henry Pleasants of the Forty-eighth Pennsylvania Infantry. Prior to the war he had been a civil and mining engineer, and when the war came, Pleasants allegedly enlisted with the hope that his own tragic life would be ended quickly. Instead he had survived the fighting to this point and now found himself dug in at the position closest to the Confederate line around Petersburg.

Situated half a mile southeast of the city, the trenches of the Forty-eighth Pennsylvania were only 130 yards from a four-gun Confederate redoubt known as Elliott's Salient, dubbed such because Brig. Gen. Stephen Elliott's South Carolinians were entrenched here.

At some point during the month of June, Pleasants either envisioned the opportunity on his own or overheard some of his men, mostly coal miners from Schuylkill County, discussing an idea for digging a tunnel under the Confederate works and blowing the line open with gunpowder. To a court of inquiry convened afterward, Pleasants claimed, "I noticed a little cup of a ravine near to the enemy's works. . . . [And] it occurred to me that a mine could be excavated."

He suggested as much to his division commander, Robert B. Potter, who passed the proposal on to the corps commander, Ambrose E. Burnside. The idea appealed to Burnside, who had an interest in technical solutions to problems, but he found that neither the army commander, George Gordon Meade, or the general in chief, Ulysses S. Grant, was particularly enthusiastic toward the scheme. In the meantime, Pleasants discussed the notion with some of the miners in his ranks and was gratified by their exuberant response. So anxious were the men to do anything to break the boredom of the siege, they began work on the tunnel on June 25 before the idea was approved.

Burnside sanctioned the work shortly after it began, but Meade did not address the matter officially. The latter approval would have given Pleasants access to the tools and supplies necessary to the task; without it, the miners were left to their own devices.

Secrecy was vital to the mine's success. So the dirt and clay excavated during the digging were hauled surreptitiously to a nearby creek or added to the Federal earthworks. Yet Confederate suspicions were aroused when Edward Porter Alexander, head of the Southern artillery, inspected the area and expected to see Union soldiers engaged in the classic siege manner of advancing their trenches. When he saw nothing of the kind opposite Elliott's Salient, he surmised that something else was afoot. As that something began to dawn on him, he rushed to Robert E. Lee's headquarters, carelessly exposing himself to fire and taking a wound in his hand. "They were coming," he reported, "but it was not above ground . . . they were coming underground. They were mining us!"

Pleasants's miners improvised wheel barrows from cracker boxes. For shoring timbers, they scrounged wood from a nearby destroyed bridge and an abandoned sawmill behind the Confederate lines. When army-issue picks proved unwieldy, Pleasants found a smithy to correct them. Stale air became a problem as the tunnel lengthened, so Pleasants devised an ingenious ventilation system. Certain measuring devices, although at hand with the army, were not made available, so Burnside requisitioned older models from Washington, which required more time.

In addition to these logistical matters, the work itself encountered the usual pitfalls of mining. At first the soil was sandy and easily moved, but then a stratum of puttylike marl was encountered. Pleasants rectified the matter by redirecting the course of the tunnel by a few degrees. Entrepreneurs among the miners took some of the marl and, according to a staff officer, "put the impression of the Ninth Corps badge on small pieces, cut it out in shape of the badge and dried it in the sun, selling them for 25 cents."

Confederate countermining efforts were halfhearted at best. Very few believed that the Federals could dig a horizontal shaft any farther than four hundred feet. Still, as the tunnel approached the Southerners' line, Pleasants occasionally stopped the work to nervously listen for countermining.

Lt. Col. Henry Pleasants (left) and Maj. Gen. Ambrose E. Burnside (right)

LOSSING'S PICTORIAL FIELD BOOK OF THE CIVIL WAR

LIBRARY OF CONGRESS

On July 17 the tunnel was estimated to be 510.8 feet long and slightly past the redoubt. From that point the miners dug left and right lateral galleries, approximately forty feet long, creating four chambers in each wing. These paralleled the main trench line and were slightly to the rear. On July 23, after moving approximately eighteen thousand cubic feet of dirt and rock, the work was completed.

Pleasants estimated that he needed six tons of gunpowder to finish the task. After waiting for four days, he received four tons. Beginning at 4 P.M. and working until 11 P.M., the men of the Forty-eighth Pennsylvania hauled 320 kegs into the tunnel in pitch darkness—lanterns or torches posed too great a danger of igniting the explosive prematurely.

Instead of shipping a premium-quality fuse line, the quarter-master supplied short pieces of common fuse. The miners had to splice these together. Their final act was to backfill the area around the gunpowder chambers so that the explosive force would not dissipate itself through the tunnel, but rather focus the power of the explosion against the Confederate position above.

Afterward it would be seen that the work of the Pennsylvanians was the easy part of the operation. Events had not gone as well in determining how best to exploit the anticipated breach created by the explosion.

According to Burnside's original plans, Gen. Edward Ferrero's division would lead the attack through the gap into the Confederate line. After penetrating the ruins of the Southern defenses, they were to

Once the mine had been completed, it was stocked with four tons of explosives. The men had to work in total darkness for fear that a spark might ignite the whole thing prematurely.

spread out, left and right, and sweep the adjoining lines of any resistance. Burnside based his choice of personnel on the fact that this division was the most rested in his corps; the three other divisions had been in the trenches and under fire for thirty-six days, averaging thirty casualties a day. Ferrero's men had been in the rear and able to drill and prepare for the attack. They were also African-American units, the only black troops in the Army of the Potomac.

While the work on the arming of the tunnel was being completed, Burnside was blindsided by Meade, who rejected his plan of attack. Meade viewed Ferrero's men not as fresh but as inexperienced. The task of charging entrenchments, he believed, required combat-hardened troops. At the same time, he thought the involvement of black troops to be somewhat reckless and argued that, if the plan failed, critics might claim "that we were shoving these people ahead to get killed because we did not care anything about them."

Burnside of course rejected Meade's reasoning and the matter was appealed to Grant. When nothing was heard from Grant's headquarters after a day, Burnside interpreted the silence as assent and resumed his original battle plan. The next day he was flabbergasted to receive word that Grant not only supported Meade's reasoning that Ferrero's men not be used, but he also scotched the move to clear the Confederate trenches and directed the attack be focused on the crest of Cemetery Hill, less than a mile behind the Southerners' line. At that time, nothing stood between the hill and Petersburg.

Almost at the last minute, Burnside convened his three other divisional commanders—James Ledlie, Robert Potter, and Orlando Willcox—and asked for a volunteer to spearhead the attack. When no one responded, he had them draw straws. Ledlie drew the short one. Of the three men, he was the least capable and seemingly had the reputation as the most incompetent divisional commander in Grant's army. None of that, however, prevented Burnside from giving him this responsibility.

More critical to the operation was the lack of instruction given to Ledlie. Burnside merely parroted Grant's and Meade's orders to occupy the hill. He instructed Potter and Willcox to follow Ledlie; the one would veer to the right, the other to the left. All other tactical matters, however, were silently left to the discretion of the commanders in the field.

Meade visited Burnside's headquarters on the eve of the attack, now slated for July 30. He addressed all the divisional commanders, stressing the importance of timing in the attack and the need for them to occupy Cemetery Hill as quickly as possible and before the Confederates could regroup. If they failed, they should return to their lines as fast as they could.

The attack would begin with the explosion of the mine at 3:30 A.M. on July 30. Grant ordered a feint on the north side of the James River to draw some of Lee's army away from the Petersburg encampment. As expected, more than twenty thousand men were shifted toward the mock battle, reducing the Petersburg defenses at least that much.

During the early morning hours of July 30 Ledlie's men awaited the signal to attack. In the forefront were several heavy artillery units, detached as infantry, but none of them had imagined they would see action in this fashion.

Complicating the situation was the absence of engineers to clear some of the Federal defensive works so that the infantry could attack across a wider front. Both Meade and Burnside should have been responsible for overseeing this, but neither acted.

Pleasants surveyed the mine one last time then went to his tent to read. He emerged at 3 A.M. with a small box of matches and made his way to the tunnel entrance. By his calculation, the ninety-eight feet of fuse would take fifteen minutes to ignite the powder. He lit it at 3:15.

There was no explosion at the anticipated time.

Fifteen minutes later Pleasants was, in the perception of one of his men, "like a maniac." At 4:10 he announced that he was going to enter the mine to investigate. Two other men—Lt. Jacob Douty and Sgt. Henry Reese—instead ran ahead of him and into the tunnel. They discovered that the fuse had gone out at one of the splices. They relit it and ran back out.

At 4:44 the earth heaved and the air exploded with the sound of a hundred cannon. The four-gun Confederate redoubt was all but obliterated.

A Michigan soldier noted, "A monstrous tongue of flame shot fully two hundred feet into the air, followed by a vast column of white smoke, resembling the discharge of an enormous cannon;

Shortly before dawn on June 30, 1864, the powder in the mine exploded in a geyser of earth and men and weapons. The Federals were almost as shaken as the surprised Confederates.

then a great spout or fountain of red earth rose to a great height, mingled with men and guns, timbers and planks, and every kind of debris, all ascending, spreading, whirling, scattering and falling with great concussion to the earth once more." Of the 300 South Carolina troops and 30 gunners in the redoubt and nearby trenches, 278 were casualties.

Immediately the Federal guns—110 cannon and 54 mortars—opened a barrage along the two miles of works in this section. The sound was deafening.

Although this expenditure of gunpowder was aimed specifically at the Southerners, the Confederates were not the only troops disoriented by the explosion and the shelling. Many of Ledlie's troops fled to the rear; most of those who remained in position were stunned. When the first elements moved forward, perhaps some ten minutes later, they had to improvise a way up and out of their trenches and advanced in small groups rather than organized ranks. After sprinting across one hundred yards of no man's land, they stopped at the edge of a twelve-foot wall of dirt, astonished at the sight before them.

Where once had stood a four-gun redoubt there was now a crater that varied from 150 to 200 feet in length. It was 60 feet wide and 30 feet deep. As the Federals maneuvered into the vast chasm, one of the first men to glimpse the wreckage observed, "The bottom and sides . . . were covered with a loose, light sand, furnishing scarcely a foothold, and for this reason, as well as that of the narrowness of the place, it was with great difficulty that the troops could pass through it."

Many men stopped once they descended into the crater. For them the moment had shifted from one of attack to one of rescue. They extracted some partially buried Southerners and gathered up those who had been dazed by the explosion and conducted them to the rear, focusing their efforts on taking prisoners. Few officers had been able to keep up with these men in the forefront. No one was there to urge the men forward, through the trenches, and on to Cemetery Hill. Those unit commanders who had entered the crater gave instead a variety of instructions, none agreeing another. Some soldiers took it

Confederate Gen. William Mahone (left) and Union Gen. George Gordon Meade (right)

upon themselves to dig in at the far side of the crater. Ledlie, the division commander, was nowhere near his men but had taken refuge far to the rear, possibly with medicinal spirits.

Beyond the crater the Northerners saw a startling expanse of trenches and bombproofs and moved into it. Some of the heavy artillery regiments found a working gun and began to put it to use against the Confederates. Other units began leapfrogging from trench to trench, advancing three hundred yards into the Southerners' line.

Confederate resistance gradually increased as the Southerners shook off the stupor that followed the explosion. Rebel batteries opened a converging fire on the ground between the crater and the Union trenches, shredding the oncoming troops with canister. Those Federals who managed to get to the crater and the trenches just beyond it quickly fell into hand-to-hand fighting.

At 6:10 A.M. word reached Lee's headquarters of the Union breakthrough. Short on men because of the feint above the James River, the Confederate commander sent word to Gen. William Mahone to pull two brigades out of the line and plug the breach.

North Carolina and Virginia regiments that had been positioned on either side of Elliott's Salient also shifted men to support the remnants of the South Carolina units originally emplaced there. "When we reached our position," a North Carolina soldier recalled, "we counted twelve United States flags in the works, and the whole field in front of the Crater was full of Yankees."

Heavy fire kept the bulk of the Federals in the crater, and the crowded conditions there blocked the Union advance more than anything else. Willcox's division found itself stalled in the trenches to the left of the depression; Potter's was caught up on the right.

Meade ordered Edward O. C. Ord's and Gouverneur K. Warren's corps into action, but they could not advance for the massed troops stalled in front and inside the crater. Ferrero's troops charged into the fray around 7:30. Their headway was blocked by a steady flow of returning wounded and panicked comrades as well as prisoners from the front. Ferrero, however, chose that his men should go to the front without him—he joined Ledlie in the rear. Meanwhile, those men who survived the shower of canister and shot moved up and out of the crater to form a ragged battle line.

Grant surveyed the fighting then went to Burnside's head-quarters. Aware that the situation was horribly out of control, he told his corps commander, "The entire opportunity has been lost. There is now no chance of success. These troops must be immediately withdrawn. It is slaughter to leave them here." Burnside wanted to argue.

Shortly after arriving at the front, Confederate General Mahone saw the confusion in the Federal ranks and called for an additional brigade from his own command. While he set up a line of battle facing the crater and awaited the arrival of these troops, he saw that several Federal officers were forming men for a charge of their own. Mahone struck at 9 A.M., before they were ready. A Virginia sharpshooter recalled, "I shall never forget the magnificent appearance of that long line of tattered uniforms as it swept in splendid form across the field in the face of a tremendous fire that with every step was thinning our ranks."

The Federals being formed to charge were assembled from Ferrero's division, perhaps as many as two hundred black soldiers. They did not shrink back from the more numerous Confederates but plowed into them. No reinforcements came up from the crater.

After a short while the African-American soldiers had to fall back. Many of the Southerners lost all control when they found that their opponents were black troops. Few were taken prisoner that were not beaten in the field, and most were killed outright. Those who escaped the onslaught of the white men's fury fled panic-stricken to the rear, touching off a stampede among other Federal troops.

Mahone managed a second assault on the Union soldiers seeking shelter in the crater, but it was less successful than the first. At 10 A.M. he met with the general in command of this sector, Bushrod Johnson, and the two agreed to launch simultaneous attacks at 1 P.M.

Confederate mortars were brought up and fired into the crater. The battery commander, Col. John Cheves Haskell, recalled, "We got closer and closer to the enemy until we were throwing shells with such light charges of powder that they would rise so slowly as to look as if they could not get to the enemy, who were so close that we could hear them cry out when the shells would fall among them, and repeatedly they would dash out and beg to surrender." The effect of the mortars was awful; hardly a Federal uniform was not covered with the blood and fragments of other men.

July heat also exacted a toll from the Union soldiers in the crater. Many had had nothing to eat since the night before and their canteens had long since been drained.

At 1 P.M. the Confederates attacked again. They charged through a barrage and into the Federals in and around the crater. Much of the combat was hand-to-hand, with the most effective weapons being bayonets and rifle butts. The bottom of the crater piled up with Union corpses. There was so little space unfilled within the chasm that one officer recalled, "Whites and blacks were squeezed so tightly together that there was hardly standing room. Even many of those killed were held in a standing position until jostled to the ground."

Word finally arrived from Burnside's headquarters that his soldiers should fall back as best they could, and many ran back to the Union lines but large numbers of prisoners were also taken. The fighting played out until midafternoon. Afterward the Southerners formed a new line—in front of the crater.

A truce was declared at 5 A.M. on August 1 to allow both sides to retrieve their wounded and dead. A Pennsylvania soldier reported that "the Confederates brought a brass band and posted it on their front line of works. We had a band on our line. So for two hours the bands played alternately, the Federals playing National airs and the Confederate Southern airs."

Mahone's two brigades had held off three Union corps: Burnside's was caught in the crater, Ord's had been forced back, and Warren's had

Had the African-American soldiers who had been drilled to exploit the opportunity created by the explosion actually been used in the assault, the outcome of the affair of the Crater might have been vastly different. At the last moment, Meade assigned other troops to the task, largely because he feared potential criticism if the plan failed.

After the fall of Petersburg, photographers roamed the siege lines outside the city. One of them created this image of the crater left by the explosion of June 1864.

never been able to enter the fighting. Throughout the day Lee was not far from the fighting, ready to step in and lead his men if necessary. The Confederate commander's presence did much to raise the fighting spirit of his men. In his dispatch to Jefferson Davis, he pronounced every one of them a hero.

In his report to Washington, Grant summarized the battle as "the saddest affair I have witnessed in the war. Such opportunity for carrying fortifications I have never seen and do not expect again to have." Federal losses were estimated at thirty-seven hundred, Confederate casualties at fifteen hundred. A court of inquiry was convened.

Burnside was relieved of command and given a leave of absence; he was never recalled to service. Ledlie took a leave of absence and was instructed upon his return to duty to go home and await further orders; they never came. Ferrero, although censured for his actions, retained his command and received a brevet promotion to major general in December for "meritorious service." Willcox was censured for not leading his men with "[more] energy" and held on to his command for the remainder of the war.

At some point during the battle, Henry Pleasants advanced as far as the crater's rim. The sight of shattered men and weapons sickened him. He felt a profound guilt for having facilitated such death and destruction. Afterward, according to his cousin and biographer, Henry Pleasants Jr., the matter left him "cold, sick at heart, disillusioned, and resentful." For his role in the battle of the Crater, Pleasants was given a brevet promotion to brigadier general during the last weeks of the war.

22

FRANKLIN

HOW A GENERAL DESTROYED HIS OWN ARMY

During the autumn of 1864 there was probably no one in the South more desperately ambitious or more desperately optimistic than Maj. Gen. John Bell Hood. At the same time he was also one of the most tragic figures in the Confederacy. Hood was not a strategist, and the price for his mistakes were not paid by him but by the army he sent into battle in the twilight hours of November 30, 1864.

Hood had made his reputation with the Army of Northern Virginia, distinguishing himself during a rise from regimental to divisional command. He had been crippled at Gettysburg, where he lost the use of his left arm, and had been further disabled at Chickamauga, where he lost his right leg. As a result, he could ride only if he was tied to his saddle, and he assuaged his pain with laudanum, which affected his judgment. In the South such injuries were viewed with much respect and sympathy, and the ambitious general exploited his reputation and appearance to gain command of one of the great armies of the Confederacy—the Army of Tennessee. At the age of thirty-three he was the youngest general to exercise such command, but it was a task to which he was not well suited.

After almost four months of constant campaigning in Georgia, Hood had abandoned Atlanta to William T. Sherman's army in early September and bivouacked his exhausted army at Palmetto Station, about twenty-five miles southwest of the city. There on September 25 Jefferson Davis reviewed the forty thousand troops and conferred with his general, whom he counseled to temper his impetuousness with prudence—in the four weeks he directed the Georgia defense, Hood had lost almost a quarter of his army. Strategically, Davis urged Hood to harass Sherman's supply line and draw the Federals out of Georgia, suggesting that he even venture into Tennessee.

This was Davis's third visit in as many years to the Army of Tennessee, and both of the earlier visits had led to battlefield failures. Consistent with his previous appearances, he responded to criticisms of the army commander by reassigning the critics. In this instance, Lt. Gen. William J. Hardee, a corps commander, was reassigned. He was replaced by Benjamin F. Cheatham, a good fighter but not a profound commander; he had never conducted a battle before.

At the same time Davis limited Hood's discretion somewhat by appointing a departmental commander to oversee and coordinate the armies in the western theater. He chose P. G. T. Beauregard, mostly because the only other available candidate was Joseph E. Johnston and Davis had less disdain for Beauregard. Although the position sounded powerful, in practice Beauregard had almost no authority, no power. By the time he assumed the post, Hood was already moving to execute the strategy prescribed by the president.

Davis returned to Richmond but made several speeches along the way that promised to reverse the setbacks in Georgia and outlined just how Hood would do it. His words were of course reproduced in Southern newspapers and reprinted in the North; Ulysses S. Grant and Sherman both commented on the matter. "To be forewarned is to be forearmed," the latter noted.

Hood's maneuvers at first perplexed Sherman. In attacking the Federal supply line between Chattanooga and Atlanta, he would thrust one way, pull back, and thrust another. His attacks were little more than raids. After a while Sherman saw that there was no design, no strategy to what the Confederate commander was doing.

Indeed there was none. Hood was a fighter through and through. He knew only that his duty was to attack; he lacked the ability to imagine any goal other than to hurt the enemy in the most direct manner he could. Against Sherman he hoped to draw him onto a battlefield of his choosing then implement the flanking tactics he had seen successfully demonstrated earlier in the war by Robert E. Lee and Stonewall Jackson. Hood, however, was no Lee. Yet on the basis of his conference with Davis, he had determined to march through Tennessee, seize Kentucky, then march to join Lee at Petersburg and defeat Grant. It was a grand scheme, but he had neither the men nor the materials necessary to execute it.

Sherman had his own plans. He wanted to march to the sea then link up with Grant and defeat Lee's army at Petersburg. To contend with Hood in the meantime, he would send George H. Thomas to Tennessee with almost twenty-seven thousand men—John M. Schofield's and David S. Stanley's infantry corps and James H. Wilson's cavalry. Additional troops would be allocated to the Volunteer State to increase Thomas's command to a formidable force. Thomas went to Nashville immediately to coordinate the effort, and Schofield and Stanley moved to Pulaski, seventy-five miles south of Nashville, to block the route of Hood's anticipated approach from Alabama.

The Army of Tennessee began the march into its namesake state along three separate routes on the morning of November 21 with slightly more than thirty thousand men—three corps led by Stephen D. Lee, Alexander P. Stewart, and Cheatham. Providing cavalry support were ten thousand horsemen under Nathan Bedford Forrest.

Hood promised his men that they would face little risk of defeat. He vowed that they would not fight in Tennessee unless the situation were to their advantage: He would not engage a numerically superior foe, and he would fight on ground of his choosing.

Scouts reported Hood's movements to Thomas in Nashville, and he ordered Schofield and Stanley to buy time until reinforcements arrived in Nashville by falling back to Columbia, forty-five miles south of the state capital. The progress of both Confederate and Union armies was hampered by cold, wet weather and intermittent snow.

Thus began a race toward Nashville. On November 23 Schofield, as commander of the joint Union force, feared that Hood was closer to Columbia than he was. Despite his worries, his men reached Columbia on November 24 and entrenched before the Confederates appeared, but Schofield then feared that Hood would flank him. As the Southerners deployed around Columbia on November 27, Schofield pulled back and across the Duck River and destroyed the bridges.

Hood was greatly encouraged to see Schofield retreating. The two men had been classmates at West Point; Schofield had been a scholar and Hood had barely graduated. He envisioned besting his colleague by leaving his wagons, most of his artillery, and the bulk of Lee's corps behind so that he could move the other two corps around Schofield and ambush him at Spring Hill, roughly eight miles above Columbia.

Schofield's army entrenched above the Duck River in anticipation of attack. This would be a fighting withdrawal, so the army's supply train and most of the artillery were sent north. During the morning of November 29, eight hundred wagons and forty guns were spread out for several miles between two divisions and progressed ponderously northward. This lackluster movement, being overseen by Stanley, Schofield's second in command, changed abruptly when firing was heard coming from Spring Hill.

Forrest's cavalry had reached Spring Hill in the late morning hours and clashed with about two hundred of Wilson's horse soldiers. The fighting was short and one-sided. Although Wilson was a talented Union cavalry commander, he had not shown his mettle thus far in supporting Schofield.

Federal brigades moved quickly to support the two-regiment garrison in the town. Their superior numbers and heavier firepower turned back the Confederate horsemen, who were also running low on ammunition. Nevertheless, Forrest managed to keep Stanley's men occupied, forcing them to throw up makeshift breastworks.

Hood approached Spring Hill at midafternoon, but he issued conflicting orders to Cheatham and two of his divisional commanders. Cheatham believed that Spring Hill itself was the objective; Patrick Cleburne and William B. Bate were ordered to block the nearby thoroughfare that Schofield's army would be using. Hood had been in the saddle since 3 A.M. He retired to one of the grand homes of the community and stayed there until the next morning, leaving Cheatham in charge. Given Hood's physical condition, he was likely in too much pain to know how exhausted he was. The laudanum would help.

Cleburne skirmished with a Union brigade southeast of the town but was turned back by heavy artillery. He halted when Cheatham ordered him to await the imminent arrival of the Stewart's corps. The latter, however, was not as close as Cheatham believed, having taken a wrong road. All Confederate efforts stalled as night fell. The Southerners encamped, trying to both dry out and warm up. In Hood's absence, neither Cheatham nor Stewart wanted to risk anything.

There are many questions about Hood's expectations. Virtually all accounts of the misstep at Spring Hill are somewhat jaded by the participants' desire to avoid culpability. No one seems to know if Hood had hoped to reach Nashville before Schofield or if he planned to pin Schofield somewhere between Spring Hill and Columbia and destroy his army. If anything, when Hood went to bed early that night in Spring Hill, he seemingly believed that Schofield's main force was still far to the south, and he most likely anticipated battle the next day. Because he failed to communicate his plans to his corps commanders, they blundered that night by leaving the Columbia pike wide open.

Schofield arrived in Spring Hill around 7 P.M. that night, ahead of his army. Normally methodical in his performance in the field, he was somewhat shaken by Hood's aggressiveness and by finding him there. The Union commander had begun to pull out from the Duck River trenches as soon as he had heard of the action at Spring Hill, but the

John Bell Hood (left) and John M. Schofield (right)

Federals did not entirely abandon the line. The units withdrew quietly, and a small rear guard remained to maintain appearances.

The marching Federals made slow progress in the darkness. Sometime after midnight they saw campfires and quickened their step until word came that these were Confederate campfires. Their approach was masked somewhat by a loud wind and the sounds of their comrades who had reached Spring Hill earlier that afternoon who were reinforcing the breastworks thrown up that day. Schofield's army marched silently past the Southerners, encamped roughly a quarter of mile off the roadway. Occasionally the Confederates fired in answer to some noise, but that had been going on all night. Others who heard them thought they were a late-arriving division, possibly Lee's, which had been in position at Columbia throughout the day. No one investigated.

One of the myths of the affair claims that Union soldiers walked up to the campfires to light their pipes. No such thing happened. Other allegations assert that many of the general officers neglected their duties to enjoy all that a quiet town had to offer.

Schofield and Stanley were thunderstruck at the seeming indifference the Southerners showed to the Union army's presence. Briefly pondering what to do, they agreed to move on, even daring to bring up the eight hundred wagons and ambulances and artillery. They were gone by daybreak.

When Hood learned that Schofield had escaped, he was livid and dressed down his commanders over breakfast. In his mind, Cheatham, Cleburne, and John C. Brown were at fault. Others have since scrutinized the embarrassment of the Army of Tennessee at Spring Hill and placed no small burden of blame on Hood. On the morning of November 30, 1864, however, Hood's assessment was the only one that mattered.

Cleburne was the brightest star in the constellation of the Army of Tennessee. He first distinguished himself at Shiloh, and thereafter the dispatches of his commanders conveyed little other than praise for his performance under fire. He might have been made a corps commander had he not espoused the idea of emancipating any slaves who would fight for the South. Although he had not been at breakfast with Hood, Cleburne was greatly offended that his commander chose to blame him for Schofield's escape, but he would pursue the matter after the conclusion of the present campaign.

Schofield halted his army at Franklin, twelve miles above Spring Hill. He had hoped to find pontoons awaiting him at the Harpeth River, but none had as yet arrived. So he put some men to work improvising bridges across the river on the bridgehead remains of three earlier spans. Other troops went about the business of reviving a line of entrenchments from an April 10, 1863, engagement and rejuvenating earthworks known as Fort Granger on the opposite bank of the river. When telegraphic communication was restored with Thomas in Nashville, Schofield indicated that he planned to get his army across the Harpeth shortly after dark. In the meantime, his men needed to gather themselves after their nightlong march.

The city of Franklin sits in a curve of the Harpeth River, and the line of works invested by Schofield's men was anchored to the river on both sides and formed an arc south of the city. The Union commander saw that the position could be outflanked if his opponent forded the river, so he made no plans to stay there. Still he positioned his men so he could withdraw without being completely vulnerable and installed artillery in Fort Granger to protect his left flank.

Bisecting the line south of the city was the Columbia pike. The defensive works were left open at the roadway, but a second line of breastworks was erected to buttress the first. Also marking the center of the line were several buildings of the Fountain Branch Carter family farm just inside the works; the main house was to the west of the pike and a large cotton gin building was to the east. The full line measured close to a mile and a half and sheltered roughly seventeen thousand troops.

Two brigades from the rear guard were then deployed on the heights to the front of the earthworks, one on Winstead Hill and the other on Breezy Hill. From there they saw Hood's army approach in two columns. At 2 P.M. the Federals on these two hills fell back to a smaller hill, known as Privet Hill and Merrill's Hill, roughly halfway toward the main line. There they prepared to skirmish and fall back.

Cheatham's and Stewart's corps had taken most of the day to march to Franklin; Lee's corps remained in Spring Hill but was to move up later. Again Hood moved in "light marching order," that is, without the encumbrances of all his wagons and artillery. Along the way the men's spirits were buoyed by the sight of discarded Federal equipment and abandoned wagons. Shortly after arriving near

Franklin and quickly surveying Schofield's position from Winstead Hill, Hood called a council of war. He ordered an immediate assault on the Federal line. Head-on.

It was an all-or-nothing gamble. Hood had seen Lee trust his fortune to fate on more than one occasion. The setting at Gaines's Mill in June 1862 possibly came to mind. There Hood himself had led a frontal assault across open ground against Federal entrenchments. The breakthrough he achieved opened the way for the string of successes known as the Seven Days' battles and marked Lee's ascendancy. Hood now perceived that he faced a similar scenario.

Stewart's corps, supported by Forrest, would advance along the Lewisburg pike, which paralleled the river, and strike the left side of the Union line. Most of Cheatham's corps would use the Columbia pike to hit the center of the Federal earthworks. The remainder of Cheatham's men would follow the Carter's Creek pike into the right side of the defenders. Cheatham, Cleburne, and Brown—the three commanders whom Hood blamed for the failure at Spring Hill—would be thrown into the area most likely to be the worst fighting, where the Union line was strongest and the ground entirely open.

Forrest was the first to object, arguing that his cavalry with a single infantry division could flank Schofield's army by crossing the river. Cleburne and Cheatham objected as well. Hood listened to none of them. Addressing Cleburne, the Confederate commander specifically ordered that his men "not fire a gun until you run the Yankee skirmish line from behind the first line of works." That was what he had done at Gaines's Mill. This army, Hood declared, had hidden so long behind the safety of breastworks during the fighting in Georgia that it had forgotten how to fight.

At 2:45 P.M. the lines of battle were formed and eighteen thousand infantrymen awaited the order to advance. The only Confederate artillery on the field were two six-gun batteries. As the men stood in the waning autumn afternoon, it was clear that the weight of the attack would be focused on the left side of the Union line—four infantry divisions and two cavalry divisions took position to the east of the Columbia pike. Against the Yankee right, Hood allotted two divisions of infantry and a single division of cavalry.

The advance began with parade-ground precision. Both Union brigades at Privet Hill fell back again, roughly halfway to the main line.

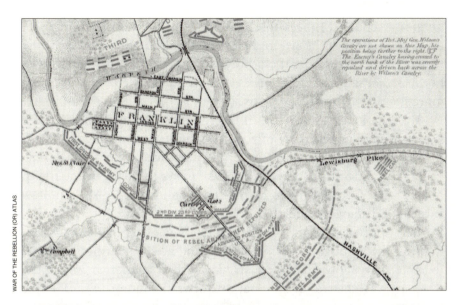

A map of the battlefield clearly shows the line of Union breastworks and highlights both the point at which the brunt of the attack occurred along the Columbia pike (the diagonal line aimed toward the center of Franklin) and the greater distance that the left side of the Confederate attack had to traverse in order to engage the enemy.

No one within the Federal line had seen a battle in the offing. Most imagined that, if anything, they were more likely to be harassed by Forrest's cavalry than assaulted by Hood's infantry. Confident of that, the majority of the Federal soldiers behind the earthworks took little notice of the Confederate movement but focused on their first hot meal in several days and pondered where to rest afterward. A sizable number were on the verge of fulfilling their term of enlistment, thus the prospect of fighting was far from their minds. To these men, Nashville was but the final step toward home.

Cleburne ventured to the vacated Privet Hill and borrowed a sniper's telescopic sight to look over the Federal position. "They have three lines of works," he said aloud. "And they are all completed." Following this surveillance, he altered his battle formation, advancing his men in column rather than in ranks abreast. Such positioning would expose as few men as possible to enemy fire; they would deploy when they were within small arms' range.

Almost an hour was needed to move into position across the open field. For the first time in combat the veterans of the Army of

Tennessee could see the whole field of action before them. The spectacle of gaunt men in tattered clothes, threadbare uniforms, some wearing captured Federal clothing, some lacking coats or shoes or both, presented an image of a ragged and dirty band of robbers more than an army preparing to attack.

Eyes looked to Winstead Hill, Hood's command post, for the signal to attack—the wave of a flag. As soon as it was given, a regimental band began playing "Dixie," another offered up "The Bonnie Blue Flag." The music was offset, an onlooker recalled, by the tramp of marching feet that rolled across the ground like the "low, hollow rumble of distant thunder."

The approaching gray wall jolted the Federals into action. A section of 3-inch ordnance rifles opened up on the advancing ranks. Confederate sharpshooters replied, striking several gunners manning the weapons with the two brigades at the forward Union position. These four thousand men were largely in the open and highly susceptible, but they had orders to hold their position. Coming straight toward them, however, were eight thousand Southerners from Cleburne's and Brown's divisions, advancing along the Columbia pike.

Confederate guns opened on the forward Union position, and the Federal battery commanders there limbered their field pieces and fled to the main Union line. When Cleburne's men were within four hundred yards, they shifted into two lines of battle and ran for-

Patrick Cleburne was the premiere divisional commander in the Army of Tennessee. He was a veteran of virtually every battle in which that army was engaged. Had he not publicly advocated the emancipation and conscription of slaves, Cleburne might have been a corps commander or even commander of the army itself. As it was, though, he fought at the head of his men at Franklin. His life was wasted as were the resources of the army on that field in the last hours of that November day.

ward with a shout of the bone-chilling Rebel Yell. The guns from Fort Granger opened on the Southerners as they charged, and the front-line Union brigades unleashed a volley when the Confederates were one hundred yards away. Momentarily staggered, Cleburne's men fell upon the Federals in hand-to-hand fighting. These Union troops had no choice but to fall back, fleeing for the safety of the breastworks. The Southerners now loosed a volley of their own then ran after the withdrawing Federals.

A wedge-shaped human mass rushed toward the Union line, Cleburne's and Brown's men mixing with the Federal infantry. At some point the shout was sounded for the Southerners to follow the fleeing Northerners into the works. The men behind the barricades held their fire, fearful of shooting down their own comrades. The situation was desperate. Finally, the units in the line fired as one, and gunners unleashed a storm of canister. The center position along the Columbia pike fell under a cloud of powder smoke, and for the moment the Confederates opened a two-hundred-yard gap in the Union line.

As soon as Schofield heard the firing and grasped that Hood was attacking along his front, he urged his quartermasters to get his wagons rolling toward Nashville—minus the ammunition wagons and ambulances. Stanley was with him, and the two men separated, with Schofield going to Fort Granger to coordinate the battle, which he anticipated would include an attack across the river, and Stanley riding to the entrenchments below the city. The battle was upon them and, at the same time, out of their hands.

Earlier that afternoon, Union Col. Emerson Opdycke's brigade had found refuge behind the Carter house. Now they charged without orders into the oncoming Confederates in a full-scale melee. To the Federals' advantage, Cleburne's and Brown's men had been scattered and tired during the lengthy run from the advance post to the main line. Opdycke's men persevered through sheer weight of numbers.

"I never see[n] men fight . . . more determined than the Rebs did," an Illinois sergeant later noted. "And I never see[n] enemy men fall so fast." The number of men crowded into the confined space around the Carter house created ranks four and five deep. Weapons were fired then passed to the rear for reloading and passed forward again.

Finally the Southerners fell back to the outside of the entrenchments. Both sides fired so rapidly that their ammunition was nearly exhausted. The dead and wounded were searched for cartridges while, among the Union ranks, others went after ammunition wagons. Those Confederate brigades trailing the first to fall on the Union line now caught up with their comrades at the breastworks.

So many Southerners were taken prisoner during this fighting that, as they were moved to the rear, Stanley feared his line had collapsed. Powder smoke so obscured visibility that one could see no farther than fifty yards. On horseback, however, Stanley presented a conspicuous target. His horse was shot down, and as he fell, Stanley was hit in the neck. He refused to seek medical treatment until he had organized the defenders around the Carter house and the cotton gin building.

Brown, Cleburne, and Stewart occupied the periphery of the works. As additional men advanced and crowded on top of the those who were still alive there, they would launch additional pushes. Of the eighteen Confederate brigades that fought at Franklin, seven fought there.

The Carter garden was hotly contested territory. One Federal officer counted as many as thirteen Confederate charges across this small patch. Part of the attraction was a set of six 12-pounder Napoleons. So many gunners were shot down while they worked the guns that, after a while, anyone in blue took on the tasks of those who were felled. Later reports claimed that these weapons unleashed 169 blasts of canister at nearly point-blank range.

This fight died down after a half-hour then resumed with a fury. Men on both sides resorted to holding their rifles up over the top of the breastworks and firing blindly. By 5 P.M. the Union line stabilized around the Carter property. On the eastern side of the pike, near the cotton gin building, the defensive line was formed in such a way as to give the Federals an angle from which to open an enfilading fire on the approaching Confederates.

In a ditch fifty yards west of the Columbia pike, Confederate Brig. Gen. Otho F. Strahl was shot while passing reloaded weapons to the firing line. He was hit twice again as he was being carried to the rear. The second of these wounds was fatal.

So many general officers and unit commanders were killed or wounded during this frontal assault that command fell to captains and lieutenants. More important, no unit commanders were able to send word of their situation to the rear, thus neither Hood nor Cheatham knew what was happening at the front. Neither man attempted to communicate with the other. Both could see the flashes of artillery and rifle fire, but they knew almost nothing of what it meant.

As darkness fell, the situation around the Carter farm had become a stalemate. The Southerners held the center of the main earthworks, and the Northerners occupied the line west of the Columbia pike.

The situation at the left side of the Union line was much different, even though only five thousand Federals faced more than fifteen thousand Confederates. Here the guns of Fort Granger proved highly effective against the flank of Stewart's corps. At this segment of the line the onrushing Southerners also had to contend with a barrier of osage orange, highly prickly underbrush, which the Union troops had improvised as abatis. Further staggering the attackers was the fact that many defenders exercised sixteen-shot Henry repeating rifles.

Confederate penetration was greatest near the Carter cotton gin, where the main elements of Cleburne's division overran a Union battery and seized loaded guns. They could not work them against the Federals, however, because the gunners had been thoughtful enough not to leave behind any friction primers. By the time some ingenious Southerners devised a way to fire the guns, they were forced back when Union reserves rushed up. Many of these arriving Federals brandished five-shot Colt revolving rifles.

During the fighting, Confederate Gen. Hiram Granbury was urging his Texas brigade into action when he was shot just below his right eye. He never knew what hit him.

Patrick Cleburne had already lost two horses in the fighting. At a point some eighty yards in front of the Federal line he was trying to swing the weight of his brigade toward the gin. At approximately forty yards from the main works, he was fighting more like a private than a divisional commander when he disappeared into a cloud of powder smoke. This most favored son of the army was struck by a single bullet just below and left of his heart.

The brigade of Brig. Gen. John Adams was entangled in the osage abatis as he tried to guide his men toward the gin. Adams was on horseback and seemingly living a charmed life. He turned his horse toward the works and tried to leap the parapet, but both horse and rider were struck. The animal crashed atop the earthwork, and Adams, hit by seven to nine bullets, fell into the inner ditch. He lived long enough to ask for a swallow of water, to thank a soldier for making a small pillow of raw cotton for him, and to ask to be returned to his lines. His last words were, "It is the fate of a soldier to die for his country."

Elements from the ten Confederate brigades arrayed here continued to focus their efforts on the cotton gin building. The recaptured Union guns were emptied repeatedly into their ranks. At one point the bodies in front of the two guns were piled so high they obstructed the muzzles. Still the Southerners broke through in hand-to-hand fighting.

Gunners switched to double and triple canister. A young Confederate, believed to be a drummer boy from Missouri, ran up to the guns and jammed a plank of wood into one of the gun barrels to prevent its use. The weapon was discharged, and the boy was no more.

Any Confederates who made it over the parapet were either shot, bayonetted, or captured. Lacking ammunition, many were forced to surrender. The fighting around the gin lasted roughly forty minutes.

On the Union right, west of the Carter house, the scene began far less chaotically. Bate's command advanced along the Carter's Creek pike, but because the line arced toward the river, these Southerners had at least a half-mile to three-quarters of a mile farther to cross than the other attacking columns. They were not in position until after the sun set, and then powder smoke from the other sectors of the fighting drifted here, obscuring what little visibility there was. When a small gust of wind cleared some of it away, the Federals found Bate's men forty yards in front of them and just as surprised as they were to encounter each other.

There were far more Union troops here than Bate expected, although some of the Federal units were comprised of men who had never seen combat. Many of these green troops fled when the fighting began. Those who remained encountered ammunition shortages, but when an ammunition wagon was brought up, their hesitancy changed to determination. Reinforcements also helped to reestablish the line.

The horse of Confederate Brig. Gen. States Rights Gist was shot out from under him. Gist sprinted toward a locust grove just to the west of the Carter house, but he was shot down after only a few steps. His men went on into the grove and into the Union line in hand-to-hand combat. They were supported by Gen. John C. Carter's brigade. Nevertheless, their losses were heavy.

Carter was shot as he rode recklessly before his men. He slumped in his saddle and was helped down by an aide. Some men managed to

Fountain Branch Carter's farm provided many landmarks to the fighting at Franklin. His home was to the west of the Columbia pike and was the scene of Emerson Opdyke's counterattack. One of Carter's sons was a captain in Hood's army. He was shot down within sight of his home and died in the house hours after the battle was over.

carry him back, but his wounds were mortal and he died ten days later. In the meantime, his troops were too shot up to accomplish anything. They occupied the ditches that fronted the earthworks. Among the casualties there was Capt. Theodrick "Tod" Carter; he fell mortally wounded just five hundred feet from the house in which he grew up.

Confederate divisional commander John C. Brown learned that he had no support on his left flank and was then badly wounded himself and carried to the rear. The attack stalled. Federal artillery was diverted to this area, and reinforcements strengthened the line. The Southerners had no choice but to fall back. Across the river, Forrest was thrown back. Hood's assault ended.

Twenty-four Confederate generals were exposed to fire on the Franklin plain. Six were killed or mortally wounded. Four were seriously wounded, and one was captured. Fifty-four regimental commanders were either killed, wounded, or captured.

Lee's corps arrived on the scene shortly after the fighting began at 4 P.M. He later insisted that, had he known of Hood's plans, he would have moved up sooner. Hood ordered him to be ready to support Cheatham's attack since his first reports from the battle were only that Cheatham had encountered "stubborn resistance." Lee would put his divisions into the fight only if such deployment proved necessary.

On the east side of the Columbia pike was the cotton gin building. Federal soldiers stripped it of most of the siding for use in the breastworks. Cleburne disappeared near here in a fog of powder smoke and was never seen alive again.

Lee met with Cheatham closer to the front, grasped the direness of the situation, and made plans for a night attack although he was not sure of where he was supposed to attack. In the last formal assault of the battle, his first division advanced around 9 P.M. over the dead and wounded in the field. Approximately thirty yards in front of the main Union line, the whole front lit up with a volley from the Federals. The Confederates were caught between the Yanks in front and their own artillery behind. They could do nothing but hug the earth and finally fall back.

The rest of the night was tense; the slightest noise solicited a flurry of shots. Both sides sent out small reconnaissance parties, and a few souvenir hunters ventured out.

Confidence was high along the Union line. Unit commanders talked of attacking in the morning and destroying Hood's army. Schofield moved to the city to take in the situation, because so much was obscured from his view at Fort Granger. There he heard of Wilson's repulse of Forrest and sent word to Thomas in Nashville, "We have whipped them here at every point."

Despite his ebullience, Schofield still saw that he was vulnerable and was concerned that his ammunition supply was low. He would pull back. Orders to that effect were issued early in the evening, stressing that the withdrawal be executed under the "strictest silence." The wooden wheels of the cannon were wrapped with blankets, and to further muffle the noise, blankets were also spread across the makeshift bridges erected earlier in the day.

Even though ambulances had been freed up by sending the sick and the wounded from Columbia and Spring Hill to Nashville by train, a large number of wounded was left behind. The evacuation was nearly compromised when a fire broke out at 11 P.M. in a livery stable in the city and spread. Flames threatened to illuminate the countryside, but the blaze was extinguished after an hourlong fight.

Union pickets pulled back at 1 A.M., abandoning the earthworks. By 2 A.M. the army was out of Franklin and the bridges were fired. By 4 A.M. all Union personnel had withdrawn except for one company, which acted as the rear guard.

Hood, unaware of the beginning of Schofield's withdrawal, called a council of war at midnight in his headquarters and announced that the army would attack in the morning. A hundred guns would open on the Federal position at daybreak, and the general assault would begin at 9 A.M. The guns were moved up at 2 A.M. just as scouts returned from the front to say that the Union army was gone. Hood ordered the guns to fire on Fort Granger, but the shots fell into the city. His troops entered the town around 4 A.M.

Surgeons and burial crews went to work. Almost every building was used as a hospital.

Hood entered the city later that morning, but he was shaken by the sight of the battlefield. "His sturdy visage assumed a melancholy appearance, and for a considerable time he sat on his horse and wept like a child," one of the men noted. When his grieving passed, he issued a statement of victory to his troops: "The commanding general congratulates the army upon the success achieved yesterday over our enemy. . . . [W]hile we lament the fall of many gallant officers and brave men, we have shown to our countrymen that we can carry any position occupied by our enemy."

A Missouri captain noted, "Two such victories will wipe out any army the power of man can organize."

The assault at Franklin was the last great Confederate charge of the war. Eighteen thousand men moved toward the Union line, more men than had been involved in Pickett's Charge at Gettysburg. Nearly seven thousand fell; seventeen hundred never got up again.

The Carnton mansion, not far from the battlefield, was used as a hospital and accommodated as many men as the house and yard could hold. On the lower verandah the bodies of three of the five generals killed at Franklin were placed—Cleburne, Granbury, and Strahl—awaiting removal to Columbia. Many soldiers paid their last respects, but they could not linger long.

Hood marched on to Nashville with nineteen thousand men. At the time, the state capital was probably the most fortified city on the continent. There Hood found Thomas waiting—with seventy thousand troops. The weather turned bitterly cold, and on December 15 Thomas marched out his troops and swept Hood away.

The gamble at Franklin had gained nothing, but an army, which the South could not afford to lose, had been wasted.

Stephen D. Lee was very generous in his assessment of his commander when he observed that Franklin was the price paid for the blunder at Spring Hill. The blunder, however, was Hood's, and the price paid was in the lives of his men. No one can ever doubt their courage or valor, but Hood will always bear the stigma of the commander who wrecked his own army.

23

FORT STEDMAN

"GOD DID NOT INTEND THAT WE SHOULD SUCCEED"

THE ARMY OF NORTHERN VIRGINIA had been trapped in the trenches around Petersburg since June 1864. With the approach of spring the next year, the prospects of Robert E. Lee's 44,000-man army, like those of the Confederacy as a whole, had grown even bleaker. At the same time, Ulysses S. Grant's besieging army had swollen to 128,000 troops, and William T. Sherman's army was progressing steadily up the eastern seaboard to join Grant. Their combined force would total at least 200,000.

In addition to the hardships of the siege, Lee was losing significant numbers of men to desertion. Almost every Southern soldier on the front line, including the commanding general, saw that the end was quite near. Lee had but two choices: do nothing and watch his army die or attack and see what might happen. Although the odds were far greater than any he had ever tempted previously—detaching Stonewall Jackson to march against John Pope and later Joseph

Hooker or George E. Pickett's charge at Gettysburg—Lee again resolved to overcome a desperate situation by taking a desperate risk.

On the morning of March 4, 1865, Lee summoned thirty-three-year-old John B. Gordon, one of his four corps commanders, to his headquarters to review the condition of the army and discuss the options facing the commander. Grant would soon be launching an offensive that the Southern army likely could not resist. Militarily, the Confederates would either have to retreat or seize the initiative from Grant by attacking first. The only other recourse was surrender.

Two days later the two men met again. Lee had since met with Jefferson Davis and reported that he believed the evacuation of Petersburg was but a matter of time. Davis, however, stressed that regardless of what happened, his government was not yet disposed to capitulate. The army had no choice but to fight.

Lee had determined that a breakthrough along the southern segment of Grant's line would force the Union commander to consolidate his army by pulling back. A portion of the Army of Northern Virginia could then pull out and join Joseph E. Johnston's Army of Tennessee and strike Sherman, possibly disabling him and preventing his linking up with Grant. Then Johnston's combined force could unite with Lee, and that joint force could take on Grant. Gordon's task was to pinpoint a weakness in the Union line for the breakthrough.

After examining the front for a week, Gordon recommended that the upcoming attack be focused on Fort Stedman, an enclosed four-

Confederate Gen. John B. Gordon masterminded the breakthrough at Fort Stedman after a series of meetings with Robert E. Lee. The plan was intricate and multilayered, requiring small teams of men to accomplish key goals for the next group to follow. To execute the attack, significant numbers of men were drawn from various points of the Confederate defenses, which weakened the Southerners' line and exposed it to collapse.

gun redoubt roughly a mile south of the Appomattox River. Only 282 yards separated the Union position from a Confederate redoubt known as Colquitt's Salient. The Federal fort was supported by one partially enclosed battery to the north and two to the south. These were imaginatively known as Batteries 10, 11, and 12. Rounding out the Union position were Fort Haskell, about a half-mile south of Stedman, and Battery 9, a half-mile north of Stedman.

The no man's land between the Confederate and Federal lines was filled with almost every siege device known to military science at the time, especially abatis and fraises. The former were lines of obstacles fashioned of harvested underbrush, and the latter were angled rows of sharpened logs placed inches apart and linked together with telegraph wire.

Gordon's plan of attack was complex and methodical. The assault would be staged to begin at night. Select groups would stealthily remove the Confederate obstructions in no man's land to open several avenues of attack. Hand-picked men would then infiltrate the Union lines and silence the Federal pickets and remove obstacles from the other half of no man's land. A third group, comprised of fifty men with axes, would then move up to create openings through the fraises in front of Stedman.

Once these avenues were opened, three groups of one hundred men each would rush into Stedman and Batteries 10, 11, and 12 and secure the positions. They would be followed by three more hundred-man groups who would secure the positions behind Stedman. This was one of the trickier parts of the mission. The ground beyond Stedman was honeycombed with trenches, covered passageways, and bombproofs, which could easily disorient an advancing force. Local guides were found to lead these squads to secure and hold the rear Union trenches.

Once the special squads had moved out, masses of Southern infantry would follow, enlarging the breakthrough by securing the trench line to the south and north. Behind the infantry would be cavalry, advancing into the Union rear and disrupting communication and coordination within the Federal lines.

Lee approved the plan on the evening of March 23. He began shifting men from across the line to give Gordon a chance to succeed. Eventually this amounted to almost a third of his total army. George E.

Pickett's sixty-five-hundred-man division was also ordered up, coming by train to Petersburg.

During the early evening of March 24, a vessel carrying Abraham Lincoln and his family anchored at the Union supply base at City Point, mere miles from Fort Stedman. There the president met with Grant, whose greatest concern was that Lee would somehow slip away from Petersburg and join Johnston. A campaign against the combined Confederate armies might last into the summer. Their evening ended with an invitation to the commander in chief to review the army the next day.

In the early morning hours of March 25 Federal listening posts reported activity around some of the obstructions in the field, but nothing appeared unusual when the noise was investigated. The usual occasional shooting across the lines all but ceased around 1 A.M.

Small parties of Confederates, carrying their rifles in the prescribed manner to indicate that they were deserting with their weapons, approached the Union pickets and were conveyed casually to the inner works. Such desertion was encouraged with offers of ten dollars for each rifle surrendered. In this instance, however, once the men were well within the Union position they turned their rifles on the Federal pickets and quietly conveyed them as prisoners back to the Confederate line.

Gordon was at Colquitt's Salient. By his side was a private whose job was to fire a shot to signal the infantry to rush toward the secured fort. In the trenches behind him were almost twelve thousand men.

The first squad began the work of clearing a path through the obstacle field. Suddenly a Federal picket called out a challenge: "What are you doing over there, Johnny? What is that noise? Answer quick or I'll shoot."

Gordon feared the worst, but the soldier next to him replied very coolly: "Never mind, Yank. Lie down and go to sleep. We are just gathering a little corn. You know rations are mighty short over here."

The crisis passed. A short while later the clearing was completed.

Gordon ordered his companion to fire the shot to launch the attack. The young man, however, hesitated a moment, feeling a moment's guilt for his deception. Gordon issued the order again. The soldier instead called out to the Federal picket, "Hello, Yank!

A section of the siegeworks from the southwestern segment of the Petersburg line shows how close the trenches were and also highlights the placement of pickets in the no man's land between the lines.

Wake up; we are going to shell the woods. Look out; we are coming." Then he discharged his weapon into the air.

The mass of men mounted the breastworks and entered the open field. Ahead of them, a single Union picket ran back to his line, shouting, "The Rebels are coming!"

Within Battery 10, gunners ran to their two 3-inch guns, which were always kept loaded, and fired into the Confederate line. The position was swarmed before they could reload.

At Fort Stedman a guard heard the ruckus at Battery 10 and ran to the four guns, discharging each in the direction of the Southern line. One of the commanders suspected that Battery 10 had fallen, and since the redoubt had an open trench connection with the batteries on either side, he tried to reposition one of his guns to cover this approach. The rest of the roused gunners rushed to the other three pieces and fired a total of twelve rounds into the Confederate works around Petersburg before they were overcome.

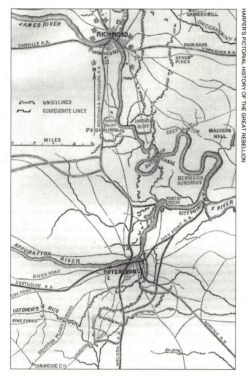

An overview of the battle lines around Petersburg and Richmond reveals the intricate system of entrenchments erected here over the course of the war and near battlefields that saw more than one engagement.

Battery 11 fell into the Confederates' hands without a shot.

The discharge of the guns strobed the open ground over which the one-hundred-man groups advanced. These storm troops scrambled into the Federal trenches and into the fort and supporting batteries. Resistance was brief.

Success was just as swift for those units targeting the camps of two infantry regiments just behind the redoubts, although there was much more hand-to-hand fighting there. After securing the position, many of the Southerners fell on whatever rations they could find.

This initial phase had achieved all but one of its goals, the seizure of Battery 12. Effectively, a thousand-foot gap had been opened in the Union line.

Frontline Union command in this sector was in the hands of Bvt. Brig. Gen. Napoleon B. McLaughlen. He was on the scene quickly, first checking with his southernmost position, Fort Haskell, and seeing that its personnel were alert and manning the guns. Advancing up the trench line to Battery 12, he found the gunners in place and then encountered one of the officers from the overrun regiments to the rear. Aware now that Battery 11 was occupied by Confederates, he ordered a counterattack and turned the mortars from Battery 12 in that direction. The Southerners abandoned the battery.

Believing that he had sealed the breach in his line, McLaughlen rode into Fort Stedman and found the situation far more confusing than he expected. He barked orders to the men, and then in the graying light of the early dawn realized that these soldiers were not of his army. At the same time the Southerners recognized they had a Union officer in their midst and took him prisoner, sending him back through their lines.

Battery 11 again fell into Confederate hands when troops pushed through the breached line and outflanked the Yankee regiments attempting to hold the position. The limited light worked to the Southerners' advantage, as they were on top of the Union units before the Northerners could discern who was rushing toward them from Fort Stedman. Those who were not taken prisoner fled back toward Fort Haskell but were overtaken and captured.

Gordon entered Stedman and saw that all had gone as well or better than he had planned. His infantry force had filled the position and expanded the pocket to the north, east, and south. He was especially interested in knowing how far his last three hundred-man squads had fared in penetrating the Union rear. The mission seemingly accomplished its goal of breaking Grant's grip on Petersburg and giving Lee the opportunity to maneuver once again.

That hope vanished with the first report from one of the special groups advancing to the east. It had not been able to achieve its objective. The guide had been separated from the group during the rush across the line, and the men had wandered into the maze of trenches and earthworks behind Stedman with no idea of where they were or where they were going. Similar reports came shortly from the other two groups.

Behind the Union line, Brig. Gen. John F. Hartranft commanded the reserve for this sector. He was aware that something was happening at Fort Stedman, but he was two miles away and had only three regiments immediately at hand and three other regiments farther to the south. Shortly after the first shots were fired, his aides rode up to investigate the situation and the regiments here were formed for battle.

Gordon saw that his position to the south was stabilized and directed the units now entering the field to the north and toward Battery 9. The oncoming Confederates had little difficulty sweeping through the trenches, but more alert Union commanders pulled back into the northern battery. Other units withdrew to the northeast until they could form a line.

Battery 9 opened fire on a huge line of approaching Southerners. The two guns were supported as other batteries were brought up from the reserve and positioned to enfilade the attackers. Likewise, Union batteries all along the Confederate pocket focused their fire on the Southerners from Battery 12 northward. One North Carolina soldier recalled that the shelling "from our right beyond Fort Stedman and the minnies from the fort near the river on our left, and with shell from the bluff in our front, our position was made, in the opinion of our commanders, untenable."

Gordon saw that the Federal forts were now fully manned. His forward units had failed, and he had received word that Pickett's division would not be coming up. "Our wretched railroad trains had broken down," he later noted. "It was impossible for me to make further headway with my isolated corps, and General Lee directed me to withdraw."

Efforts to take Fort Haskell collapsed at daylight. Hartranft had sent one of his regiments there to solidify the line and then established a defensive line to the east to block the Confederates from seizing a sizable supply depot. This latter line was pushed back and reformed twice, buying valuable time while additional units could be brought forward. These reinforcements halted the Southern advance, curtailing its advance to the north and northeast of Fort Stedman.

Hartranft inspected the situation to the south and found the Union line beginning to stabilize and saw that his distant three regiments had moved up. He shifted units to fill the gaps and began to move in strength to regain the occupied positions.

Gordon had already begun to pull his men back. The Yankee fire now made it a rout. For a counterassault, Hartranft formed nearly four thousand men across an arc a mile and a half long. They began to move forward just before 8 A.M. when orders came up to delay any action until additional troops arrived. It was an order Hartranft couldn't obey. He later explained, "I saw that the enemy had already commenced to waver, and that success was certain. I, therefore, allowed the line to charge; besides this, it was doubtful whether I could have communicated with the regiments on the flanks in time to countermand the movement."

The advancing Federals had little difficulty in reclaiming the batteries and Stedman. Within the fort a Southerner looked out from a bombproof and caught the eye of a Union captain. When the Federal officer approached to take him prisoner, he found that he had captured thirty-five officers and men who had sought refuge there. A squad of Pennsylvania soldiers seized a Confederate flag and waved it in celebration, which drew fire from a Union battery farther to the rear. The Rebel banner was immediately put down.

Other Union commanders surmised that the force gathered at Colquitt's Salient had to have been shifted there from other points along the southern segment of the Confederate line. They exploited the weakened front and overran several picket lines, but they could not break through the main line. The seized positions were braced for a counterattack, and Confederate efforts succeeded in regaining only a few of these.

At City Point, Lincoln was informed there had been "a little rumpus up the line." He, Grant, and their families and guests took a special train at noon for a review of the troops at Patrick Station and George Gordon Meade's headquarters. Shortly before their arrival, fifteen hundred prisoners from the Fort Stedman fighting were marched into a holding area nearby. Lincoln was briefly informed of

Large numbers of Confederates were captured as a result of the breakthrough. At the time of the attack, Abraham Lincoln was visiting Ulysses S. Grant and witnessed groups of prisoners being processed away from the front.

the morning's battle then proceeded to the reviewing area. One of the Confederate prisoners, seeing the Union president and the casualness of his visit, recalled, "All of us Confederates agreed with one accord that our cause was lost."

In a letter to Jefferson Davis, Lee reported: "I was induced to assume the offensive from the belief that the point assailed could be carried without much loss and [with] the hope that [by our] seizure of the redoubts in the rear of the enemy's line . . . Grant would . . . be obliged so to curtail his lines that upon the approach of Genl Sherman, I might be able to hold our position with a portion of the troops, and with a select body unite with Genl Johnston and give him battle. . . . I fear now it will be impossible to prevent a junction between Grant and Sherman, nor do I deem it prudent that this army should maintain its position until the latter shall approach too near."

Confederate losses were estimated at four thousand men, including dead, wounded, and captured. Federal casualties reached about two thousand for both the defense of Fort Stedman and the later action involving the assault on the Southern line.

As Grant analyzed the action, he realized that this was Lee's last offensive effort at Petersburg. To attempt anything like it again would risk annihilation. Still he anticipated that Lee would withdraw, hoping to find a way to join forces with Johnston. As events played out, he was correct, but Lee was too far away from Johnston to hope to link up with him. Within two weeks of the attack on Fort Stedman, the Army of Northern Virginia would be surrendered and the war would be over for all practical purposes.

Long after the war, John B. Gordon encountered a Union veteran of the battle for Stedman who asked him why he believed the assault failed. "I'll tell you why," the old general replied. "God did not intend that we should succeed. He did not intend that the Southern Confederacy should be an accomplished fact. He caused the axle of the tender of the last section of the train that was to bring the troops north of Richmond to break, thus delaying that entire body of troops [Pickett's division] from reaching us. Had they arrived I believe that we should have captured City Point that morning. God did not intend that we should succeed."

SELECTED BIBLIOGRAPHY

Abel, Annie Heloise. *The American Indian As Slaveholder and Secessionist.* Cleveland: A. H. Clark Co., 1915.

———. *The American Indian in the Civil War, 1862–1865.* Cleveland: A. H. Clark Co., 1919.

American Annual Cyclopaedia and Register of Important Events of the Year 1862. New York: D. Appleton & Co., 1863.

American Cylopaedia. New York: D. Appleton & Co., 1858.

Arnold, James R. *Shiloh 1862: The Death of Innocence.* Osprey Military Campaign Series, no. 54. Oxford, England: Osprey, 1998.

Bailey, Anne J. *The Chessboard of War: Sherman and Hood in the Autumn Campaigns of 1864.* Great Campaigns of the Civil War. Lincoln: University of Nebraska Press, 2000.

Bailey, Ronald H. *Forward to Richmond: McClellan's Peninsula Campaign.* Alexandria, Va.: Time-Life Books, 1983.

Bohannon, Keith S. "One Solid Unbroken Roar of Thunder: Union and Confederate Artillery at the Battle of Malvern Hill." In *The Richmond Campaign of 1862: The Peninsula and the Seven Days,* ed. Gary W. Gallagher, 217–49. Military Campaigns of the Civil War. Chapel Hill: University of North Carolina Press, 2000.

Casdorph, Paul D. *Prince John Magruder: His Life and Campaigns.* New York: Wiley, 1996.

Cozzens, Peter. *The Darkest Days of the War: The Battles of Iuka and Corinth.* Chapel Hill: University of North Carolina Press, 1997.

———. *General John Pope: A Life for the Nation.* Urbana: University of Illinois Press, 2000.

———. *The Shipwreck of Their Hopes: The Battles for Chattanooga.* Urbana: University of Illinois Press, 1994.

Daniel, Larry J. *Shiloh: The Battle That Changed the Civil War.* New York: Simon and Schuster, 1997.

Davis, William C. *Battle at Bull Run: A History of the First Major Campaign of the Civil War.* Garden City, N.Y.: Doubleday, 1977.

————, and the Editors of Time-Life Books. *Death in the Trenches: Grant at Petersburg.* The Civil War, vol. 22. Alexandria, Va.: Time-Life Books, 1986.

————, and the Editors of Time-Life Books. *First Blood.* The Civil War, vol. 2. Alexandria, Va.: Time-Life Books, 1983.

Domer, Ronald G. "Rebel Rout of Streight's Raiders." *America's Civil War* (September 1996): 30–36.

Eisenhower, John S. D. *Agent of Destiny: The Life and Times of Winfield Scott.* New York: Free Press, 1997.

Eisenschiml, Otto, and Ralph Newman. *The American Iliad: The Epic Story of the Civil War As Narrated by Eyewitnesses and Contemporaries.* Indianapolis: Bobbs-Merrill, 1947.

Encyclopedia Americana. 30 vols. New York: Americana Corp., 1957.

Faust, Patricia L., ed. *Historical Times Illustrated Encyclopedia of the Civil War.* New York: Harper & Row, 1986.

Garrison, Webb. *Friendly Fire in the Civil War.* Nashville: Rutledge Hill Press, 1999.

————. *Love, Lust, and Longing in the White House.* Nashville: Cumberland House, 2000.

Harper's Encyclopedia of U.S. History. 10 vols. New York: Harper, 1901.

Johnson, Robert U., and Clarence C. Buel, eds. *Battles and Leaders of the Civil War.* 4 vols. Reprint, New York: Castle Books, 1956.

Johnson, Swafford. *Great Battles of the Confederacy.* New York: W. H. Smith Publishers, 1985.

Johnson, Timothy D. *Winfield Scott: The Quest for Military Glory.* Lawrence: University Press of Kansas, 1998.

Klein, Maury. *Days of Defiance: Sumter, Secession, and the Coming of the Civil War.* New York: Alfred Knopf, 1997.

Korn, Jerry, and the Editors of Time-Life Books. *The Fight for Chattanooga.* The Civil War, vol. 17. Alexandria, Va.: Time-Life Books, 1983.

Lang, J. Stephen. *The Complete Book of Confederate Trivia.* Shippensburg, Pa.: Burd Street Press, 1996.

Long, E. B., and Barbara Long. *The Civil War Day by Day: An Almanac.* Garden City, N.Y.: Doubleday, 1971.

Longacre, Edward G. "All Is Fair in Love and War." *Civil War Times Illustrated* (June 1969).

Lossing, Benson J. *Pictorial Field Book of the Civil War.* 3 vols. Hartford: T. Belknap, 1870–76.

McDonough, James Lee. *Shiloh: In Hell Before Night.* Knoxville: University of Tennessee Press, 1977.

————, and Thomas L. Connelly. *Five Tragic Hours: The Battle of Franklin.* Knoxville: University of Tennessee Press, 1983.

McPherson, James M., ed. *Battle Chronicles of the Civil War 1863.* Grey Castle: Civil War Times Illustrated, 1989.

Marvel, William. "The Crater: July 30, 1864." *Civil War* (April 1998): 17, 20–22.

Miles, Jim. *Forged in Fire: A History and Tour Guide of the War in the East, from Manassas to Antietam, 1861–1862.* The Civil War Explorer. Nashville: Cumberland House, 2000.

Miller, Francis T., ed. *Photographic History of the Civil War.* 10 vols. New York: Review of Reviews, 1911.

Moore, Frank, ed. *The Rebellion Record.* 12 vols. New York: Van Nostrand, 1868.

Nevin, David. *The Road to Shiloh: Early Battles in the West.* The Civil War, vol. 4. Alexandria, Va.: Time-Life, 1983.

Newell, Clayton R. *Lee vs. McClellan: The First Campaign.* Washington, D.C.: Regnery, 1996.

Page, Dave. *Ships versus Shore: Civil War Engagements Along Southern Shores and Rivers.* Nashville: Rutledge Hill Press, 1994.

Pollard, Edward A. *The Lost Cause.* New York: E. B. Treat & Co., 1867.

Razza, Michael S. "The Man Behind the Mine: The Short, Unhappy Life of Henry Pleasants, Mastermind of the Petersburg Mine, Reached a Fitting and Tragic Climax at the Crater." *Civil War* (June 1996): 22–27.

Robertson, James I., Jr. *Stonewall Jackson: The Man, the Soldier, the Legend.* New York: Macmillan, 1997.

———, ed. *Journal of the Southern Historical Society.* 49 vols. Richmond, 1876–1944.

Ropes, John Codman. *The Army Under Pope.* Campaigns of the Civil War, vol. 4. New York: Scribner, 1881. Reprint, Harrisburg, Pa.: Archive Society, 1992.

Scientific American, vol. 6, no. 19. New York: Munn & Co., 1862.

Sears, Stephen W. *Controversies and Commanders: Dispatches from the Army of the Potomac.* Boston: Houghton Mifflin, 1999.

———. *To the Gates of Richmond: The Peninsula Campaign.* New York: Ticknor & Fields, 1992.

Sifakis, Stewart. *Who Was Who in the Civil War.* New York: Facts on File, 1988.

Still, William N., Jr. *Iron Afloat.* Columbia: University of South Carolina Press, 1985.

Suhr, Robert Collins. "Small But Savage Battle of Iuka." *America's Civil War* (May 1999): 42–49.

Sutherland, Daniel E. *The Emergence of Total War.* Civil War Campaigns and Commanders Series. Edited by Grady McWhiney. Fort Worth: Ryan Place Publishers, 1996.

Sword, Wiley. *The Confederacy's Last Hurrah: Spring Hill, Franklin, and Nashville.* Modern War Studies. Lawrence: University Press of Kansas, 1992.

———. *Shiloh: Bloody April.* 1974; reprint, Dayton, Ohio: Morningside House, 1988.

The Confederate Veteran. 40 vols. 3-vol. index. Reprint; Wilmington, N.C.: Broadfoot, 1986–88.

Thomas, Emory M. *Robert E. Lee: A Biography.* New York: Norton, 1995.

Trudeau, Noah Andre. *The Last Citadel: Petersburg, Virginia, June 1864–April 1865.* Boston: Little, Brown and Co., 1991.

U.S. Congress. Joint Committee on the Conduct of the War. *The Battle of Ball's Bluff.* 1863. Reprint, Millwood, N.Y.: Kraus Reprint, 1977.

———. *The Battle of Bull Run.* 1863. Reprint, Millwood, N.Y.: Kraus Reprint, 1977.

U.S. Navy Department. *Official Records of the Union and Confederate Navies in the War of the Rebellion.* 30 vols. Washington, D.C.: Government Printing Office, 1894–1927.

U.S. War Department. *The War of the Rebellion: A Compilation of the Official Records of the Union and Confederate Armies.* 128 vols. Washington, D.C.: Government Printing Office, 1880–1901.

Van Doren Stern, Philip. *The Confederate Navy: A Pictorial History.* New York: Da Capo Press, 1962.

Warner, Ezra. *Generals in Blue.* Baton Rouge: Louisiana State University Press, 1964.

Werlich, Robert. *"Beast" Butler: The Incredible Career of Major General Benjamin Franklin Butler.* Washington, D.C.: Quaker Press, 1962.

INDEX